S. Freeman, sc

Major General James Wolfe

from a scarce contemporary print engraved by R. Houston

OLD QUEBEC

THE FORTRESS OF NEW FRANCE

BY

GILBERT PARKER

AND

CLAUDE G. BRYAN

WITH ILLUSTRATIONS

New York

THE MACMILLAN COMPANY

LONDON: MACMILLAN & CO., Ltd.

1903

Norwood Press
J. S. Cushing & Co. — Berwick & Smith Co.
Norwood, Mass., U.S.A.

CONTENTS

CONTENTS

LIST OF PLATES

¹ Inscription on plate for 2nd Governor of Canada 1766, *read* Lieutenant-Governor of Canada 1766.

LIST OF ILLUSTRATIONS

LIST OF ILLUSTRATIONS xiii

MAPS

NOTE

THE student of the history of the ancient capital of Canada is embarrassed, not by the dearth but by the abundance of material at his disposal. The present volume, therefore, makes no claim to originality. It is but an assimilation of this generous data, and a simple comment upon the changing scenes which were recorded by such ancient authorities as the Jesuit priests and pioneers in their *Relations*, and by the monumental works of Francis Parkman, whose researches occupied more than forty years, and whose picturesque pen has done for Canada what Prescott's did for Mexico. Admiring tribute and gratitude must also be expressed for the years of careful study and the unfaltering energy by which the late Mr. Kingsford produced his valuable *History of Canada*. Nor can any one, writing of Quebec, proceed successfully without constant reference to the historical gleanings of Sir James Le Moine, who has spent a lifetime in the romantic atmosphere of old-time manuscripts,

and who, with Monsieur l'Abbé Casgrain, represents, in its most attractive form, that composite
citizenship which has the wit and grace of the old
régime, with the useful ardour of the new.

THE AUTHORS.

OLD QUEBEC

CHAPTER I

EARLY VOYAGES

LIVING in the twentieth century, to which the utter-most parts of the earth are revealed, and with only the undiscovered poles left to lure us on, we cannot fully appreciate the geographical ignorance of the Middle Ages. The travels of Marco Polo had only lately revealed the wonders of the golden East, and in the West the Pillars of Hercules marked earth's furthest bound. Beyond lay the *mare tenebrosum*, the Mysterious Sea, girding the level world. England was not then one of the first nations of the earth. She was not yet a maritime power, she had not begun the work of colonisation and empire : the fulcrum of Europe lay further south. But as our Tudor sovereigns were making secure dominion in " these isles," the Byzantine Empire was moving slowly to its end, and favouring circumstances were already making Italy the centre of the world's commerce and culture. There the feudal system, never deeply rooted, was declining slowly, and Italian energy and enterprise now having larger opportunity, seized the commerce of the East as it received vast impulse from the Crusades, and this trade became the source of Empire.

Venice, Genoa, and Pisa were now great emporiums of Oriental wares, were waxing rich on a transport trade which had no option but to use their ports and their vessels. Inland Florence had no part in maritime enterprise, but was the manufacturing, literary, and art centre of mediæval Europe. Her silk looms made her famous throughout the world, her banks were the purse of Europe, and among her famous sons were Dante, Petrarch, Boccaccio, Macchiavelli, Michael Angelo, Leonardo da Vinci, Galileo, Amerigo Vespucci. For the development of their commerce, the cities of the North had grouped themselves into the great Hanseatic League, with branches in Bruges, London, Bergen, and Novgorod. Commercialism had everywhere become the keynote of the closing Middle Ages, inspiring that maritime enterprise which was soon to outline a new map of the world.

The main route between the West and East had hitherto been by way of the Red Sea and the Euphrates, and it was controlled by the Italian cities. Italy had, therefore, no interest in finding a water route to the East which would rob her of

this profitable overland traffic.   But the experience
of her sailors made them the most skilful of the
world's navigators and the readiest instruments of
other nations in expeditions of discovery.   Thus
Columbus of Genoa, Cabot of Venice, and Verrazzano of Florence are found accepting commissions
from foreign sovereigns.

   " The discoveries of Copernicus and Columbus,"
says Froude, " created, not in any metaphor, but in
plain language, a new heaven and a new earth."   The
new theory of Copernicus was, indeed, one of the
choicest flowers of the Renaissance, and though
timidly enunciated, it revolutionised the world's
geography.   Further, the discovery of the polarity
of the magnet, and the invention of the astrolabe,
gave to the mariners of the fifteenth century a
sense of security lacking to their fathers, while the
kindling flame of the New Learning led them upon
the most daring quests.   The Portuguese were the
first to enter on the brilliant path of sea-going
exploration which distinguishes this century above
all others.   By 1486 they had already found
Table Mountain rising out of the Southern sea, and
hoping always for a passage to the East, had named
it the Cape of Good Hope.   Spain soon followed
her rival into these unknown regions, a policy due
mainly to the enthusiasm of Isabella of Castile, who,
in spite of the conservative apathy of the Council

of Salamanca, was eager to become the patroness of Christopher Columbus.

Although the Northmen of the tenth century had been blown almost fortuitously upon the shores of Nova Scotia, by way of Iceland, Greenland, and Labrador, the discovery of North America must always be set to the credit of Christopher Columbus. From the age of fourteen he had been upon the sea, and his keen mind was stored with all the nautical science afforded by the awakened spirit of the time. To this practical equipment he added a romantic temperament and a habit of reflection which carried him to greater certainty in his convictions than even that attained by his correspondent, the learned Toscanelli. Assuming that the world was round — no commonplace of the time — he determined forthwith to reach India by sailing westward. His bones lie buried in the Western hemisphere, which his intrepidity revealed to an astonished world.

As soon as Columbus, in the name of Ferdinand and Isabella, had opened the gates of the New World, ships from England and France began to hasten westward across the Atlantic. The Cabots, holding to the North, discovered Newfoundland in 1497; Denis of Honfleur explored the Gulf of St. Lawrence in 1506; and a few years later Verrazzano coasted along the North Atlantic seaboard in four

ships fitted out for him by the youthful Francis of
Angoulême. This voyage was practically the beginning of French enterprise in the New World.

On Verrazzano's return to Dieppe, he sent the
King a written account of his travels, and France
was presently burning with excitement over the
abundant riches of the New World. Spain, meanwhile, had been reaping the wealth of the West
Indies, and Hernando Cortés was laying a stern
hand upon the treasures of Mexico. And now disasters at home were, for a time, to rob the fickle
Francis of all ambition for transatlantic glory. In
the contest for the crown of the Holy Roman Empire he had been worsted by Charles V., and shortly
afterwards the strength of France was hopelessly
shattered at Pavia, the King being carried back a
prisoner to Madrid. But when, at last, the peace
of Cambrai had somewhat restored tranquillity to
France, Philippe de Brion-Chabot, a courtier at the
Louvre, decided to follow up Verrazzano's almost
forgotten exploit of ten years before, and Jacques
Cartier became the instrument of this tardy resolution.

Jacques Cartier was born at St. Malo, the white
buttress of Brittany. Daring Breton fishing-boats
had often sailed as far as the cod-banks of Newfoundland, and it is not impossible that Cartier himself
had already crossed the Atlantic before he was commissioned by Chabot. From a child he had lived

upon the sea.   He was forty years old when he received his commission, and on the 20th of April,
1634, he set sail from his native town.   Holding a
northern course he came at length to Newfoundland,
and having passed through the Straits of Belle Isle
and across the Gulf, he erected a white cross at
Gaspé, and sailed on westward till Anticosti came in
sight.   It was then August, and as constant westerly
winds delayed his further course, he decided to return to France.   Unfortunately, however, he did
not leave until he had lured on board his ships two
young Indians, whom he carried back as trophies,
sowing thereby the seed of future trouble.

His countrymen were deeply stirred by his report.
Beyond a doubt the great Gulf up which he had
sailed was the water route to Cathay, and France
could hardly await the arrival of spring before
sending another expedition.   By the middle of
May, 1635, Cartier was ready to embark on a second voyage, and on this occasion no less than three
ships were equipped, numbering among their officers
men of birth and quality — gentlemen in search of
adventure, others eager to mend broken fortunes,
and all bent on claiming new lands for France and
for the faith.   Assembling in the old cathedral they
confessed their sins and heard the Mass ; and on the
19th of May the dwellers of St. Malo saw the sails
of the *Hermine*, *La Petite Hermine*, and *Emerillon* melt

into the misty blue of the horizon. Almost immediately a fierce storm scattered the ships, and they only
came together again six weeks later in the Straits of

JACQUES CARTIER

Belle Isle. This time Cartier coasted along the north
shore of the Gulf; and to a bay opposite Anticosti
he gave the name of St. Lawrence, upon whose
festival day it was discovered. Then for the first

time a white man entered "the great river of Canada."

With the kidnapped Indians for pilots, the three caravels passed by the cañon of the Saguenay, mysterious in its sombre silence. Presently the rocky cliff of Cap Tourmente towered above them, and at length they glided into safe anchorage off the Isle of Bacchus.[1]

To the savage Indians the mighty vessels of France were marvels from another world, and the river was soon swarming with their birch-bark canoes. The story of the two braves who had been carried away to France filled them with grave wonder, and the glittering costumes of Cartier and his officers seemed like the garments of gods. The great chief, Donnacona, waiving regal conventions, clambered upon the deck of the *Hermine*, where Cartier regaled him with cakes and wine, and with a few beads purchased the amity of his naked followers. Then Cartier set out in a small boat to explore the river.

Above the Island of Bacchus he found himself in a beautiful harbour, on the farther side of which the great river of Canada boomed through a narrow gorge. On the left of the basin the broader channel of the river passed out between the Isle of Bacchus and a range of wooded heights; while on

[1] Now the Island of Orleans.

his right, a tower of rock rose majestically from the foam-flecked water. Among the oak and walnut trees that crowned the summit of this natural battlement clustered the bark cabins of Stadaconé, whence, as wide as eye could range, the Lord of Canada held his savage sway.

This Algonquin eyrie seemed only accessible by a long detour through the upland, in which the rocky heights gradually descended to the little river of St. Croix. Thither Cartier and his companions made their way, and then, for the first time, white men gazed upon the green landscape spread beneath that high promontory. On the north and east the blue rim of the world's oldest mountains, then as now, seemed to shut off a mysterious barren land; on the south and west the eye met a fairer prospect, for beyond a sea of verdure the sun's rays glistened upon the distant hills of unknown, unnamed Vermont. Between these half-points of the compass the broad St. Lawrence rolled outward to the sea, and the discovering eye followed its bending course beyond the Isle of Bacchus and past the beetling shoulder of Cap Tourmente. In the summer of 1635 Cartier stood entranced on this magnificent precipice; and to-day the visitor to Quebec gazes from the King's Bastion upon the same panorama, hardly altered by the flight of nearly four centuries.

But Quebec had yet for many years to await its

founder. Cartier's mission was one of discovery, not colonisation ; and he resolved to push further up the river to Hochelaga, an important village of which the Indians had told him. But Donnacona soon repented of the information he had given, and left nothing undone to turn Cartier from his purpose. As a last resource the magicians of Stadaconé devised a plan to frighten the obstinate Frenchman, but the crude masquerade arranged for that purpose provoked nothing but amusement. A large canoe came floating slowly down the river, and when it drew near the ships the Frenchmen beheld three black devils, garbed in dogskins, and wearing monstrous horns upon their heads. Chanting the hideous monotones of the medicine men, they glided past the fleet, made for the shore, and disappeared in the thicket. Presently, Cartier's two interpreters issued from the wood and declared that the god Coudouagny had sent his three chief priests to warn the French against ascending the river, predicting dire calamities if they should persist. Cartier's reply to the Indian deity was brief and irreverent, and he forthwith made ready to depart.

The *Hermine* and *Emerillon* were towed to safer moorings in the quiet St. Croix, and with the pinnace and a small company of men Cartier set out for Hochelaga. The journey was long and toilsome, but by the beginning of October they came to a beautiful island, the site of Montreal. A thousand

Indians thronged the shore to welcome the mysterious visitors, presenting gifts of fish and fruit and
corn.   Then, by a well-worn trail, the savages led
the way through the forest to the foot of the mountain, and into the triple palisades of Hochelaga.

The early frosts of autumn had already touched
the trees, and Cartier, having accomplished his exploration, hastened back to Stadaconé, where he set

MANOIR DE JACQUES CARTIER À LIMOULON

about making preparations for spending the winter.
A fort was hastily built at the mouth of the St.
Croix.   But the exiles were unready for the violent
season that soon closed in upon them, almost burying their fort in drifting snow and casing the ships
in an armour of glistening ice.   Pent up by the
biting frost, and eking out a wretched existence on
salted food, their condition grew deplorable.   A
terrible scurvy assailed the camp, and out of a
company of one hundred and ten, twenty-five died,
while only three or four of the rest escaped its

ravages. The flint-like ground defied their feeble spades, and the dead bodies were hidden away in banks of snow. To make matters still worse, the Indians grew first indifferent, and then openly hostile. Cartier was sorely beset to conceal from them the weakness of his garrison. At last, however, a friendly Indian told him of a decoction by which the scurvy might be cured. The leaves of a certain evergreen were put to brew, and this medicine proved the salvation of the decimated company.

By and by came the spring; and when at last sun and rain had loosed the fetters of ice, Cartier determined to return to France. Before the ships weighed anchor, however, Donnacona and four of his companions were enticed on board, and with these sorry trophies the French captain turned his prows homeward. At midsummer-time the storm-battered ships glided once more into the rock-bound harbour of St. Malo.

Five years elapsed before France sent another expedition into the New World. The perennial conflict with Charles V. kept the French king's mind fixed on his home dominions, and Chabot, Cartier's former patron, had fallen upon evil times. At last, however, a new adventurer appeared in the person of the Sieur de Roberval, a nobleman of Picardy. The elaborate but almost incomprehensible text of the royal patent described the new envoy as Lord of

Norembega, Viceroy and Lieutenant-General in
Canada, Hochelaga, Saguenay, Newfoundland, Belle
Isle, Carpunt, Labrador, the Great Bay, and Baccalaos.
Under him Cartier was persuaded to take the post
of Captain-General. The objects of the enterprise
were discovery, colonisation, and the conversion of

ARRIVAL OF JACQUES CARTIER AT QUEBEC, 1535

the Indians; albeit the instruments for this pious
purpose were more than doubtful, their five ships
being freighted for the most part with thieves and
malefactors recruited from the prisons of France.

An unexpected delay occurring at St. Malo, it
was determined that Cartier should sail at once, and
that Roberval should follow as soon as possible with
additional ships and supplies. Accordingly, on the

23rd of May, 1541, Cartier again spread his sails for the West, and after a stormy passage arrived in the St. Lawrence. The uncertain attitude of the Indians, however, prompted him to establish his colony further westward than Stadaconé, and he continued his course up the river and dropped anchor at Cap Rouge.

Summer and autumn passed away and brought no sign of Roberval. A gloomy winter further damped the spirits of the colonists at Charlesburg-Royal; and when the ice had gone out of the river, Cartier gathered his company back into the ships and set sail again for France. At Newfoundland he encountered the belated Roberval. High words were exchanged, and, as a result, the fiery Viceroy sailed alone to New France; and Cartier, bidding Canada a last farewell, held on his way to St. Malo.

Francis Parkman transcribes from the manuscript of Thevet the following incident which marked Roberval's voyage: — " The Viceroy's company was of a mixed complexion. There were nobles, officers, soldiers, sailors, adventurers, with women, too, and children. Of the women, some were of birth and station, and among them a damsel called Marguerite, a niece of Roberval himself. In the ship was a young gentleman who had embarked for love of her. His love was too well requited, and the stern Viceroy, scandalised and enraged at a passion which scorned concealment and set shame at defiance, cast anchor by the haunted island (the Isle of Demons), landed his indiscreet relative, gave her four arquebuses for defence, and with an old woman nurse who had pandered to the lovers, left her to her fate. Her gallant threw himself into the surf, and by desperate effort gained the shore, with two more guns and a supply of ammunition. The ship weighed anchor, receded, vanished; they were left alone. Yet not so, for the demon-lords of the island beset them day and night, raging round their hut with a confused and hungry clamouring, striving to force the frail barrier. The lovers had repented of their sin, though not abandoned it, and Heaven was on their side. The saints vouchsafed their aid, and the offended Virgin, relenting, held before them her protecting shield. In the form of beasts and other shapes abominably and unutterably hideous, the brood of hell, howling in baffled fury, tore at the branches of the sylvan dwelling; but a celestial hand was ever interposed, and there was a viewless barrier which they might not pass. Marguerite became pregnant. Here was a double prize — two souls in one, mother and child. The fiends grew frantic, but all in vain. She stood undaunted amid these horrors, but her lover, dismayed and heart-broken, sickened and died. Her child soon followed; then the old woman nurse found her unhallowed rest in that accursed soil, and Marguerite was left alone. Neither reason nor courage failed her; and when assailed by the demons, she shot at them with her gun. They answered with hellish merriment, and thenceforth she placed her trust in Heaven alone. There were foes around her of the upper, no less than of the nether, world. Of these the bears were the most redoubtable, yet as they were vulnerable to mortal weapons, she killed three of them — all, says the story, 'as white as an egg.'

"It was two years and five months from her landing on the island, when, far out at sea, the crew of a small fishing-craft saw a column of smoke curling upward from the haunted shore. Was it a device of the fiends to lure them to their ruin? They thought so, and kept aloof. But misgiving seized them. They warily drew near, and descried a female figure in wild attire waving signals from the strand. Thus, at length, was Marguerite rescued, and restored to her native France, where, a few years later, the cosmographer Thevet met her at Natron, in Perigord, and heard the tale of wonder from her own lips."[1]

Meanwhile, Roberval sailed on up the St. Lawrence, and established himself at Cap Rouge, in the deserted forts of Charlesburg-Royal built by Cartier. But the inexperience and imprudence of

---

[1] Parkman's *Pioneers of France*, p. 203.

Francois Xavier de Laval.

First Bishop of Quebec.

the haughty Viceroy soon put his establishment
in sore straits. Ignorance of physical conditions
and disregard of natural laws of health had always
been the chief cause of suffering among these transatlantic exiles, and Roberval now added a lament-
able want of perception and solicitude. Unlike
Cartier, the inexorable Viceroy did not recognise his

CAP ROUGE

colonists as companions in privation, but ruled them
with a rod of iron. The pillory, the whipping-post,
and the scaffold were distressing features in his
system. Then came winter, famine, and the scurvy.
Fifty of the settlers died, and by spring even the
headstrong Roberval was ready to forsake his enterprise. His departure ends the earliest period of
French adventure in America.

c

Thenceforth, for more than half a century, France writhed in civil war, and spared no vessel to explore the great river of Canada.   For all these years New France was left to its aboriginal inhabitants and to fate.

CHAPTER II

THE name of Champlain must ever stand before all
others in the history of Quebec. He was the founder
of the city, and for more than a quarter of a century
he was its very life. If repeated disappointment and
misfortune could have brought this great empire-
builder to despair; if obstacles apparently impossible
to overcome could have turned the hero from his
purpose, Quebec would not be to-day the oldest city
in the western hemisphere. As it was, his character
gave the keynote not only to the great fortress-capi-
tal, but to the whole history of New France. He
was an embodiment at once of the religious zeal
and of the mediæval spirit of romance which carried the Bourbon lilies into the trackless wilderness of North America, at a time when English
colonisation contented itself with a narrow strip on
the Atlantic seaboard.

Samuel de Champlain was born in 1567 at the
small seaport of Brouage, on the Bay of Biscay.

His father was a captain in the French navy, in which profession the son also received early training. In the conflict between the King and the rebellious Duc de Mercœur and the League, Champlain was found on the Royalist side ; and Henry the Fourth rewarded his faithful subject with a pension and a place at court.   But the war in Brittany was not long over before Champlain became restless.   The spirit of adventure beat strong in his veins, and at length he determined upon a project which, while it should serve the purpose of the King, was also well spiced with peril.   Proceeding to Cadiz, where his uncle was Pilot-General of the Spanish marine, Champlain obtained command of one of the ships in Don Francisco Colombo's fleet, bound for the West Indies.   On this voyage he was absent from France more than two years, visiting not only the West Indies, but also Mexico and Central America.

On his return, these travels gave him an unusual importance at the French court; and when, in 1603, the aged De Chastes, Governor of Dieppe, decided to seal his pious life with an enterprise for the King and for the Church, the adventurous Champlain became the instrument of his purpose.

De Chastes' two small vessels set sail from Honfleur, one commanded by Pontgravé, the other by Champlain.   The voyage was long but uneventful.

Pontgravé's former trading-post at Tadousac had been abandoned, and they held their lonely way up the St. Lawrence, past the mantling rock of Stadaconé, on to the wooded heights of Hochelaga. Cartier's Indian village of sixty-eight years before had disappeared — undoubtedly swept from existence by the relentless Iroquois.   At this point, however,

The old boy looks surprised

CHAMPLAIN

the foaming St. Louis rapids barred their way, and the caravels were turned homeward.   With wind and current down the river, and out through the Gulf, in due season they came safely to Havre de Grace.

In their absence the Sieur de Chastes had died; but De Monts, another courtier at the Louvre, succeeded to the patent for colonising in the New World.   Exploration was not to rest, and Champlain and the Baron de Poutrincourt accompanied the new

Deputy in his Acadian expedition of 1604. Once more the Atlantic was crossed. Passing Cap la Hêve the explorers sought a suitable site for their colony along this coast, and when they reached the beautiful basin of Annapolis, hemmed in by a circle of wooded hills, the artistic Poutrincourt was charmed, and forthwith obtained from De Monts a private grant of the surrounding country. He established his demesne here, naming the place Port Royal, while Champlain and De Monts, continuing their way around the Bay of Fundy, came at length to the bleak island of St. Croix, where they founded their colony.

There is no need to present fully the vicissitudes of the tiny settlement. Scurvy and the rigours of the first winter carried off thirty-five colonists out of a total of seventy-nine. The winter of 1606–1607 was happily much less severe; moreover, Champlain's " Ordre de Bon-Temps," and Lescarbot's wit and gaiety contributed to cheer the shivering exiles. In the spring, however, the first ship from St. Malo brought bad news from France. The enemies of De Monts at home had triumphed, and had persuaded the King to cancel the charter of the Deputy. In a way this contretemps led to the founding of Quebec.

Although De Monts was no longer Lieutenant-General of Acadia, he was yet unwilling to give up the scheme which appealed so strongly to his

adventurous nature.   On his return to Paris, his
influence had been sufficient to secure for one year
a monopoly of the new fur trade.   Champlain,
cherishing the memory of the voyage of the
previous year, persuaded him that the valley of the
St. Lawrence would serve his purpose better even
than Acadia, and between them they planned an
expedition in which profit and adventure were evenly
mingled.   Two ships were fitted out — the one
commanded by Champlain, the other by the elder
Pontgravé.   The latter was to revive the old trading-
station of Tadousac, while Champlain was to establish,
further inland, a fortified post from which expeditions
might set forth to find the hoped-for passage to
Cathay.

Pontgravé sailed from Honfleur on the 5th of
April, 1608, Champlain following on the 13th of
the same month.   His was the first ship to carry a
permanent colony to New France.   Crossing the
wide gulf by Anticosti, the little vessel of Champlain
stopped at Tadousac to do a timely service for his
colleague who was now further up the river.   The
stately grandeur of the scene was not new to
Champlain.   Five years before he had glided past
the yawning cañon through which the dark Saguenay
rushed down from the north ; he had gazed upon the
blue sky-line of the Laurentian mountains ; in the
caravel of De Chastes the surging tide had carried

him past the Isle of Bacchus and the milky cataract
of Montmorency.

Anon the channel narrows; on the left are the
Heights of Levi, and on the right a frowning cliff
shoulders far into the stream. Here ancient Stadaconé stood; but the Iroquois passed over it long
since, and the village is gone. On this spot
Champlain decided to establish his post, and what site
could be more suitable than that found by the Breton
mariners as they rounded the point of Orleans?
They had entered a beautiful harbour where an
armada might safely ride at anchor. On their left
the Heights of Levi formed the southern boundary of
the glistening basin; on their right, a tiny river
murmured through the lowlands; and beyond it a
rugged promontory thrust into the current a tower
of rock, commanding the narrow channel into which
the mighty St. Lawrence was here compressed. The
solitude of a forest wilderness now hung over the
site of Stadaconé. On the narrow wooded strand
at the base of this rocky eyrie, Champlain made a
landing.

Trees were felled, and in the clearing the log
foundations of " L'Habitation " were laid. Ere the
summer ended it was completed; and a sketch from
Champlain's own unskilled pencil has preserved its
grotesque likeness. First of all there was a moat,
then a staunch wall of logs, with loopholes for

MONTMORENCY FALLS

musketry, and, inside, three buildings and a court-
yard. Over all rose a dove-cot, quaintly mediæval,
and prettily symbolical of Champlain's peaceful
invasion. But Indians were Indians, and two or
three small cannon were accordingly mounted on
salient platforms on the river-side. A large storehouse
was also built inside the palisade; and presently
Champlain laid out a flower garden.

In preparing against foes without, however, Champlain had taken no thought for foes within. Not
all of the little company had the same enthusiasm as
their leader, and a plot was set on foot to destroy
him, and sell Quebec to the Spaniards and the
Basques. Fortunately the fidelity of his pilot saved
Champlain from assassination. Warning reached
him in time, and he dealt fearlessly and rigorously
with the mutinous crew. The four ringleaders were
decoyed on board a pinnace from Tadousac, and
seized and put in irons. The body of the chief
conspirator swung next morning from the cross-
trees, and his three companions were sent back to
the galleys of France. A free pardon for the minor
malcontents secured their loyalty from that time
forward.

In September, Pontgravé set sail for France, and
Champlain and his twenty-eight companions made
ready for the winter. Frost and snow came early
that year, and a devastating scurvy invaded the

Habitation. The improvident Montagnais huddled in their birch tepees about the fort, raving for food, and perishing with disease; while of the twenty-eight Frenchmen there were only eight despairing survivors to greet the returning spring. On the 5th of June, however, Pontgravé's ship again arrived at Quebec, to the joy of Champlain and his stricken companions.

Summer warmed their enthusiasm anew, and the dauntless explorer now thought only of pressing on westward to Cathay. To further this project, he consented to ally himself with the Hurons and Algonquins in an attack upon the Iroquois, and for several days their dusky allies swarmed in and around Quebec. At length, towards the end of June, the war-party set out. Champlain embarked in a shallop with eleven men, armed with arquebuse and match-lock, sword and breast-plate; and the painted, shrilling foresters swarmed up the river in their bark canoes. From the St. Lawrence they passed into the Iroquois River.[1]

After destroying one of the Mohawk towns, the victorious raiders returned to Quebec. Champlain, " the man with the iron breast," had cemented his alliance with the northern tribes, and from this time forth Quebec became the great emporium for the fur trade of the continent.

In 1613 Champlain's enthusiasm was kindled by

[1] Now the Richelieu.

the tale of one Nicolas de Vignau, who claimed to have traced the Ottawa to its source in a great lake, which also emptied itself through a northern river into an unknown sea. Champlain set off with Vignau and three others to establish this new route to Cathay. In two birch canoes they proceeded up the St. Lawrence and into the rushing Ottawa. Portaging around the seething Chaudière, they came at length to Allumette Island. Here the old Algonquin chief, Tessouat, received them ; but he presently convinced Champlain that there was no such northern route as he looked to find. Whereupon Vignau confessed his imposture, and Champlain generously let him go unpunished.

Meanwhile, De Monts had wearied of his New World enterprise, and to secure the interests of his colony Champlain was constrained to make annual voyages to France. In 1612 he found a protector in the Comte de Soissons, who appointed the discoverer his deputy in New France. Soissons, however, died in the same year; but fortunately the Prince of Condé, by whom he was succeeded, was also well-disposed, and retained Champlain as his lieutenant.

Up to this time Quebec had realised only an elementary form of colonisation. The entire population numbered less than fifty persons, and the city consisted of the fortified post at the foot of the cliff, with a few cabins clustering about the log palisades.

But on his visit to France in 1615, Champlain took
a step forward in his policy.   Hitherto the dwellers
at Quebec had been transients.   They came not to
take up residence, but to trade, intending to return
again to France as soon as possible.   The fear of a
death unshriven likewise contributed to tentative
settlement ; and to meet the latter want, Champlain
resolved to establish a church in his colony.   Four
Récollet friars — Franciscans of the Strict Observance — were easily persuaded to return with him to
Quebec.   Burning with holy zeal, they confessed
their sins, received absolution, and embarked at
Honfleur on the 24th of April, 1615.   A month later
they arrived at Tadousac, and sailed on to Quebec.
Every new arrival increased the surprise of the
bewildered Indians, who gazed with suspicion upon
the four mendicant friars, in their coarse, gray
soutanes girt at the waist with the knotted cord
of St. Francis of Assisi, and wearing peaked *capotes*
and thick wooden sandals.

   The site of the first church in New France was
selected without delay.   It stood on the strand near
the Cul-de-sac, a little distance from the Habitation.
Its construction was simple and speedy, and before
the end of June the half-hundred citizens of Quebec
knelt upon the bare ground and reverently listened
to the first Mass ever said in Canada.   The guns of
the ship in the harbour, and the cannon on the ram-

parts, boomed forth in honour of the event.   That day the priesthood began its long *régime*.   The colonial policy of New France had now been definitely shaped.   Henceforth this new Power would stride into the wilderness with the crucifix in one hand and the sword in the other — for God and for the King;

BONNE STE. ANNE (OLD CHURCH)

by baptism, binding the heathen to the faith, and by co-operation with the native tribes against the Iroquois, making Quebec the heart and soul of the vast Indian country, whose boundaries no one knew, and whose wealth none could divine.

In pursuance of this policy, Father Dolbeau, with much suffering, accompanied the roving Montagnais to their northern hunting-grounds.   Their wander-

ings were so wide that, before he returned, the priest
had encountered the Esquimaux of Labrador. Meanwhile, Père Joseph made his way to the Sault St.
Louis, where a mighty concourse of savages was
assembled ; and when the war-conference was ended
he went back with the Hurons to their villages.
Champlain and Étienne Brulé, the most daring bush-
man in New France, followed him thither by way of
the Ottawa, Lake Nipissing, French River, and the
Georgian Bay.   Thus Lake Huron was discovered.
Then, from Cahiagué, the Huron capital, set out the
memorable war-party of 1615, which came near to
altering the fate of the Colony.   Up the Severn,
across Lake Simcoe, thence by portage route to the
valley of the Trent, they arrived at Lake Ontario.
Crossing to the south shore, they hid their canoes in
the forest and were soon in Iroquois territory ; but
when they came within sight of the Onondaga town,
Champlain was no longer able to control his naked
allies, and in spite of his precautions they rushed the
palisade, only to be beaten back and scattered.   The
muskets of the twelve Frenchmen alone saved a
rout, Champlain himself being wounded ; and with
much chagrin the dispersed Hurons made their way
back to Lake Ontario.   They refused even to escort
their wounded leader to Quebec as they had promised, and he was obliged to spend the winter in the
lodge of one of the chiefs.   He hunted and fished

with the Hurons, and in one of these expeditions he was lost in the forest for several days, being only saved by that wonderful resource which marked his character. When the spring came again Champlain set off for Quebec, guided by his kind host Durantal. He reached the fort in July, after an absence of a year, and the inhabitants, who had long since believed him dead, assembled in the Récollet church for a special thanksgiving service — nor without good reason, for upon the inveterate ruler and leader depended the destiny of France in America.

The condition of the little colony had not improved during the absence of the governing and inspiring spirit. From the force of circumstances, it did not at once improve upon Champlain's return. These first settlers of Quebec, whose food and living were easily got, and with no ambition to work or trade, idled their time away. Gambling and drinking were their common diversions, the more reckless spirits taking to the woods and adopting the savage life of the hunting tribes. These became the famous *coureurs de bois*, the picturesque vagrants who were destined in the succeeding years to constitute so serious a "problem" in the administration of New France. At first Champlain could do little more than hold his colony together. Intelligent as his purposes were, he received no help from the Court of France or from the Viceroy De Monts,

D

though the importance of the enterprise of colonisation was set before Europe with every circumstance
of national pride and no detail of responsibility.

A painful evidence of the slight importance which
the Louvre attached to New France is furnished by
the frequent and easy changes in its patronage to
which reference has already been made. On the
imprisonment of Condé, the young Duc de Montmorency purchased for a song the Lieutenancy of
New France, and he in turn sold it to his nephew,
Henri Lévis, the Duc de Ventadour. All except
De Ventadour had been moved by the lust of gain;
in his case, however, the motive was religious — to
win the infidels of the New World to the faith of the
Old. The Jesuits were his chosen instruments; and
accordingly, in the summer of 1625, Charles Lalement, Enemond Masse, and Jean de Brébeuf,
landed at Quebec. No guns boomed a welcome to
the disciples of Loyola. No salvos of artillery hailed
their arrival. Their reception was even distressing.
In the temporary absence of Champlain, the Calvin-
ist Émery de Caen was in charge of the fort, and in
the violence of his heresy refused them shelter. The
inhabitants, likewise, declined to admit the newcomers to their homes. In despair at such treatment
the three Jesuits were on the point of returning to
France, when the hospitable Récollets invited them
to the convent at Notre Dame des Anges. In Sep-

tember the Jesuits made a clearing on the opposite
side of the St. Charles, and here they began to build
a convent of their own.   Thus had the forty-three
French exiles, who now made the permanent population of Quebec, a sufficiency of both Récollets and
Jesuits for their spiritual guidance.   Lalement soon
became the keeper of Champlain's conscience, and
from this time forward the Jesuits were to have
their way in New France.

In 1627 Richelieu's policy of absolutism was extended also to the New World.   Revoking the
charter of De Caen the Huguenot merchant, he organised the Company of One Hundred Associates,
of which he was himself the head.   In return for
sovereign powers and a perpetual monopoly of the
fur trade, this society was to people New France
with artisans and colonists, whom they were pledged
to provide with cleared lands for agriculture and to
maintain.   Huguenots, moreover, were to be for
ever excluded from the colony.

For a time the new company took an honest view
of its obligations — but only for a time.   Within a
year or so, Quebec was again on the verge of starvation; and in the spring of 1629 the famished inhabitants were eagerly awaiting the Company's ships
from France.   By July their patience was almost
worn out, when at last the watchers at Cap Tourmente brought the news that a fleet of six vessels

had reached Tadousac. Quebec could scarcely await their arrival, and the more eager inhabitants prepared to meet the ships down the river. But suddenly two Indian canoes swung round the point of Orleans. These made hot haste for the rock, and breathlessly announced that the fleet in the river was a hostile English squadron, and that a fishing village had already been pillaged and destroyed. Joy now became consternation. Unknown to the distant colony, war between France and England had been declared.

Quebec was not left long in suspense, for next day the messengers of the English admiral, Sir David Kirke, himself a Huguenot refugee, arrived with a demand for surrender. The heart of the valiant Champlain was wrung. He had inspected his empty magazine and the rickety fort which the improvidence of the Company had allowed to fall into ruin. But even the weakness of his starved and paltry garrison did not affect his fortitude. Kirke's envoy was courteously dismissed, with the bold assurance that Quebec would defend itself to the last man. Champlain still clung to the hope that supplies would arrive from France; and even as he uttered his bold defiance, De Roquemont's convoy and fleet of transports had entered the Gulf of St. Lawrence. Quebec strained eager eyes for the succouring sail. Night and day the tiny garrison stood to the guns, resolving to spend their remaining fifty pounds of gunpowder with equal fervour in welcome of friend or foe.

But weeks wore into months, and misery and de-spair proportionately increased. Here were nearly a hundred persons huddled in a decayed fortress in the wilderness, with seven ounces of pounded pease for a daily ration. By and by this supply also failed, and the starving inhabitants were driven into the wood in search of acorns and roots. Then came the news, which Champlain had long been dreading, that De Roquemont's fleet had fallen into the hands of Sir David Kirke. The last hope of saving Quebec was now brushed away. But the English fleet did not yet summon the garrison to surrender, and in-stead of making immediate assault, Kirke continued to blockade the River and the Gulf.

Another winter dragged by, and spring came again. The people continued to starve, ever hoping that the enemy would raise the siege. This hope was not to be fulfilled. On the 19th of July three English ships sailed up the river, and with the apathy of despair the gallant Champlain and his sixteen famished soldiers watched them anchor in the basin. The bitter end was come.

Next day, the 20th of July, 1629, the English flag floated, for the first time, over the fortress of Quebec. " There was not in the sayde forte at the tyme of the rendition of the same, to this examinate's knowledge, any victuals, save only one tubb of bitter roots" — such is the evidence of one of Kirke's captains. This, in brief, is the story of the first of the five sieges of Quebec.

When Lewis Kirke, the Admiral's brother, took possession of the city in the name of King Charles, he treated his captives with high courtesy. The French inhabitants were given the option of remaining in peaceful possession of their homes, or being transported back to France. Louis Hébert, the chemist, and his relatives the Couillards, the only two families of colonists in the strict sense of the word, elected to remain on their small holdings. Champlain and the Jesuits, choosing to return to France, embarked in the ship of Thomas Kirke, who was sailing down the river to join his brother's fleet at Tadousac. When they were opposite Mal Baie, about twenty-five leagues below Quebec, a strange sail bore in sight. She proved to be a French ship which had stolen past Tadousac with succours for Quebec. The *George* immediately gave chase, a sharp fight ensued, but in the end the Frenchman struck his flag, and the new prize was borne down the river.

Sir David Kirke now continued homeward with his prisoners. They reached Plymouth in October, and from here the devoted and patriotic Champlain went to London to urge the French ambassador to seek the restitution of Quebec. Its capture had

actually occurred after the declaration of peace, and
on that ground was held invalid. Champlain pleaded
well and in the end prevailed. It was not, however,
until 1632 that the fortress was restored to France
by the Treaty of St. Germain-en-Laye; and it is
probable that the mercenary Charles held such a
concession cheap when weighed in the scale with
four hundred thousand golden crowns, the promised dowry of Henrietta Maria.

During the three years of English occupation
Quebec had made no progress. The Indians had
found in the newcomers a spirit in rough contrast
with the forbearance and good-fellowship of the
French. Disliking the brusqueness of the new
rulers, the Algonquins now shunned the city. Even
the fort had been burned to the ground, and the
Hébert homestead alone made a sweet oasis in a
desert of neglect and dilapidation.

Such was the condition of the settlement in the
summer of 1632, when Émery de Caen again sailed
into the harbour. He had come to take over
possession from the English. Despite his old
antipathy, his fierce Calvinism, he now brought
with him — in some sense the price of his commission — the Jesuits Père de Noué and Père le
Jeune; and joyfully the exiled French gathered at
the house of honest Hébert to hear Mass after the
lapse of three years.

It is not clear why the Huguenot De Caen was chosen to retake possession of Quebec. The expedition was fitted out at his own expense; and for recompense, a monopoly of the fur trade was granted him for one year. At the end of that time the Company of One Hundred Associates was to resume the privileges of its charter. Thus it happened that, in 1633, Champlain was reappointed Governor of New France by the astute Richelieu.

With three vessels Champlain set sail on the 23rd of March, and two months later he look over the command of Quebec from De Caen. The next two years passed placidly for the city. The Indians rejoiced to have " the man with the iron breast " back in their lodges, and the harbour swarmed once more with friendly canoes. Meanwhile, trade increased with the Indians, and the settlement became a genuine commercial colony. On one occasion as many as seven hundred Hurons flocked to Quebec with their hunting trophies, and at length every midsummer came to be marked by an Indian Fair. Père le Jeune's *Relation* gives a quaint description of one of the annual visits of the tribes. On the 24th of July, 1633, the harbour was dotted with fur-laden canoes from the Ottawa and from Lake Huron. Landing at the Cul-de-sac, the dusky braves took possession of the strand below the rock, where they hastily set up their portable huts of birch-bark. "Some," says

the Jesuit chronicler, " had come only to gamble or
to steal; others out of mere curiosity; while the
wiser and more businesslike among them had come
to barter their furs and sacks of tobacco leaves."
The second day of the visitation was marked by a
solemn conclave of the chiefs and the officers of
Fort St. Louis — a smoking pow-wow for the exchange of compliments and wampum.

The courtyard of the fort witnessed this garish
function. The chiefs and principal men of each
village grouped themselves together. Some were
garbed in beaver skins, others in the shaggy hide of
the bear. Still others were guiltless of apparel, and
all bore themselves with an excessive dignity bordering on burlesque. Brébeuf, Daniel, and Davost stood
by in their sable vestments; and in the midst of all
was Champlain surrounded by the soldiers of his
garrison. The next two days were given up to trade
— a beaver-skin exchanging for a tin kettle, a bright
cloth, or a string of beads. On the fifth day a huge
feast was given, by means of which savage appetites
forced the French to disgorge a moiety of their
profit. But before another dawn the Indians had
vanished, and Quebec smiled to see its storehouses
full of furs.

By this time the little settlement had more than
ever taken on the appearance of a mission. The
Récollets had virtually been excluded from New

France, the influence of the Jesuits having permeated
even the official atmosphere of Fort St. Louis. It
has been claimed that, in his younger years, Champlain was a Huguenot. It is more likely he was a
Catholic of a liberal type; and certainly in his last
years a Jesuit became his spiritual adviser. Both
the soldier and the merchant gave way to the priestly
influence in the purposes of Government. The
cross was to precede the sword of empire on the
march into the wilderness.

In the midst of peace and progress a heavy loss
was now to befall Quebec. Champlain, beyond sixty-
eight years of age, lay prostrate in the fort. His
last illness had come upon him, and on Christmas
Day, 1635, the father of New France passed away.
Soldiers, priests, and settlers sorrowfully followed his
remains to the little church on the cliff, Notre Dame
de la Recouvrance, which Champlain himself had
founded in honour of the restitution of the city, and
where he had renewed so often his faith and hope
and courage.

A great spirit had crossed the bourne. The whole
history of Canada has no fairer pages than those
which deal with the deeds of the founder of Quebec.
His was a character great and unselfish, often mistaken, but always high-minded and just; not free from
the credulity that characterised his generation, but
with a spirit of romantic endurance which leaves the

New World still his debtor ; with a love of high em-
prise unsullied by lust of gain or by cruelty or vain-
glory.   Like Moses, he went forth into a land of
promise ; and, like Moses, the place of his sepulchre
is not known.   It is, however, recorded that his remains were placed *" dans un sépulcre particulier."*
During the administration of Montmagny a small
chapel adjoining Notre Dame de la Recouvrance came
to be known as " Champlain's Chapel," and for a long
time this was believed to mark the founder's tomb.
But in 1856 an excavation at the foot of Breakneck
Stairs revealed a curious vault containing human
bones ; and later investigation has led to the belief
that the last resting-place of Champlain was a rocky
niche part way down Mountain Hill, in full view of
the strand upon which his early Habitation was built.

CHAPTER III

THE Indians with whom the French explorers first came in contact were of the Algonquin family. Under different tribal names this race spread itself over the Atlantic seaboard from Carolina to Hudson's Bay, and farther west than the Great Lakes. In the comparatively small area now forming northern New York lived the Iroquois, or Five Nation Indians, who, like the Helvetii of old, outstripped all the other tribes in valour, and at the time of the arrival of the Europeans were engaged in reducing their Algonquin foes to subjection. The Hurons, who figure so prominently in early Canadian annals, were of Iroquois stock; but owing to their situation in the Georgian Bay peninsula, and their alliance with the neighbouring Algonquins, they became the especial object of Iroquois enmity, and the feud went on till they were exterminated.

The story of this conflict so closely concerns the history of Quebec, that the period intervening

between the death of Champlain and the establishment of Royal Government has been described as the
Heroic Age of New France. Indeed, on looking back
over the trials of that period, it seems incredible
that the colony was able to weather the storms of
Iroquois savagery by which it was swept. But this
dark misery was so clearly the outcome of French
colonial policy, that a reference to the underlying
principles of that system is necessary.

The French idea of colonisation was propagandism.
True, it was not actually born of that deep principle,
but rather of high adventure and of the alluring
mystery of discovery. Religion, however, very soon
became its prevailing impulse. The expedition of Verrazzano had its *raison d'être* in nothing higher than
the cupidity of Francis I., who was dazzled by legends
of Mexican gold and Peruvian silver; but religion
inspired Cartier to his great adventure ten years later.

The Old World was in the throes of the Reforma-
tion. With shafts of heresy, Luther in Germany
and Calvin in France were assailing the Catholic
Church, and devout Catholics like Cabot had conceived the idea of requiting the Church for her losses
in the Old World by religious conquests in the New.
Roberval's voyage had been likewise undertaken for
discovery, settlement, and the conversion of the
Indians. The aged De Chastes, the patron of
Champlain, had been animated almost entirely by a

religious motive, and the explorer's own frequent declaration was that "the salvation of a single soul is worth more than an empire."

Such sentiments alone were enough to explain the friendship of Champlain with the Hurons and Algonquins, on whose lands he had settled his colony, and to whom the French owed something at least in the way of assistance or protection. But apart from sense of a religious obligation, he was forced to depend on the Indians to guide him through the country he wished to explore, and their goodwill was also necessary to develop the fur trade for the great companies. It was natural, therefore, that Champlain should enter into alliance with the neighbouring tribes, whose amity meant so much to the struggling settlement. But New France was destined to reap bitter fruits from this seeding.

The offensive and defensive bond against the Iroquois almost cost the colony its existence. It was, in fact, another Hundred Years' War with a foe as implacable as death itself. The constant aim of the French was to organise and harmonise the tribes against their common enemy, and to establish a league of which Quebec would be the heart and head. All this was in direct contrast with the English system, which took no account whatever of the Indian tribes. The English colonists in Connecticut, New Hampshire, and Virginia displaced the Indian; the

French made him part of their system. New France was a trading colony, New England an agricultural colony. The French, with few exceptions, did not go to the New World to make a home, but to secure fortunes; the English colonists went to the New World to settle; they bore with them their household gods.

For a hundred years or more, New France was dependent on Old France for provisions; and even up to the death of Champlain, there were, in fact, only two plots of ground under cultivation by French settlers — that of Louis Hébert in Upper Town, and the small farm of the Récollets on the St. Charles. In New England, the settlers first of all cleared the land, laid out their farms, and stored their provisions against the winter season. They traded with the Indians and acquired wealth, and for their greater convenience they made purchases in the Old World. | Thus, from the first days almost, the New England Colonies were self-contained, while New France depended on Europe to a degree amazing and pathetic. This fact strikes the keynote of the French *régime*, explaining, as it does, most of the trials and tribulations of New France in its perennial warfare with the Iroquois, and in the later friction with New England.

Nor is it astonishing that New France never became self-reliant. From first to last her natural growth was throttled, either by the greed of the fur companies or by the mistaken paternalism of the Bourbons. The Company of One Hundred Associates, which Richelieu founded in 1624, was no improvement on the previous administrations of New France, in spite of its elaborate charter and the fact that Richelieu himself was at the head of it. The fur companies were doubly politic in discouraging agriculture, for the purchase of peltries thus became practically the sole industry of the colony, while at the same time the people were left dependent upon the stores of the company for food. The colonisation of New England was intensive, the colonisation of New France extensive; New England cleared and built as occasion demanded; New France merely established bases from which to penetrate the wilderness. Before the death of Champlain, the white crosses which her pioneers were wont to set up were to be found as far west as Lake Huron, and before the close of the seventeenth century they dotted the trackless forests from Michillimackinac to New Orleans. It is not surprising, then, that the Indians became an important factor in the history of Canada.

M. de Montmagny, Champlain's successor, arrived in the spring of 1636. He was a Knight of Malta, a brave soldier, and a religious fanatic. During the twelve years of his administration, Quebec was almost constantly defending itself against

Philip de Champagne.   Freeman.

Cardinal de Richelieu

from the Versailles Gallery

the Iroquois. Redoubled efforts to convert the
Indians also mark this period. The first of these
efforts was the pious project of M. de Sillery, a
Knight of Malta. De Sillery had wearied of the gay
court of Fontainebleau, and in 1637 he supplied
the means whereby the Jesuit Le Jeune established
a hostel for converted Algonquins. The site chosen
was a few miles up the river from Quebec; and
although Iroquois hostility soon made havoc of the
mission, the spot is known to this day as Sillery
Cove.

In the same year, 1637, the Jesuits began a
wooden structure in the rear of the fort, resolving
to devote the six thousand crowns donated by
the Marquis de Gamache, to the founding of a
school for Indian children, and a college for French
boys. Father Daniel brought down the first pupil
from the Huron country, when he returned to
Quebec, and the interpreter Nicollet skilfully induced
several other Indian families to send hostages to the
Jesuit seminary. But the untamed savage drank
shyly at the fountain of learning, and Father Le
Jeune relates of the dusky scholars that one ran
away, two ate themselves to death, a fourth was
kidnapped by his affectionate parent, and three others
stole a canoe, loaded it to the gunwale with such
commodities and food as they could lay hands upon,
and escaped up the river. The indefatigable Jesuits,

E

however, were not to be discouraged, and they still wrote with delight of their savage province. Their ardent *Relations* were sent regularly to France, and the hearts of princesses in the Faubourg St. Germain, and of nuns in the convents of Montmartre were alike fired with zeal for the Canadian mission.

"Is there no charitable and virtuous lady," pleaded Le Jeune, "who will come to this country to gather up the blood of Christ by teaching His word to the little Indian girls?" Thirteen nuns in a single convent straightway vowed their lives to the far-off mission; but the touching appeal of the Jesuit father sank deepest of all in the heart of the fever-stricken Madame de la Peltrie.

A review of the early life of Madame de la Peltrie makes it easy to understand how her mind was readily inflamed by the tearful *Relations des Jesuits.* As a child religious ecstasy had possessed her ardent mind; and her father, a gentleman of Normandy, was continually striving against her inclinations for the cloister. Twice he carried her back from a convent whither she had fled, and by a series of devices at length contrived a happy marriage for her. At twenty-two she was left a widow and childless, and once more the fervour of her early years consumed her. She resolved afresh to be a nun. Her father entreated and, under threat of disinheritance, commanded her to marry again. Meanwhile,

what was being done in Canada came to her knowledge, and increased her ardour tenfold. A Jesuit,
of whom she sought counsel in her dilemma, suggested
a casuistical compromise. Through him a formal

MARIE DE L'INCARNATION

marriage was arranged, and the death of her father
soon afterwards left herself and her revenues free for
pious enterprise in New France.

Repairing to the Ursuline Convent at Tours,
Madame de la Peltrie made choice of three nuns to
share with her the bliss of founding a convent at

Quebec. The most remarkable of these was the devout Marie de l'Incarnation. At this time the latter was forty years of age, tall, stately, and forceful in appearance, and with a history as romantic as that of Madame de la Peltrie herself. At seventeen she had made an unhappy marriage. Two years later her husband died, and left her with an infant son. She gave the child into the charge of her sister, and devoted herself to solitude and religious meditation. Visions, ecstasies, rapture, and dejection took alternate possession of her mind. Fastings and the severest forms of discipline henceforward made up the melancholy routine of the life of the " holy widow." Love for her child for a long time kept her from taking the veil, but at length, by prayer and fasting, she emancipated herself from this maternal weakness of the flesh, and was rapturously received by the Ursulines of Tours. Yet in spite of the vagaries of her devout mind, Madame de l'Incarnation possessed a singular aptness for practical affairs. Several of her early years had been spent in the house of her brother-in-law, where she had displayed an amazing talent for the ordinary business of life. A knowledge of this trait had doubtless led the Jesuits to press her appointment as Superior of the new Ursuline Convent which Madame de la Peltrie proposed establishing at Quebec. Meanwhile, the Duchesse d'Aiguillon, Richelieu's niece, had also been moved by the pleadings from

Quebec, and she determined to found a Hôtel-Dieu. Three nuns of the Hospital were entrusted with this project.

The ship bearing Madame de la Peltrie, the three Ursulines, and the three Hospitalières set sail from Dieppe early in May, 1639. The excitement and activity of the outer world must have contrasted strangely with the peacefulness of their quiet cloisters; yet the frail nuns were buoyed up by a marvellous enthusiasm and a noble faith. This faith, however, was destined to be sorely tried. Winds and waves beset them on the way, icebergs struck terror into their spirits, and it was not till the middle of July that the leaking ship came to anchor in the harbour of Tadousac. Thence they proceeded in small boats up the river; and on the 1st of August the welcoming cannon of Fort St. Louis boomed forth, and Quebec was *en fête* in honour of so notable an arrival.

Pending the erection of a suitable building at Quebec, the nuns of the Hospital established themselves at the mission palisade of Sillery, and the Ursulines began their work in the small wooden structure on the river's brink below the rock. An outbreak of smallpox among the Indians soon overcrowded their wretched tenement, and infected savages came thither only to die. Worn out with labour, the indefatigable nuns continued bravely to contend with the disease and suffering around them, and the monuments of their high endurance and beautiful devotion are to be found to-day in the ivy-clad cloisters in Garden Street, where the gentle Ursulines still minister to the maidens of French Canada; and in the pretentious hospital on Palace Hill where nuns still care tenderly for the sick and dying, and read the inspiring history of their order back to 1639.

About the middle of the seventeenth century a stranger in Quebec would have been surprised to find that the city lacked nothing so much as people. Reversing the natural law of supply and demand, it built churches before it had worshippers, schools before it had scholars, and hospitals before it had patients. The purpose was to attract settlement by preparing beforehand for the wants of colonists. These early establishments have, however, justified themselves by a continuous and permanent history, and Quebec is now, as it was nearly three centuries ago, a city of churches and convents. The bells rang then, as now, from morning till night, Gregorian chants streamed out through convent windows, and the black-robed priest was the soul of all.

Montmagny rebuilt in stone the fort on the precipice, and spared nothing to give the place a formidable appearance. For safety the church and presbytery of the Jesuits stood close to the parapet.

The Ursulines, with less caution, began to build their tiny convent in the neighbouring woods. The first Hôtel-Dieu was rising on the cliff overlooking the valley of the St. Charles, and not far away was the new farm of Louis Hébert, the chemist — all together making a picture of progress. Champlain's first

URSULINE NUNS OF QUEBEC (SALLE D'ÉTUDE, NOVICIAT)

Habitation had fallen to ruin, but a few wooden tenements still remained to mark the earliest settlement in Lower Town, and the Church of the Récollets told the tale of past perils and an unfailing faith. A league or so up the river was the Algonquin mission of Sillery, with its clustered cabins and rude oratory, surrounded by a palisade.

Montmagny was a *dévoté* surrounded by a suite as pious as himself. Through these amenable spirits

the Jesuits were supreme not only in matters of
religion, but in matters of state. Indeed, in this
ecclesiastically governed community there was little
distinction between sacred and secular matters. The
church was the centre of affairs. A stake was planted
before the sacred edifice bearing a placard of warn-

JESUITS' COLLEGE AND CHURCH
(Latter destroyed by fire, 1807)

ing against blasphemy, drunkenness, and neglect of
the Mass. A pillory, with chain and iron collar, and
a wooden horse, stood close by — suggestive means
of religious correction.

Even the recreations of the people partook of a
religious character. The feast of St. Joseph, the
patron saint of New France, was celebrated with

pious display. On May-Day the young people of Quebec tripped about a maypole surmounted by a triple crown in honour of Jesus, Maria, and Joseph. The annual visits of the Company's ships from France, however, temporarily disturbed the calm of the monastic city. The genuflexions of drunken sailors were seldom in honour of St. Joseph; and the ribald humours of visiting mariners profaned for a season the quiet rock of Quebec.

CHÂTEAU ST. LOUIS, 1694

But throughout this missionary period the hatchet of the Iroquois was suspended over the city. Their dreaded war-cry rang all too often through the adjacent forests, and their stealthy tomahawks found victims even under the guns of Fort St. Louis. So daring became the incursions of the implacable savages that the settlers did not dare to till their lands. To pass from one post to another without a strong escort meant risk of death or capture; and capture was more dreaded than death itself. Every year had its tale of surprises and massacres.

The sleepless sentries on the ramparts, and the staunch palisades of the fort seemed insufficient protection against a foe as silent as an arrow and as swift in speeding upon its victim. At this time also the Jesuit missions among the distant Hurons were suffering unknown horrors; but the tale of their disasters is for another chapter.

Successive governors of Quebec — Montmagny, D'Ailleboust, and D'Argenson — pleaded with the home authorities to send reinforcements for their feeble garrison, by whom alone Quebec hoped to escape the ever-dreaded catastrophe. Through press of home affairs, and official neglect and indifference, these requests continued to be disregarded. Reprisals were taken against the Iroquois whenever opportunities occurred; but even these were all too rare.

In May, 1660, an Iroquois captive was brought to Quebec. A stake was erected in the *Place d'Armes*, and in the sight of the populace the Indian was burned to death. A deed of this nature, occurring with the apparent sanction of the religious governor of a civilised community, must be taken to reflect the terrible pressure of suffering which made such inhuman reprisals possible. The savage nature of this vengeance was softened to the eyes of many by the poor casuistry of the Jesuits, who gave out, and believed, that the soul of the Mohawk would go straight to Paradise on the wings of his unwelcome baptism.

This particular Indian met his fate with the wonderful fortitude of his race, but not with their stoic silence. Instead, he breathed out threatenings, and promised the fell destruction of the pale-faced interlopers. Even now, he told them, hundreds of his kinsmen were gathering upon the Ottawa and St. Lawrence for the final effacement of Quebec, and with hideous fury the baptized savage called down upon them the wrath of his gods.

Forthwith Quebec became deeply alarmed. The desultory attacks of the Iroquois were now to be exchanged for a deliberate assault in which the whole strength of the Five Nations should be thrown into the struggle. The Ursulines and nuns of the Hôtel-Dieu forsook their convents to take refuge in the fortified college of the Jesuits, whither the fugitives from the surrounding settlements also fled. A company of soldiers took up their quarters in the Ursuline Convent, the re-doubts of the fort were strengthened, and barricades were erected in the streets of Lower Town. All night long sentries paced the parapets, peering anxiously into the surrounding darkness, and straining their ears for the creeping tread in the thicket.

After several days of watching, however, no Iroquois appeared, and the inhabitants began to breathe freely again. The more courageous returned to their deserted homes and farms, but the timid still clung to the blockhouse. The panic had also spread to Ville Marie,[1] and the imminence of this danger produced one of the most brilliant exploits which Canadian history records — a feat of daring closely resembling, and not surpassed by, the achievement of Leonidas in the Pass of Thermopylæ.

The story is one of the finest in the picturesque pages of Parkman, part of whose narrative is here transcribed.

Adam Daulac, or Dollard, Sieur des Ormeaux, was a young man of good family, who had come to the colony three years before, at the age of twenty-two. He had held some military rank in France, and it was not long before he set on foot a remarkable Indian enterprise. Sixteen young men caught his spirit, struck hands with him, and pledged their word. They bound themselves by oath to accept no quarter, made their wills, confessed, and received the sacrament. After a solemn farewell, they embarked in several canoes, well supplied with arms and ammunition. Descending the St. Lawrence, they entered the mouth of the Ottawa, crossed the Lake of Two Mountains, and slowly advanced against the current of the river. A few days later they

---

[1] Now Montreal.

reached the foot of the formidable rapid called the
" Long Sault," where a tumult of waters foaming
among ledges and boulders barred their onward way.
Besides, it was needless to go farther. The Iroquois
were sure to pass the Sault, and could be fought
here as well as elsewhere.

THE URSULINES' CONVENT

Just below the rapid stood a palisade fort, the
work of an Algonquin war-party of the preceding
autumn. It was a mere enclosure of trunks of small
trees planted in a circle, and was already ruinous.
Such as it was, the Frenchmen took possession. They
made their fires and slung their kettles on the neighbouring shore. Here they were soon afterwards
joined by a small party of friendly Indians, consisting
of about forty Hurons from Quebec, under their brave

and wily chief Étienne Annahotaha, and five Algonquins led by Mituvemeg. Daulac made no objection
to their company, so they all bivouacked together.

In a day or two their scouts came in with tidings
that two Iroquois canoes were coming down the
Sault. Daulac had only time to set his men in
ambush before the advance canoes of the enemy
swept down the river. A few of the Iroquois escaped
the Frenchmen's volley, and fleeing into the forest,
they reported their mischance to their main body,
200 in number, on the river above. Thereupon
a fleet of canoes suddenly appeared, bounding down
the rapids, filled with warriors eager for revenge. The
allies had barely time to escape to their fort, leaving
their kettles still slung over the fires. The Iroquois
made a hasty attack, but being repulsed, they withdrew and fell to building a rude fort of their own
in the neighbouring forest. This gave the French
breathing-time, and they used it for strengthening
their defences. They planted a row of stakes within
their palisade, to form a double fence, and filled the
intervening space with earth and stones to the height
of a man, leaving twenty loopholes or more, at each
of which three marksmen were stationed.

Their work was still unfinished when the Iroquois
were upon them again. They had broken to pieces
the birch canoes of the French and their allies, and
kindling the bark, rushed up to pile it blazing against

the palisade; but so brisk and steady a fire met them that they recoiled, and at last gave way. Again and again, however, they came on, each time leaving many of their bravest fighters dead upon the ground. At length, their spirits dashed, the warriors drew back. A canoe was hastily sent down the river to call to their aid five hundred Iroquois who were mustered near the mouth of the Richelieu.

Meanwhile, the defenders of the fort were harassed night and day with a spattering fire and a constant menace of attack. Thus five days passed. Hunger, thirst, and want of sleep wrought fatally on the strength of the French and their allies, who, pent up together in a narrow prison, fought and prayed by turns. Deprived as they were of water, they could not swallow the crushed Indian corn which was their only food. Some of them, under cover of a brisk fire, ran down to the river and filled such small vessels as they had. But this meagre supply only tantalised their thirst, and they now dug a hole in the fort, to be rewarded at last by a little muddy water oozing through the clay.

On the fifth day an uproar of unearthly yells from seven hundred savage throats, mingled with a clattering salute of musketry, told the Frenchmen that the expected reinforcement had come. Soon a crowd of warriors mustered for the attack. Cautiously they advanced, screeching, leaping, and firing as they came on; but the French were at their posts, and every loophole darted its tongue of fire. Besides muskets, they had heavy musketoons of large calibre, which, scattering scraps of lead and iron among the throng of savages, often maimed several of them at one discharge. The Iroquois, astonished at the persistent vigour of the defence, fell back discomfited. The fire of the French had told upon them with deadly effect. Three days more wore away in a series of futile attacks; and during all this time Daulac and his men, reeling with exhaustion, fought and prayed, sure of a martyr's reward.

At length the Iroquois determined upon a grand final assault. Large and heavy shields, four or five feet high, were made by lashing together three split logs with the aid of cross-bars, and covered with these mantelets a chosen band advanced, followed by the motley throng of warriors. In spite of a brisk fire they reached the palisade, and crouching below the range of shot, hewed furiously with their hatchets to cut their way through. Daulac had crammed a large musketoon with powder, and lighting a fuse, he tried to throw it over the barrier, to burst like a grenade among the savages without; but it struck the ragged top of one of the palisades, fell back among the Frenchmen and exploded, killing and wounding several of them. In the confusion which followed, the Iroquois got possession of the loopholes, and thrusting in their guns, fired on those within. In a moment they had torn a breach in the palisade, then another and another. The brave Daulac was struck dead, but the survivors kept up the now hopeless fight. With sword, hatchet, or knife, they threw themselves against the throng of enemies, striking and stabbing with the fury of madmen, till the Iroquois, despairing of taking them alive, fired volley after volley and shot them down. All was over, and a burst of triumphant yells proclaimed the dearbought victory.

To the colony it proved salvation. The Iroquois had had fighting enough. If seventeen Frenchmen and a handful of Indian allies, behind a picket fence, could hold seven hundred warriors at bay so long, what might they expect from many such fighting behind walls of stone? For that year they thought no more of capturing Quebec and Ville Marie, but returned to their villages dejected and amazed, to howl over their losses, and nurse their dashed courage for a day of vengeance.

F

CHAPTER IV

"AD MAJOREM DEI GLORIAM"

If on its material side French colonial policy took account of the Indian, it did so much more on its religious side. Quebec was the farthest outpost of Catholicism. New France was for ever to be free from the taint of heresy, allowing none but Catholic settlers within her gates; and Huguenots, as we have seen, were specifically excluded. The Indians were to be rescued from heathen darkness and led into the sacred light of the Church. Jesuit missions thus became a salient feature in the early history of Quebec, the nerve centre of the movement being the palisaded convent on the little St. Charles.

To go back in review. On the retrocession of Quebec by the English, under the Treaty of St. Germain-en-Laye, in the time of Champlain, the influence of the Jesuits was sufficient to secure for themselves the undivided control of the Canadian mission. Returning to Quebec in 1632, Father Le

Jeune and his two companions had established themselves in the half-ruined convent of Notre Dame
des Anges, built by the Récollets sixteen years
before. The log stockade enclosed two buildings,
the smaller of which served as storehouse, stable,
and workshop, and the larger as chapel and refectory.
Four tiny cells opened off the latter, and in these the
fathers lodged, while the lay brothers and the workmen found apartments in the garret and the cellar.
The regimen of this crude establishment was severely
ascetic. The day began with early Mass and closed
with evening prayers. The intervening time was
spent by the laymen in cultivating the little clearing,
and by the fathers in hearing confessions at the fort
a mile away, or in struggling with the Algonquin
idiom, by the vague assistance of one Pierre, an
Indian proselyte, who, in weakness of flesh, ran away
when the season of Lent drew near.

The strength of the Jesuits was increased in the
spring of 1633 by the arrival of four new priests.
Of these the most remarkable was Jean de Brébeuf,
the descendant of a noble family in Normandy, and
destined to prove his own nobility by an intrepid
zeal and an almost incredible courage.

Le Jeune's distressful experiment with a band of
wandering Algonquins had convinced the Jesuits that
their schemes of mission-conquest could not bear
much fruit if they were confined to the vagrant

tribes of the north.   Farther west in the peninsula
of the great lakes lived Indians of fixed habits and
domicile, and otherwise further advanced towards civilisation than the improvident hunting tribes round
about Quebec.   Of these the most notable were the
Hurons.   As long before as 1615 the Récollet Le
Caron had gone among them, and several years later
Brébeuf had made the perilous lodges of Ihonatiria
his habitation, but had at length returned to France.
On his coming to Quebec again in the spring of
1633, Brébeuf anxiously turned his thoughts towards
his former mission, awaiting only a favourable opportunity to forsake the comparative safety of the city
of Quebec for the gloomy shores of Lake Huron
and "the greater glory of God."

Midsummer brought the annual swarm of Hurons
to the trading fair at Quebec.   For a week the all
but naked savages overran the little settlement, their
animal curiosity almost driving the French to dis-
traction, and their casual peculations causing much
annoyance.   But their presence was a necessary evil,
if the Fur Company was to declare its dividends.
Hence long-suffering courtesy became essential both
to the peace of the city and to future interests so
much at stake.

A powerful consideration with the community was
the anxiety of the Jesuits to go back with the Indians
to their villages on Lake Huron.   Champlain, when

governor, had espoused this project in the most
seductive of his speeches. " These are our fathers,"
he had announced to the sixty chiefs gathered for the
nonce in the quadrangle of the Fort. " We love
them more than we love ourselves. The whole
French nation honours them. They do not go
among you for your furs. They have left their
friends and their country to show you the way
to the happy hunting-grounds. If you love the
French, as you say you do, then love and honour
these our fathers, and care for them in your distant
villages."

But the wind bloweth where it listeth, and the
Indian mind was no more sure. Above all else it
lacked definiteness; it was touched by rhetoric.
Champlain's auditors had been thrilled with deep
emotion. They were for embarking at once with
the Jesuits. Then they had faltered, and by the
next day they had decided to depart without them.
For another year, therefore, the fathers had remained
at Notre Dame des Anges, studying the Huron
language for future use, and caring meantime for the
spiritual welfare of the half-hundred French residents
of Quebec.

The summer of 1634 once more saw the city given
over to the visiting Hurons. The old persuasive
palaver was repeated, and this time with more success.
When the trading fair was over, Brébeuf, Daniel, and

Davost set off with the savage fleet, each in a
different canoe, facing a journey of nine hundred
miles fraught with many perils, but with none so
ominous as the sullen and menacing mood of their
heathen conductors.

Week after week they pressed toilfully up the St.
Lawrence and Ottawa; barefooted they struggled
over the rocky portages, with a pittance of pounded
maize for their daily ration, and mother-earth for
their nightly couch. Davost's guide robbed and
abandoned him at an island in the Upper Ottawa.
Daniel was likewise deserted; but the giant Brébeuf
yielded to no hardships, and surpassed even the
seasoned savages in strength and endurance. On
the shore of the Georgian Bay, however, his guide at
length abandoned him. But Brébeuf had been here
in a former year, and his instinctive woodcraft guided
him twenty miles through the forest to the palisaded
village of Ihonatiria.

" Echom has come again," cried the inhabitants, as
they recognised the towering figure of the Jesuit who
had departed from them five years before; and they
opened again their lodges to the missionary.

After days of anxious waiting, Brébeuf had the
joy of seeing Daniel and Davost arrive at Ihonatiria.
The hardships and dangers they had endured, and
the indignities they had suffered from their brutal
guides, were only outweighed by their zealous delight

in reaching at length the scene of their devoted
labours.   The Hurons aided them in the construction
of a log mission-house ; and when the fathers had

MONUMENT TO THE FIRST CANADIAN MISSIONARY

decorated the interior with highly-coloured pictures
of the saints and the glittering regalia of the Church,
the red men filled it to overflowing.   A striking clock
and a magnifying glass, however, were the chief objects

of wonderment, and the credulous Indians regarded the priests as the workers of miracles. This awe and respect the fathers turned to good account, gathering the children into the mission-house for daily instruction. With a mind also to the physical welfare of their flock, they succeeded in reconstructing the palisades and fort of the Huron village.

Yet with all the outward respect in which the Jesuits were held, their doctrines made little or no impression upon the Indian mind. The adult Hurons had a superstitious fear of baptism, and shunned the sign of the cross as a spell. Under these difficulties the Jesuits laboured, saving stricken children from a dark hereafter by the furtive administration of the dreaded sacrament.

With what boldness they dared to assume, Brébeuf and his companions condemned the infernal practices of the so-called medicine-men, whose accomplishments ranged from the curing of snake-bites to the casting out of devils. To them all diseases of the body called for much the same treatment, varied only in the proportion of vehemence allowed in their incantations and at medicine-feasts. The disgraceful orgies attending these "cures" led the priests to interfere : a policy which enraged the sorcerers of the tribe, and presently put the lives of the missionaries in jeopardy.

The summer of 1635 was marked by a great

drought. The maize and beans withered in the sun; and in spite of the hoarse invocations of the medicine-men and the fierce efforts of the tribal rain-maker the sky stayed cloudless. Thereupon the Jesuits were accused. The cross upon the mission-house had frightened the bird of thunder[1] away from Ihonatiria. Such were the charges which the sorcerers brought against the Jesuits; and the super-stitious Hurons believed that they were true. How-ever, a timely vow was made to St. Joseph, the chosen protector of the Hurons, and in answer to their ardent prayers the rain fell in welcome torrents — so Brébeuf writes — and calamity was averted for a time.

Meanwhile the work of the Jesuits extended. With headquarters still at Ihonatiria, they made visits to the neighbouring villages; and for the greater success of the mission, new priests were drawn from Quebec. By 1640 those labouring among the Hu-rons and the neutral nation further south num-bered thirteen.

It is not possible within the limits of a single chapter to portray the character and follow the

---

[1] The Indian belief regarding thunder was as follows : " It is a man in the form of a turkey-cock. The sky is his palace, and he remains in it when the air is clear. When the clouds begin to grumble, he descends to the earth to gather up snakes and other objects which the Indians call *okies*. The lightning flashes wherever he opens or closes his wings. If the storm is more violent than usual, it is because his young are with him and aiding in the noise as well as they can." — *Relation des Jesuits*, 1636.

fortunes of all those heroic souls, who gave up home and country and worldly ambition to bury themselves in the unknown wilds of the West, and to walk with their lives in their hands among the cannibal tribes of

BRÉBEUF

New France. The motto which Ignatius Loyola had adopted for his order was, "Ad Majorem Dei Gloriam," and in their perilous missions its members practised absolute obedience to quasi-military discipline. To name but four, Brébeuf, Lalement, Garnier, and

Jogues were all destined to tragic deaths, and the story of their martyrdom is one of the most sorrowful in the history of the land.

The suffering caused by the pestilence of 1637 was

Gabriel Lalement Soc. Jesu

LALEMENT

much more severe than those periodical afflictions by which the Indians were visited. Virulent smallpox was a feature of the plague, and the pious offices of priests and the incantations of the medicine-men alike proved unavailing. Clearly, some black spell had been cast upon the nation. First it was ascribed to a serpent, then to a spotted frog, then to a demon in the muskets of the French. The Jesuits were accused of compassing death by magic. The striking clock, which aforetime had merely astonished them, was now an engine of calamity; and the litanies floating out through the windows of the mission-house were fatal incantations. Yet the Indians were afraid to lay hands upon these dealers in death. Awe held them back from wreaking their sinister designs upon the fearless men who went as ever into the pestilential tepees, that through the mystic drop and sign they might rescue the poor victims from an eternity of woe.

At length it became clear to the Jesuits that fear alone would not much longer stay the hatchets of the now hopeless Hurons. Daily they expected to meet a violent death, and a letter, still extant, drawn up by five priests in the form of a last testament, shows the unfaltering fortitude of men whose dearest ambition was a martyr's death. The intervention of a squaw saved Du Peron from the tomahawk uplifted to brain him; an unseen hand delivered Ragueneau; Le Mercier and Brébeuf confounded their assailants with the courage of their demeanour; and only Chaumont suffered, being assaulted and severely wounded. Knowing, however, that their death had been finally decided upon, the Jesuits gave a *festin d'adieu* — one of those farewell feasts which Huron custom enjoined

on those about to die; and the courageous resignation
of this band of martyrs filled even the tents of the
ungodly with a superstitious awe. Once more the
annihilating blow was averted; and from this time
forward the peril threatening the Jesuit mission came
not from the Hurons themselves, but from their
implacable enemies, the Iroquois.

The year 1640 was drawing to a close when, after
a few years' respite, the terrible war-whoop of the
Five Nation Indians again rang through Canadian
woods. Quebec was continually threatened by the
Mohawks, whose highway of attack was the river
Richelieu; and the Hurons were assailed by the
Western tribe of the Iroquois confederacy. The pestilence of 1637 had ruined Ihonatiria, and for greater
security the Jesuits resolved upon a large central
establishment, in lieu of small missions in the several
Huron villages. They chose for a site the mouth of
the river Wye, which empties into Matchedash Bay.
Here, in 1639, they built the mission of Ste. Marie.
In the extreme peril of Indian warfare, the Hurons
fled thither for food and baptism; and the hunger of
three thousand neophytes and refugees soon put the
fortified mission on short rations.

Isaac Jogues and a score of Huron warriors were
despatched to Quebec for food and clothing. They
reached the city in safety, although the St. Lawrence
was closely beset by hostile Iroquois. Returning in

twelve canoes laden with necessaries for the destitute Ste. Marie, Father Jogues and his companions fell into the hands of a Mohawk war-party. Some were killed on the spot, and the others were carried up the Richelieu and across Lake Champlain to a more awful fate. First they were made to run a gauntlet of Mohawk war-clubs ; then they were placed upon a scaffold, where the women lacerated them with knives and clam-shells, and the children applied fire-brands to their naked bodies. This torture was repeated in each of the three Mohawk villages. Goupil, a lay brother, was soon afterwards murdered, and Jogues lived the life of a slave until some Dutch settlers on the Hudson effected his ransom and put him on board a ship bound for France.

In the following year, however, Jogues came back to Quebec, and on behalf of the suffering city he undertook to negotiate a peace with the Mohawks. Armed with gifts and belts of wampum, he set out fearlessly to face his former tormentors. For a short time the wampum saved him, but he was soon obliged to return to Quebec. The French, however, were determined to win the Iroquois, politically and religiously, and no danger was great enough to check them. Accordingly, in the late summer of 1646, Jogues was again despatched to the post which by this time had come to be known as the Mission of the Martyrs ; and at last, on the 18th of October, he was foully murdered in the lodge of a Mohawk chief.

In the preceding winter Anne de Nouë, a Jesuit of noble descent and frail physique, set off from Quebec to minister to the garrison at Fort Richelieu. In spite of his sixty-three years, he did not shrink from the perils of frost and snow which lay before him. On his snow-shoes and with a few days' provisions he set forth upon the path of sacrifice. A blizzard overtook him on the frozen river, he lost his way, and some days later his martyred body was discovered kneeling in the snow.

Meanwhile the dangers farther west were not decreasing. Iroquois attacks and Huron reprisals were ever threatening the Jesuit missions, and the last great blow was soon to fall. In the summer of 1648 an Iroquois war-party crept up to the gates of St. Joseph. Most of the warriors had gone to Quebec, but the palisade still contained Father Daniel and close upon a thousand women and children and old men. An early Mass had crowded the chapel, and the priest, clothed in full vestments, was exhorting the neophytes to be strong in the faith, when the dreaded war-cry rang through the village. The panic-stricken Hurons sought in vain to save themselves from stark slaughter, but Daniel met his death calmly at the door of his burning church. Seven hundred prisoners were taken, and

the retiring Iroquois left of St. Joseph only a heap
of ruins.

The destruction of the mission was, however, but
the prelude to the final extinction of the Huron nation.
Terror-stricken they awaited the blow, in spite of the
efforts of the Jesuits to rouse them to strong defence.
All winter a formidable war-party of the Mohawks
and Senecas roved through the Huron woods, and in
early spring they fell upon St. Ignace and St. Louis.
The first village was burned with no show of resistance,
and its four hundred inhabitants were either tomahawked or kept for torture. Only three escaped, and
these fled to St. Louis, about a league away. Here
Brébeuf and Lalement endeavoured to rally the
panic-stricken villagers. By sunrise the invaders
were upon them. Brought to bay, the Hurons
fought bravely. The giant Brébeuf stood in the
breach and cheered them by his hopeful courage.
Twice the Iroquois fell back, but at their third
advance drove in the shattered palisade. Those of
the Hurons who still lived were made prisoners;
the two Jesuits were bound together, and the
clustering cabins of St. Louis were given to the
flames.

Returning to the ruins of St. Ignace, the Iroquois
made preparations for the despatch of their prisoners.
Brébeuf and Lalement were stricken to the soul by
the carnival of blood ; yet their own martyrdom

was to be made the most cruel of all. Brébeuf was first bound to a stake, all the while continuing to speak words of comfort to his fellow-captives. Enraged by this behaviour, the Iroquois tore away his lower lip and thrust a hot iron into his throat. No sound or sign of pain escaped the tortured priest. Then Lalement was also led out, that each might witness the other's pangs. Strips of bark smeared with pitch enveloped the naked body of Lalement, and after making him fast to a stake they set the bark on fire. Round Brébeuf's neck a collar of red-hot hatchets was hung; and in mockery of baptism the savages poured kettles of scalding water upon the heads of both. Brébeuf was scalped, his tormentors drinking the blood, thus to endow themselves with his unflinching courage. After four hours the noblest Jesuit of all was dead; but Lalement was kept alive for seventeen hours, until a pitiful hatchet ended his voiceless misery. So died two men whose memory has ennobled the history of the land for which they laboured, and adds to the fame and honour of their race.

At Ste. Marie, Bressani, Ragueneau, and their French companions awaited the Iroquois onslaught. But the fugitive Hurons, gathering for a last resistance, had checked the Iroquois' further advance, and after a fierce battle the latter

G

withdrew southward with an army of wretched captives.

That day the Hurons as a nation ceased to exist. Abandoning their remaining villages, they dispersed in small bands to roam northward and eastward, while a few established themselves at Isle St. Joseph, thinking to protect themselves here from their inveterate foes. As for the Jesuits, Garnier and Chabanel still laboured among the Tobacco nation farther to the south; but they too became the victims of the Iroquois before this fatal year was over.

Famine and the rigours of winter presently worked sad havoc upon the little band to whom Ragueneau now ministered at Isle St. Joseph, and in the spring renewed attacks of the Iroquois led the Hurons to decide upon a remarkable enterprise. This was to migrate to Quebec and take refuge under the guns of Fort St. Louis.

On the 10th of June all was ready for the departure, the sorrowing Hurons bidding good-bye to the home of their fathers, and the Jesuits to the country consecrated by the blood of their martyrs. Proceeding by the Georgian Bay, Lake Nipissing, the Ottawa and the St. Lawrence, the fleet of canoes reached Quebec before the end of July, 1650. And while Quebec was ready to open her gates to the sorrowful remnant of a once great nation, her own

position was sorely beset. Food was scarce and
lodgings scarcer in the palisaded city. However,
the Ursulines and the nuns of the Hospital made
every effort to provide shelter for the exiled race,
and the Jesuits themselves bore the chief burden
of their converts. In the following year, 1651,
four hundred more Hurons found their way to
Quebec, and together they established a settlement
on the Island of Orleans. Here, in sight of the
protecting ramparts of the city, this decimated people
lived for a time secure. But the Iroquois were set
upon nothing less than their annihilation, and in 1656
they made a descent upon the quiet island and carried off many captives. The terrified Hurons were
then removed to the city itself and lodged in a square
enclosure almost adjoining Fort St. Louis. A map
of 1660 places the "Fort des Sauvages" on the site
of the present *Place d'Armes*. Here they dwelt for
about ten years in the same uncertain security enjoyed
by Quebec itself. Then they removed to Ste. Foye,
four miles west of the city, and again changing their
abode six years later, they founded the village of
Old Lorette.

Standing to-day on Dufferin Terrace, the observer
sees spread beneath him the picturesque Côte de
Beaupré, a graceful upland losing itself in the
Laurentian foot-hills. A shining spire in the middle
distance arrests the eye. It marks the village of

Ancient Lorette, a nine miles' drive from Quebec, where a pitiful moiety of Canada's noblest Indian tribe ekes out an existence by the making of baskets and beaded moccasins, and by that nonchalant culture of the soil which still marks the primitive man.

CHAPTER V

In the year 1660 the French population of Quebec numbered something over six hundred. The fur company continued to drive a fair trade in peltries, but the prosperity of the city itself was woefully retarded by the constant menace of the Iroquois. The Baron d'Avaugour held the office of Governor, and his strong sense of military authority brought him into conflict with the Church, by this time become the real controller of the State. This revered power was still further to impose its authority and influence through and by the person of François-Xavier Laval, the first Bishop of Canada, a man of as great ability as piety, an ecclesiastical statesman trained in the school of Mazarin. His career gives significance to a later epoch.

The fur traders had always found brandy their most attractive commodity in dealing with the thirsty savage; and Père Lalement gives a sad picture of the misery entailed. " They have brought themselves to nakedness," he writes, " and their families to beggary. They have even gone so far as to sell their children to procure the means of satisfying their raging passion. I cannot describe the evils caused by these disorders to the infant Church. My ink is not black enough to paint them in proper colours. It would require the gall of the dragon to express the bitterness we have experienced from them. It may suffice to say that we lose in one month the fruits of the toil and labour of thirty years." Accordingly, the Church now decided to prohibit it entirely, and a law was passed making it a capital offence. Two men paid the extreme penalty ; and a woman also was condemned to the scaffold. When, however, the clergy interfered to save her, the rigorous but consistent D'Avaugour declared he would punish no more breaches of this law. Brandy now flowed like water, and the thunder of the pulpit was henceforth disregarded. Exasperated by this treatment, the priests carried their grievance to the Louvre, where they received little satisfaction.

In the same year a deputy of another sort journeyed to France. Pierre Boucher's mission was to lay before the King the desperate condition of the colony, particularly in the matter of defence. Louis XIV. had but recently ascended the throne of the Bourbons, and Richelieu and Mazarin had been in turn succeeded by Colbert as the royal

adviser. The envoy from Quebec was presently
received at the Court, and the tale of suffering and
neglect which he unfolded convinced Colbert that
the Company of One Hundred Associates was
scandalously evading the obligations imposed by

COLBERT

its charter. Accordingly, in 1663, a royal edict
went forth revoking its powers and privileges. This
was a turning-point in the history of New France;
for although the company founded by Richelieu was
succeeded by an unwieldy corporation of Colbert's

design, from this time forward the Crown itself took over the control of the distant colony.

The Grand Monarch, indeed, took a finely comprehensive view of his position. He held himself in every sense the father of his people, and by a nice condescension the citizens of Quebec were included in the patriarchal fold. The far-away city on the borders of the world was no longer to be abandoned to the avaricious whims of a trading company: the King himself would now take it under his royal care. Daniel de Rémy, Sieur de Courcelles, was appointed Governor, with Jean Baptiste Talon as Intendant; and the valorous Marquis de Tracy was commissioned to New France as the King's personal representative, with instructions to settle the domestic friction of the colony, and to deal a fatal blow to the Iroquois, the " scourge of Canada."

On the 30th of June, 1665, De Tracy's caravels cast anchor in the basin of Quebec, the ships of De Courcelles and the Intendant being still at sea. The cannon of Fort St. Louis boomed a welcome down the gorge of the St. Lawrence, while the eager burghers crowded the ramparts and prepared to welcome the most distinguished company in the most brilliant pageant yet seen upon the soil of New France.

The royal pennant flew at the flag-ship's mast-head, and the decks were thronged with the brilliant uniforms of the regiment of Carignan-Salières, whom the King had sent to destroy the enemies of New France. In the midst stood the stately Marquis, gorgeous in viceregal robes and attended by a suite of nobles and gallants from the court of Fontaine-bleau. The mysteries and wonders of the West had stirred the romantic minds of the volatile courtiers, and the mission to convert New France to the Catholic faith gave to De Tracy's expedition the complexion of a mediæval crusade.

Presently the gaily-decked pinnace drew in to the landing-stage of the Cul-de-sac, where stood the notables of the New World city. Bishop Laval in pontificals, surrounded by the priests of his diocese, awaited the royal envoy at the top of Mountain Hill, which was then the only practicable highway between the Lower and the Upper Town. To-day the visitor landing at the quay reaches the terrace by the same route; but the present graceful declivity of Mountain Hill is little like the tortuous pathway of corduroy by which De Tracy and his glittering retinue made their toilsome way to the public square by the Jesuits' College. First came a company of guards in the royal livery, then four pages and six valets, and by the side of the King's Lieutenant-General, resplendent in gold lace and gay ribbons, walked the young nobles of his train. The cathedral bells pealed forth joyously, and the *Te Deum* began a day of public rejoicing.

The vessels bearing the new Governor and Intendant, however, suffered the most hapless violence. Talon's ship was 117 days at sea, and De Courcelles' was hardly more fortunate; but at length they, too, cast anchor beneath the rocky battlement, and Quebec was now flooded with soldiers of the regiment of Carignan-Salières. These bronzed veterans of Savoy came to New France fresh from the Turkish wars, and the sight of their plumed helmets and leathern bandoleers, as they marched through the narrow streets, promised the colonists a speedy riddance of their enemies. The health of Louis XIV. was nowhere in his broad dominions drunk more heartily than in Quebec.

At the close of the year extensive preparations were made for the chastisement of the Iroquois. De Courcelles had determined upon a stroke of almost foolhardy boldness: to march over the snow into the country of the Mohawks, a distance of three hundred leagues. Thick ice had formed on the St. Lawrence, and on the 9th of January the audacious Governor set off at the head of his fiery columns.

Officers and men alike shared the burdens of transport, but the soldiers of Europe were embarrassed by the unaccustomed snow-shoes which

the deep snow forced them to use. Some got
no farther than Three Rivers, but the more hardy
held their way up the valley of the Richelieu to
Lake Champlain and across the Hudson. An
unfortunate circumstance, however, had deprived
them of guides, and all efforts to find and surprise the Mohawk towns proved unsuccessful.
Wandering by mistake beyond Saratoga Lake, they
came near to the Dutch village of Corlaer,[1] where,
half-frozen and half-starved, they bivouacked in
the neighbouring woods. A few days later envoys
appeared from Albany to demand why the French
had invaded the territories of the Duke of York;
and then, for the first time, De Courcelles learned that
the New Netherlands had passed into English hands.

De Courcelles' explanation was courteously accepted, and having been supplied with provisions,
he prepared to retrace his steps to Quebec. His
intended victims, the Mohawks, harassed the retreat,
killing and taking prisoners; while sixty of his men
perished from hunger and exposure before he came
in sight of the St. Lawrence, and many more fell
before he reached Quebec.

In spite of apparent failure, however, this expedition, like that undertaken by Daulac, had a good
effect upon the Iroquois, who had come to regard
themselves as too remote for French assault.

[1] Now Schenectady.

They now sent embassies to Quebec seeking a treaty of peace, an idea to which, naturally, the French were not opposed. But the occasion was too much for Iroquois malice and lust of blood; for even whilst terms were under discussion, a band of French hunters was set upon by the Mohawks. The Marquis de Tracy, now thoroughly aroused to the sufferings of his countrymen, determined to strike a sudden and crushing blow. The Iroquois deputies, still in Quebec praying for peace, were seized and imprisoned, and a formidable force once more prepared to invade the country of the Five Nations.

It was in early October, 1666, that De Tracy and De Courcelles left Quebec at the head of thirteen hundred men. Of these, six hundred were regulars of Carignan-Salières, an equal number were irregulars from Quebec, under command of Répentigny, and a hundred Indian scouts from the missions ranged the woods. A hundred rugged colonists, commanded by the brave Charles le Moyne, joined the advancing column at Montreal. With confidence this imposing force swept on to annihilate the enemies of New France.

At the mysterious sound of the French drum-beat the Mohawks of the first village fled in terror, and the invaders pressed on to the second, third, and fourth towns, to find them also deserted.

At Andaraqué, their largest village, the Mohawks prepared to make a final stand; but the first appearance of the French army and the roll of their " devil-drums " as they emerged from the forest put the savages to instant flight.   Andaraqué, the last native stronghold, being thus abandoned, with its stores of corn and winter supplies, the French took what provisions they needed for their return journey, set fire to the town, and having planted on the site a white cross in the name of the King, they turned their faces homeward.   The remaining Indian villages were given to the flames, and although the Mohawks had escaped with their lives, the French were content to leave them to the severities of coming winter.

This policy was successful, for by the time spring came again, not only the Mohawks, but their four confederate nations, were anxious to make a sincere peace with the avenging soldiers of New France. Hostages were exchanged, several representative chiefs remaining in Quebec.   The Jesuits again undertook the Mission of the Martyrs, desiring both to win the savages into the fold of the Church and at the same time to wean the Iroquois from their friendliness towards the colonies of England, with whom the French were soon to enter into deadly conflict for the mastery of the North American continent.

The Marquis de Tracy, having in due time fulfilled

the King's commission, embarked for France, and with him departed the glittering *entourage* which for almost two years had cast upon the court of Quebec some reflection of the glories of Versailles. The regiment of Carignan-Salières was disbanded, but its officers, for the most part, elected to remain in Canada and accept the gift of seigneuries which the King distributed on conditions of fealty and homage. The soldiers settled on the fiefs as *censitaires*, and became the retainers of the seigneurs. The feudal system, with all its antique forms, was thus imported into French Canada, further to cripple her progress in the race with the English colonies, where the individual was allowed to develop freely, evolving his own laws, and creating conditions best suited to his new estate. Talon became the royal instrument of a system which had its beginning and end in the maintenance of kingly authority.

CHAPTER VI

THE NOBLESSE AND THE PEOPLE

THE Canadian seigneur held his lands of the King, and the *habitants*, or cultivators of the soil, held theirs of the seigneur upon the performance of specific duties and the payment of *cens et rente*. These tributes varied curiously in kind and amount; and on St. Martin's Day, when the *censitaires* commonly liquidated the obligations of their tenure, the seigneurie presented an animated scene. Here were gathered all the tenants, bearing wheat, eggs, and live capons to pay for their long narrow farms, at a rate ranging from four to sixteen francs.

The annual delivery of his handful of *sous* and his bundle of produce did not, however, complete the obligations of the *censitaire*. Throughout the year he must grind his grain at the seigneur's mill, paying one bushel in every fourteen for the service, bake his bread in the seigneur's oven, work for him one or two days in the year, and forfeit one fish in every eleven to the lord of the manor. Military

95

service, however, was no part of the *habitant's* duty as a tenant; for the judicious Colbert, jealous always for the power of the monarchy, had clipped this ancient feature from Canadian feudalism, and given absolute military control of the country to the Governor at Quebec. The seigneur's judicial powers varied according to the importance of his fief. Barons were empowered to erect gallows and pillories, but the ordinary judicial powers of a Canadian seigneur were confined to Middle and Low justice, which comprehended only minor offences.

The solicitous interest of Louis XIV. in the affairs of New France promised much for the country's prosperity; and every ship sailing to the St. Lawrence carried out a fresh batch of emigrants. For all of these the King paid out of his own pocket, and it cost him a pretty penny to respond to Intendant Talon's persistent appeals for more settlers. Agencies were established at several points in France to recruit colonists, and grants of money and land were held out as inducements to new settlers. In this way the King and Colbert managed to send out about three hundred men each year. But, as might be expected of emigration state-aided and scarcely voluntary, Quebec became a city of men chiefly, there being few women besides cloistered nuns. There had always been a demand for wives, but now that the soldiers and officers of the Carignan-Salières had elected to remain in the country, the scarcity of women induced a matrimonial famine.

Talon speedily apprised Colbert of the situation, and the most comely inmates of the refuge hospitals of Paris and Lyons were summoned to fill this void. In 1665 one hundred of the " King's girls " arrived in Quebec, almost instantly to be provided with partners ; and although the supply was doubled in the following year, it yet remained below the conjugal demand.

To supply the needs of the seigneurs also became a real problem. Talon, with grim humour, demanded a consignment of young ladies ; and in 1667 he was able to announce as follows : " They send us eighty-four girls from Dieppe and twenty-five from Rochelle ; among them are fifteen or twenty of pretty good birth ; several of them are really *demoiselles*, and tolerably well brought up." Amusing evidence, however, of the exceeding delicacy of such a market is found in a letter, in which the match-making Intendant alludes to the supply of the year 1670. " It is not expedient," he ungallantly writes to Colbert, " to send more *demoiselles*. I have had this year fifteen of them instead of the four I asked for."

La Hontan, writing a few years later, cannot refrain from exercising keen but slanderous wit at the expense of these fair cargoes from Quebec so gladly received. His description, albeit scandalous,

H

is amusing : " After the regiment of Carrigan was disbanded, ships were sent out freighted with girls of indifferent virtue, under the direction of a few pious old duennas, who divided them into three classes. These vestals were, so to speak, piled one on the other in three different halls, where the bridegrooms chose their brides as a butcher chooses his sheep out of the midst of the flock. There was wherewith to content the most fantastical in these three harems ; for here were to be seen the tall and the short, the blond and the brown, the plump and the lean ; everybody, in short, found a shoe to fit him. At the end of a fortnight not one was left. I am told that the plumpest were taken first, because it was thought that, being less active, they were more likely to keep at home, and that they could resist the winter cold better. Those who wanted a wife applied to the directresses, to whom they were obliged to make known their possessions and means of livelihood before taking from one of the three classes the girl whom they found most to their liking. The marriage was concluded forthwith, with the help of a priest and notary, and the next day the Governor caused the couple to be presented with an ox, a cow, a pair of swine, a pair of fowls, two barrels of salted meat, and eleven crowns in money."

On their part the girls were permitted to reject any suitor who displeased them ; and at these annual marriage fairs the contest for favour was keen on both sides. But the paternalism of the Grand Monarch went even farther than the mere enlistment of wives for the colonists. Bounties were offered on early marriages; and the maid who married before she was sixteen received the " King's gift " of twenty livres, in addition to her ordinary dowry. Bachelors who refused to marry were rendered as uncomfortable as possible, and were taxed for their abstinence or timidity. Children were likewise made a good asset, and blessed was the man whose house was full of them. Thus runs an edict of the time: " . . . In future all inhabitants of the said country of Canada who shall have living children to the number of ten, born in lawful wedlock, not being priests, maids, or nuns, shall each be paid out of the moneys sent by His Majesty to the said country a pension of three hundred livres a year, and those who shall have twelve children, a pension of four hundred livres, and that, to this effect, they shall be required to declare the number of their children every year in the months of June and July to the Intendant of justice, police, and finance, established in the said country, who, having verified the same, shall order the payment of said pensions, one-half in cash, and the other half at the end of each year."

It was not by accident but by design that an aristocratic class was created in French Canada. The perpetual contrast between the English and the French systems of colonisation was but the difference between natural evolution and artificial construction. The Canadian aristocracy was a consistent detail of the latter and in keeping with Louis' ambitious scheme of personal government. The caste system grafted upon the stem of the colonial plant was a picturesque adornment to the life of Quebec, but a doubtful experiment from any other point of view, as time proved.

For the most part the Canadian *noblesse* were either officers of the disbanded Carignan-Salières regiment, or *gentilhommes* who had come to the New World in search of adventure or gain. In both cases they were unsuited to the hard and restrictive conditions of a rugged country. The soldiers steadfastly refused to beat their swords into ploughshares or their spears into pruning-hooks, and most of them accepted a state not far removed from actual want, rather than stain their martial hands with manual labour. The leisured class thus became the starving class, and the King's annual subsidies alone kept these families from destitution. Many of them were also in receipt of the bounties granted to large families — an ineffective resource, inasmuch as hungry children but consumed the supply and renewed the demand. Disdaining work of any sort, the Canadian *gentilhomme* yet gave himself airs that were in amusing contrast to his shabby

coat and empty stomach.   The world, he held, owed
him a living without the labour of his hands, and to
him "the world" was Louis the perpetual almsgiver.

The official correspondence of the period describes
in some detail the pangs of these ill-conditioned
gentry.   "Two days ago," writes the Governor of
Quebec in 1686, "Monsieur de Saint-Ours, a
gentleman of Dauphiny, came to me to ask leave to
go back to France in search of bread.   He says that
he will put his ten children in charge of any one who
will give them a living, and that he himself will go
into the army again.   His wife and he are in despair;
and yet they do what they can.   I have seen two of
his girls reaping grain and holding the plough.
Other families are in the same condition.   They
come to me with tears in their eyes.   All our married
officers are beggars; and I entreat you to send them
aid.   There is need that the King should provide
support for their children, or else they will be tempted
to go over to the English."

Nor was this impecunious *noblesse* merely a passive
burden to New France, for the dignified hardships of
their estate soon bred active conditions equally distressing to those in authority.   Having no induce-
ment to remain peacefully at home, the sons of
the seigneurs took to the woods, often enticing
the more unsettled of their own *habitants* to follow
them thither to a life of unbridled freedom and

outlawry.   Reckless bushrangers, they carried on an illicit trade with the Indians, diverting peltries from the fur company at Quebec, and demoralising the savage proselytes of the missions. In this unfortunate way the *gentilhomme* and his children compromised with labour and managed to keep body and soul together.

Harsh edict and cruel ordinance were repeatedly launched against the practices of these well-bred offenders, but the ready covert of the forest made the evasion of the King's justice an easy matter. Moreover, the Church, while it suffered much from such children, did not venture to reprove too strongly their flagrant excesses, lest they should thenceforth dispense altogether with her sacraments ; for a furtive life in the wild woods did not prevent the superstitious *coureurs de bois* from occasionally coming to confession or to Mass.

A royal edict ordered that any person going into the woods without a license should be whipped and branded for the first offence, and sent for life to the galleys for the second ; while a third offence was punishable by death. The whole criminal code of Quebec was, indeed, of a piece with this ; and an obvious feature was the quasi-religious character of most of the offences. The edict against blasphemy read as follows: " . . . All persons convicted of profane swearing or blaspheming the name of God,

the most Holy Virgin, His Mother, or the Saints,
shall be condemned for the first offence to a pecuniary
fine according to their possessions and the great-
ness and enormity of the oath and blasphemy;
and if those thus punished repeat the said oaths, then
for the second, third, and fourth time they shall be
condemned to a double, triple, and quadruple fine;

OLD BISHOP'S PALACE (AT THE TOP OF MOUNTAIN HILL)

and for the fifth time they shall be set in the pillory
on Sunday or other festival days, there to remain
from eight in the morning till one in the afternoon,
exposed to all sorts of opprobrium and abuse, and
be condemned besides to a heavy fine; and for the
sixth time they shall be led to the pillory, and there
have the upper lip cut with a hot iron; and for the
seventh time they shall be led to the pillory and

have the lower lip cut; and if, by reason of obstinacy and inveterate bad habit, they continue after all these punishments to utter the said oaths and blasphemies, it is our will and command that they have the tongue completely cut out, so that thereafter they cannot utter them again." [1]

A citizen who had the temerity to eat meat during Lent without priestly permission was condemned to be tied three hours to the public stake, then led to the door of the church, there on his knees to ask pardon of God and the King. For approving of the execution of Charles I. by his English subjects, one Paul Dupuy was held to have libelled the monarchy and to have encouraged sedition. He was condemned to be dragged from prison by the public executioner, led in his shirt, with a rope about his neck and a torch in his hand, to the gate of the fort, there to beg pardon of the King; thence down Mountain Hill to the pillory of Lower Town to be branded on the cheek with a fleur-de-lis, and set in the stocks. Poor Dupuy's crime was not yet expiated, for, according to the remainder of the sentence, he was to be "led back to prison and put in irons till the information against him shall be completed." [2] Convicts and felons were sometimes tortured before being strangled. The execution usually took place

---

[1] *Edit du Roy contre les Jureurs et Blasphémateurs*, 1666.
[2] *Jugements et Délibérations du Conseil Supérieur.*

at *Buttes-à-Neveu*, a little hillock on the Plains of
Abraham, — afterwards to become more justly celebrated and less notorious, — and the dead body,
enclosed in an iron cage, was left hanging for months
at the top of Cape Diamond, a terror to children and
a gruesome warning to evildoers.

NEW PALACE GATE

The people of Quebec were regularly apprised of
the laws under which they lived.   On Sundays after
Mass the ordinances of the Intendant were read at
the doors of the churches.   These related to any
number of subjects — regulations of inns and markets, poaching, sale of brandy, pew-rents, stray hogs,
mad dogs, tithes, domestic servants, quarrelling in

church, fast driving, the careful observance of feast days, and so on.

Law-breakers were tried by the Superior Council, which met for that purpose every Monday morning in the ante-chamber of the Governor's apartment at Fort St. Louis. The Governor himself presided at the Round Table, the bar of justice; on his right sat the bishop, and on his left the Intendant, the councillors sitting in order of appointment. Such at least was the *venue* until about 1684, when the old brewery which Talon had built in Lower Town on the bank of the river St. Charles was transformed into a *Palais de Justice*. The altered structure served also as a residence for the King's judicial proxy, and was commonly known as the Palace of the Intendant.[1] It was an imposing mixture of timber and masonry, and at the close of the seventeenth century was the most considerable building in Quebec. While lacking the glorious site of the Castle of St. Louis, in point of interior decoration it far eclipsed this château of the Governor.

The present dilapidated tenements clustering about the foot of Palace Hill can, of course, give no idea of the natural position of the ancient *Palais de l'Intendant*. La Potherie, who visited Quebec in 1698, and Charlevoix, who writes in 1720, describe this district as the most beautiful in the city. Instead

---

[1] The declivity above its site is still known as Palace Hill.

INTENDANT'S PALACE

of the crowded quays of to-day there was a terraced lawn bordered with flower gardens; and where now the winches creak and rattle, and the railway engines hiss and scream, birds sang among willow-trees, and the Angelus echoed through a quiet woodland. Across the St. Charles lay the well-ordered grounds of the Jesuit monastery, and farther to the west the lonely spire of the General Hospital peeped through the ancient trees.

Such were the pleasing *environs* of the block of buildings which went by the name of *Le Palais*. In form it was almost a square, each side measuring about one hundred and twenty feet. An arched gateway, facing the sheer cliff, led into a large court-yard in which were situated the entrances to the Intendant's residence, the Court of Justice, the King's stores, and the prison. Soon it was also to be the site of *La Friponne*, the scene of the ribald revels of Bigot.

CHAPTER VII

FRONTENAC AND LA SALLE

THE picturesque figure of Count Frontenac now
enters upon the stage of Canadian history. Broken
in health, De Courcelles had asked to be recalled;
and ominous signs of Iroquois hostility showed the
need of a strong man for the dangerous post of
governor. This strong man was Frontenac, whose
courageous and vigorous administration in a period
of *Sturm und Drang* has induced Goldwin Smith to
call him "the Clive of Quebec."

Born in 1620, of ancient Basque family, he was
the son of a distinguished member of the household
of Louis XIII., the King himself being the child's
godfather. Frontenac's youthful passion was to be
a soldier, and at the early age of fifteen he went
to the war in Holland to serve under the Prince
of Orange. Within the next few years he took a
distinguished part in the sieges of Hesdin, Arras,
Aire, Callioure, and Perpignan. At twenty-three
he commanded a Norman regiment in the Italian

R.S.

CANADA
and the
NORTH AMERICA
1680-178?

English Mile
0   50   100   200   300

L. Winnipeg

L. Nipigon

Lake of
the Woods

C A N A

Lake Superior

L. Nippissing

R. Ottawa

Ft. Michillimachinac

Georgian Bay

Lake Huron

R. Trent

R. Wisconsin

Green B.

Fox R.

Simcoe

Ft. Front

R. Mississippi

Lake Michigan

Ft. Niagara

L. Ontario

R.
Oswe

L. St. Clair

L. Erie

LeBoeuf

I R O Q U O I S

Ft. Miami

Ft. Venango

Ft. Crévecoeur

R. Illinois

PENNSYLVAN

Missouri R.

Ft. Duquesne

Ft. Necessity

Ft. Cumberland

R. Ohio

Monongahela

MARY

Wabash R.

R. Ohio

Alleghany Mountains

VIRGINIA

L O U I S I A N A

Williamsburg

Arkansas R.

NORTH CAROLINA

35°

SOUTH
CAROLINA

R. Mississippi

G E O R G I A

Florida

New Orleans

Gulf   of   Mexico

90°   85°   80°   Longitude Wes

50°   45°   40°   35°   30°

S

70°   65°   60°   50°

Str. of Belle Isle
50°

Anticosti

R. St. Lawrence
guenay   R. St. Lawrence

Gulf of
St. Lawrence   Newfoundland

Cabot Strait   Miquelon
St. Pierre

I. of St. John
(Pr. Edward I.)   Ile Royale
(C. Breton I.)   45°

R. St. John   Louisbourg

Port Royal   Halifax
(Annapolis)   Chebucto Harb.
B. of Fundy   C. La Hève

Casco B.
Salmon Falls
R. Merrimac
Boston
Nantasket

N

WOLFE'S
CAMP

Montmorency

MONTCALM'S CAMP
Beauport   R. Montmorency

HARDY'S
CAMP

R. St. Charles   VAUDREUIL

FRENCH LINES   R. St. Lawrence
40°

General
Hospital

MONCKTON'S
CAMP

Lorette

Quebec

BATTLE OF
SEPT. 13. 1759

St. Foye.

Anse du Foulon
(Wolfe's Cove)

The Environs of
QUEBEC
1759.

Sillery

English Miles

Cap
Rouge   0 1 2 3 4 5 6 7

35°

LOUISBOURG
to show the sieges of 1744 & 1758.

Scale

0   ¼   ½   ¾   1 Mile

N

GRAND BATTERY

Louisbourg Harbour

Lighthouse Pt.

GRIFFIN'S BASTION

ISLAND BATTERY

Louisbourg

WOLFE'S
LANDING
PLACE   30°

Freshwater
Cove

Gabarus   Bay

70°   65°   60°

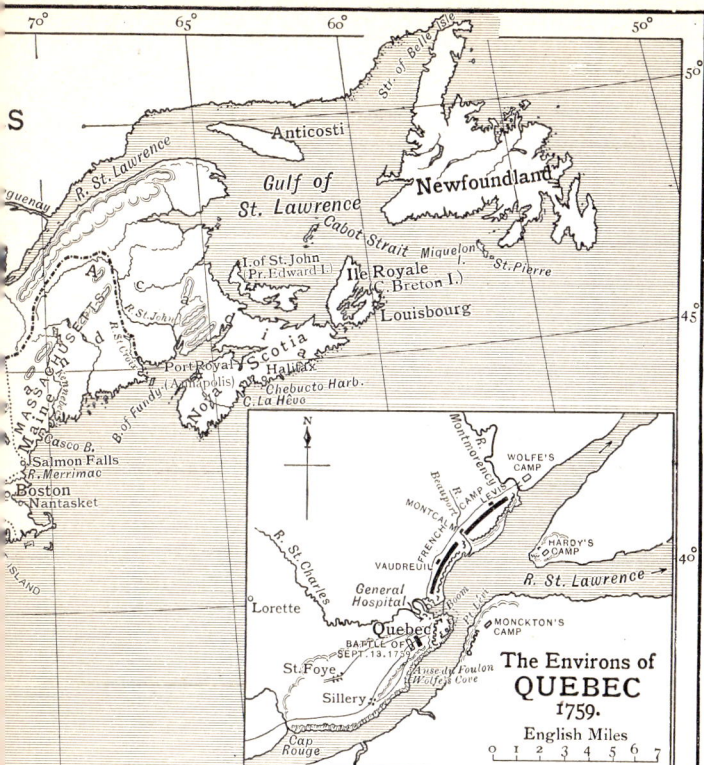

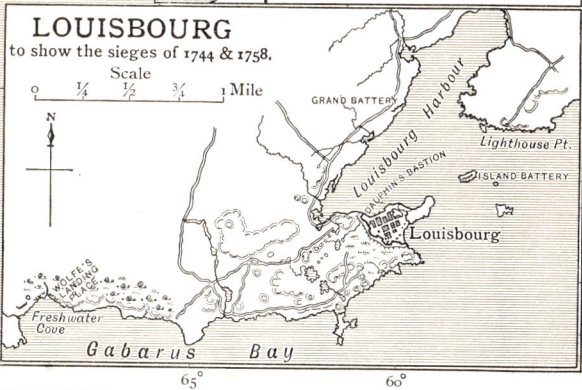

Walker & Cockerell sc.

wars, and at twenty-six he was raised to the rank of Maréchal de Camp. This was wonderful progress in the profession of war, even in an age when war was the sport of kings and soldiers fought for the mere love of fighting. Frontenac at least was one of these devotees, and when, in 1669, a Venetian embassy came to France to beg for a general to aid them against the Turks in Candia, the great Turenne selected him for this honourable duty.

Returning from the campaign in Candia with increased honour and distinction, Frontenac was appointed Governor of New France in 1672. The text of the royal commission indicates the extent of the activities which Frontenac had crowded into a life of fifty-two years, giving him his full title as: "*Louis de Buade, Comte de Palluau et Frontenac, Seigneur de l'Isle Savary, Mestre de camp du régiment de Normandie, Maréchal de camp dans les armées du Roy, et Gouverneur et Lieutenant-Général en Canada, Acadia, Isle Terreneuve, et autre pays de la France septentrionale. . . .*"

There appear, however, to have been reasons other than his eminence which led to the New World appointment of Frontenac. Far back, in 1646, he had contracted an unfortunate marriage. The dashing brigadier-general of twenty-eight had won the immature affections of Anne de la Grange-Trianon, a maid of sixteen. Her father's opposition

to the match made it necessary for the lovers to re-
sort surreptitiously to the little Church of St. Pierre
aux Bœufs, which had the privilege of uniting
couples without the consent of their parents.   But
Frontenac and his bride were ill-mated.   Both were
possessed of imperious tempers and wayward minds.
For a time they held together, then suddenly they
separated — Frontenac to find a soothing excitement
in the clash of arms, and the precocious Comtesse
to divert herself in the brilliant *salons* of Mademoiselle de Montpensier, the grand-daughter of Henry
of Navarre.

The memoirs of the Duc de Saint-Simon allude
with a humorous sympathy to Frontenac's appointment: " He was a man of excellent parts " — writes
this garrulous chronicler — " living much in society,
and completely ruined.   He found it hard to bear
the imperious temper of his wife ; and he was given
the government of Canada to deliver him from
her, and afford him some means of living."   A
more scandalous report of the motive which sent
Frontenac to Quebec is to be found in a whimsical ditty which gained quiet currency in the
Louvre —

> " Je suis ravi que le roi, notre sire,
> Aime la Montespan;
> Moi, Frontenac, je me creve de rire,
> Sachant ce qui lui pend ;

FRONTENAC

Et je dirai, sans être des plus bestes,
      Tu n'as que mon reste,
                  Roi,
      Tu n'as que mon reste.''

Be these things as they may, Frontenac came on
the scene of his new dominion with the evident purpose of devoting himself to its best interests.
The city turned out in its best finery to welcome
the new Governor ; but to the lifelong courtier, bred
in the household of royalty itself, this display appeared primitive and garish.   As he recalled the
usual brilliance of even the provincial courts of
France, the rude and rugged walls of Castle St.
Louis loomed before his critical eye in depressing
contrast.   And yet in his reception spectacular
features were not entirely wanting.   The Hurons
from ancient Lorette flocked to the city to greet their
new white chief; the *coureurs de bois* in bold
effrontery came to take the measure of their new
antagonist; the sombre Jesuits with much misgiving
hailed the arrival of so virile an executive ; and the
soldiers of the garrison acclaimed the gallant bearer
of such prowess with salvos of artillery and a *feu de
joie.*

Once duly installed, Frontenac could see no reason
why even the wilderness-colony of New France should
forgo the rightful forms and functions of a royal
province.   His mind wandered back regretfully to

the old days of the Estates General, which the kings
of France were carefully burying in the cemetery of
disuse.   Technically they still existed, although the
makers of absolute monarchy gave them no place in
the machinery of government.   Loving pomp and
circumstance, Frontenac conceived the idea of re-
producing the Estates General in New France.

The Jesuits were more than ready to constitute
the order of the clergy, the small groups of *gentilhommes* made eager nobles, while the Quebec *bour-
geoisie*, although they had never played the part
before, called themselves the *Tiers État*, and meekly
awaited the further pleasure of the commanding
Frontenac.

By and by all was ready, and heralds posted at
the door of the Jesuits' church, which had been gor-
geously decorated for the occasion, sounded the
assembly.   Frontenac, brilliantly apparelled, took
his place upon the dais ; the gallant *noblesse*, in various
attire, grouped themselves protectingly about his
person ; the sable Jesuits looked critically on ; while
the Third Estate hung breathlessly upon the gracious
motions of his Excellency.   A sunbeam from Versailles had fallen upon the rock in the wilderness, and
Quebec once more basked in the splendour of a
royal province.

One person of eminence, however, looked askance
at the assembled " States."   The Intendant Talon

too well knew the temper of the King to play with this fire so like to kindle his wrath. A disciple of Colbert, he knew that all constitutional or traditional forms standing in the path of absolutism were doomed to destruction.

As for Frontenac, he went his own unheeding way until a letter came from Colbert in this

OLD ST. LOUIS GATE

strain : " Your assembling of the inhabitants to take the oath of fidelity, and your division of them into three estates, may have had a good effect for the moment; but it is well for you to observe that you are always to follow, in the government of Canada, the forms in use here ; and since our kings have long regarded it as good for their service not to convoke the States General of the kingdom, in order, perhaps, to abolish insensibly this ancient usage, you, on your part, should very rarely, or to speak more correctly, never, give a corporate form to the inhabitants of Canada. You should even, as the colony strengthens, suppress gradually the office of the syndic who presents petitions in the name of the inhabitants; for it is well that each should speak for himself, and no one for all."

Thus at one fell swoop perished the only chance which ever came to French Canada of growing into a self-governing colony and of working out its own destiny. The physical conditions and administrative necessities of the land were, indeed, from first to last, misapprehended by its distant rulers.

For a time Frontenac nursed the chagrin natural to a proud and haughty nature thwarted in its purposes. Straightway he fell foul of Talon, and the latter withdrew to France. It was natural also that he should quarrel with the Jesuits and the Bishop, for where there was any question of mastery, he was always ready to contend. As an instance, the Bishop had pronounced the sale of brandy to the Indians a sin; and in view of the fact that the traffic was licensed under royal authority, Frontenac with his accustomed vehemence pronounced the prohibition seditious. He accused the Jesuits of keeping the Indians in perpetual wardship, and of thinking more of beaver-skins than of souls.

The next conflict was with a foeman well worthy

of his steel. An officer named Perrot had been appointed Governor of Montreal through the influence of Talon, his uncle by marriage; and as it was a matter of common knowledge that Perrot was the patron and shared the profits of the *coureurs de bois*, the enmity of Frontenac was roused against him, gaining vigour from the fact that Perrot carried his head too high. Bizard, another officer, was despatched with three guardsmen to Montreal, to arrest one Lieutenant Carion, who had assisted certain notable *coureurs de bois* in their escape from justice; and Perrot, frenzied by this trespass upon his own domain, seized the Governor's officers. On hearing of such a reprisal, Frontenac's wrath was kindled sevenfold. He knew, however, that Perrot was only to be apprehended by strategy, and accordingly a letter was despatched, inviting him to come to Quebec to explain the affair. Perrot, already alarmed at his own boldness in resisting vice-regal authority, obediently set out for the court of Frontenac, attended by a Sulpitian priest, the Abbé Salignac de Fénelon.

High words marked the interview of Frontenac and Perrot, and as a result the latter found himself a prisoner in Château St. Louis. In due time he was brought before the sovereign council and convicted of obstructing the King's justice. He was confined for almost a year, and then, as the priests

also joined in protest against the autocratic gover-
nance of Frontenac, it was judged prudent to refer the
matter to the King. Perrot was accordingly taken
from prison and shipped to France for a new
trial. The result, however, was the vindication of
Frontenac, both Louis and Colbert being determined to uphold the royal authority. Perrot was
sentenced to three weeks in the Bastile, after which
he tendered submission to Frontenac, and was again
commissioned Governor of Montreal.

Henceforth friendship took the place of enmity,
and the two governors now conspired to patronise
the *coureurs de bois*. These were halcyon days
for the picturesque banditti, whose periodical visits
disturbed the wonted calm of the saintly city. The
inhabitants shut themselves up in their houses while
these bacchanals ran riot in the streets, bedecked in
French and Indian finery, and making hideous both
day and night with their ribald *chansons*. Yet even
these roystering forest rovers were destined to bear a
part in building up French empire in the West.

The *coureurs de bois* were in fact the most
intrepid explorers of New France, and their rovings
were turned to account under the tactful guidance
of Talon. Talon's aim was to occupy the interior
of the continent, control the rivers which watered it,
and hold this vast forest domain for France against
all other nations ; and for this Imperial work he

enrolled the daring Jesuit priests and the adventurous fur-traders.   His chief reliance, however, was upon those Frenchmen whose civilised *ennui* had driven them to the restless life of the woods.

In the pursuit of this "forward" policy, the Jesuits had already established missions on Manatoulin Island, at Sault Ste. Marie, at Michillimackinac, at La Pointe on the western end of Lake Superior, and at Green Bay near the foot of Lake Michigan.   These remote posts were visited from time to time by Indians from the far west, who brought news of a great river flowing southwards.   Talon's enthusiasm for enterprise in the unknown west was doubled by the report, and he forthwith despatched an expedition under the leadership of Joliet and Père Marquette to take possession of the Father of Waters.

Louis Joliet was a native French Canadian, born at Quebec in 1645.   His exceptional brilliancy while a student at the Jesuits' College attracted the attention of Talon ; but at the age of seventeen, the forest proved more alluring than the priesthood, and he became an adventurous fur-trader.   His companion, the Père Marquette, was a fearless Jesuit, who in 1670 had undertaken a mission at the western end of Lake Superior.   The destruction of this post, however, sent him back to Michillimackinac, where he was working when ordered westward with Joliet.

Leaving St. Ignace in the middle of May, 1673,

the two voyageurs proceeded to the head of Lake Michigan, ascended the Fox River, portaged to the Wisconsin, and on the 17th of June reached the Mississippi. They descended this broad and rapid stream as far as the mouth of the Arkansas. It now seemed clear that the great river emptied, not into the Vermilion Sea[1] as was currently conjectured, but into the Gulf of Mexico ; and fearing to fall into the hands of the Spaniards, the explorers decided to re-trace their steps. They reached Green Bay before the end of September, and here the Jesuit remained to recruit his failing strength, while Joliet kept on his way to Quebec. Nine years were to pass by be-fore the navigation of the Mississippi, thus begun, was to be completed by the greatest of all Canadian adventurers.

Robert Cavelier, Sieur de la Salle, was born at Rouen, of a family of wealthy merchants, on the 2nd of November, 1643. As a child he was sent to a Jesuits' school ; and although, like Joliet, he soon abandoned all idea of entering the priesthood, he nevertheless retained a pious enthusiasm which gave a mediæval colouring to the stirring romance of his after-life. With a small allowance from his family, La Salle embarked for Canada in 1666. Through his brother, a priest of St. Sulpice, he was granted a feudal fief at Lachine, and under his

[1] Gulf of California.

resolute occupation the hitherto dangerous seigneury became a strong bulwark for the trembling settlement of Montreal. Young, gallant, and winning, La Salle drew the Indians about him by his dashing courage and by the magnetism of his person ; and, whether

ROBERT CAVELIER DE LA SALLE

through weakness of flesh or strength of spirit, he disappeared among them and withdrew from civilisation for the space of three years, a term which he employed in achieving mastery of Indian dialects and gaining knowledge of their character. On his return to Quebec in 1673, he found favour in the eyes of Frontenac, and an inexplicable sympathy united the proud veteran of a hundred fights and the debonair *coureur de bois*, beneath whose dreamy countenance the Governor read reckless valour and invincible determination.

In 1677 La Salle was despatched to France to procure royal authority for following up the explorations of Joliet and Marquette.   He also applied for a patent of nobility ; and as this request was strongly supported by Frontenac, he was made seigneur over a large tract of land, including the fort of Cataraqui,[1] and was empowered to build and occupy other forts in furtherance of exploration.   The opening sentences of this instrument show the King's anxiety to extend his vast dominions in the New World : " Louis, by the grace of God, King of France and Navarre, to our dear and well-beloved Robert Cavelier, Sieur de la Salle, greeting.   We have received with favour the very humble petition made us in your name, to permit you to labour at the discovery of the western parts of New France ; and we have the more willingly entertained this proposal since we have nothing more at heart than the exploration of this country, through which, to all appearances, a way may be found to Mexico. . . ."

To La Salle the commission was full of promise, for his ardent mind was filled with bold designs.   He foresaw a time when French enterprise, leaving the rugged civilisation on the banks of the St. Lawrence,

---

[1] Later called Fort Frontenac, and the site of the present city of Kingston.

would seize upon the rich valley of the Mississippi; a
fortified post at the mouth of the Father of Waters
would hold the interior of the continent against the
Spaniards; and the peltries and buffalo hides of the
great West would fill his forts with gold. With
Henri de Tonty, La Motte de Lussière, Father
Hennepin, and thirty men, La Salle hastened to
Quebec in the summer of 1678, and without loss
of time he organised his first expedition to the
distant Mississippi.

The story of that enterprise is a tale of disaster
which has few parallels in history. A perilous passage over Lake Ontario in a ten-ton vessel brought
them to Niagara. Above the falls they built *The
Griffin*, a schooner of forty-five tons, to carry the
necessities of the Mississippi settlement westward
by way of the Great Lakes. This vessel was lost by
some obscure calamity, and the conjecture is that she
foundered in Lake Michigan. La Salle now found
himself at the head of a mutinous company stranded
at Fort Crèvecœur on the Illinois, facing a winter
with practically no provisions. Six of his men
deserted, and on two occasions treachery all but
deprived him of his life.

In the circumstances La Salle saw only one possible course before him : to return to Fort Frontenac
for fresh supplies and material for further progress.
Leaving Tonty his trusted lieutenant in charge of

Fort Crèvecœur, he set out with an Indian guide and four Frenchmen. The hardships and disasters of the journey deprived him of his companions, one by one, but he pressed on alone. " During sixty-five days he had toiled almost incessantly, travelling about a thousand miles through a country beset with every form of peril and obstruction. . . . In him an unconquerable mind held at its service a frame of iron, and taxed it to its utmost endurance. The pioneer of Western pioneers was no rude son of toil, but a man of thought, trained amid arts and letters." [1]

This first chapter of his reverses, however, was not yet completed; for even while La Salle was getting succour for his company on the Illinois, a letter arrived from Tonty telling him of the mutiny of the garrison and the wilful destruction of Fort Crèvecœur with all it held. The calamitous news would have killed the spirit of any one less courageous than La Salle; but the bold explorer, whose whole life was a long grapple with adversity, prepared with all haste to return to the rescue of Tonty, who, he hoped forlornly, had survived the mutinous treachery. By the 10th of August he was ready, and with a new outfit and twenty-five men he set out once more for the distant Illinois.

After three months of toil and hardship he came again to Fort Crèvecœur. Anxiety for Tonty and

---

[1] Parkman, *La Salle and the Discovery of the Great West*, chap. xiv.

his faithful companions had consumed him all the way. Yet he was unprepared for the shocking sight that met his eyes. The once populous town of the Illinois was now a valley of dry bones; the bodies of women and children strewed the plain, and the charred trophies of Illinois warriors hung tragically upon blackened stakes. Such were the terrible marks of an Iroquois visitation.

Wolves ran howling away as the Frenchmen drew near, and voracious buzzards wheeled overhead. Anxiously La Salle sought among the revolting remnants for any sign of Tonty; but none was to be found, and although the relief expedition continued for weeks and months to search for their missing comrades, it was spring before the explorer heard with joy that his lieutenant had found refuge among the Pottawattamies. Meanwhile, his resources for the Mississippi expedition had been again dissipated, and once more he returned to Fort Frontenac for fresh supplies.

Soon, for the third time, the persistent adventurer set his face towards the west. His company now included twenty-three Frenchmen and eighteen Indians, equipped with all the care his former experiences could suggest. Summer had gone before his plans were completed; but all seasons were alike to La Salle, and in the early autumn his expedition began. Lake Huron was reached in October,

Fort Miami a few weeks later, and on the 6th of February their canoes glided out of the Illinois into the eddying current of the Mississippi.

Down past the turbid Missouri they swept, and beyond the mouth of the Ohio. Every day brought them newer signs of spring, and every day saw the spirits of La Salle rising at the happy consciousness of fulfilled ambition. On the 13th of March they encamped near the mouth of the Arkansas, and three hundred miles below they were well received by the Natchez Indians. On the 6th of April the great river divided before them into three wide channels: La Salle followed that of the west; Tonty took the middle course; and D'Autray descended the eastern passage. On the 19th of April the three parties met on the Gulf of Mexico. A cross bearing the arms of France was set up, and the country was named Louisiana after the Grand Monarch.

The Louisiana of to-day conveys no idea of the vast tract of country defined by La Salle's proclamation of 1682. To the explorer it meant the extent of the mighty continent, stretching westward from the Alleghanies to the Rockies, and north and south from Lake Superior to the Gulf of Mexico. All former accessions of territory were small beside it, and to his eyes it seemed the fertile Canaan of French enterprise. Yet the very magnitude of this new success made for the undoing of New France, by scattering her feeble forces over the length and breadth of a continent and distending her line of defence so far that it could be easily pierced. La Salle, however, was driven irresistibly forward by the hot ambition which ruled him. His romantic vision pictured a greater New France in the valley of the Mississippi, governed by himself — a prosperous trading colony shipping cargoes of beaver-skins directly to Europe by way of the Gulf of Mexico. Quebec, however, was the home of his enemies. His former reverses had shattered the faith of creditors, while the Canadian merchants envied him the monopoly of the Western trade. They heaped calumny upon his enterprises, labelled him a *coureur de bois*, and persistently wrecked his schemes. Final success enabled La Salle in a measure to disregard these annoyances; but when the new Governor, La Barre, went the length of seizing Fort Frontenac — thus cutting off the far west from its supplies — and even declared him an outlaw, La Salle, although he had but lately recovered from a fever, made up his mind to carry his cause to France.

In the spring of 1684, therefore, the weatherbeaten woodsman of the New World stood before the throne of the Grand Monarch; and although the Court had greater terrors for him than the Canadian forests, yet

K

he was able to set forth the rights of his case with the honest boldness of a frontiersman and the force of a cultured intellect. Louis followed his words with deepest interest, and was moved to carry out a purpose which for some time had possessed his mind. Within three months four armed vessels, bearing nearly four hundred men, set sail from Rochelle for the Gulf of Mexico. A new commission empowered the explorer to establish a fort on the southern gulf, from which to harass the Spaniards, and to fortify a base near the mouth of the Mississippi for the effective control of Louisiana.

But the story of this, the final enterprise of La Salle, is a sickening record of disaster. After a stormy passage three of the four vessels reached St. Domingo, the *St. François* having fallen a prey to Spanish buccaneers. At St. Domingo a violent fever threatened the leader's life and mind, and delayed further progress for almost two months. At length, near the end of December, they entered the Gulf of Mexico; but the uncertainties of its navigation were further increased by dense fogs; and when, after days of anxious searching, the fleet came to anchor off a low-lying marshy coast, La Salle had sailed four hundred miles beyond the mouth of the river he sought. Unaware of his mistake, he determined to land and build a temporary fort; but the frigate

Aimable, laden with stores, was wrecked upon a reef; Beaujeu, the recreant commander of the *Joly,* deserted his leader and made sail for France, and presently La Salle was left with only the little frigate *Belle.* Soon afterwards this vessel also sank beneath the stormy waters of the forbidden sea.

Thus, by accident and by disease the imposing expedition which had left Rochelle in the midsummer of 1684 was now reduced to a wretched band of starvelings, huddled together on the malarial sands of the Mexican gulf. In this last extremity La Salle saw one hope of salvation, and the magnitude of his new project was characteristic of the invincible adventurer whom fate had so often buffeted in vain. At the head of half his followers he boldly set out for Canada overland, hoping to bring back succour to the desolate maroons who still remained at Matagorda Bay.

Throughout his undertakings the virile mind of La Salle had always held his fellows in willing or unwilling subjection. The weak were glad to lean upon his strength, and to these he was the " guardian angel." [1] To others, however, his fine reserve and distinguished manner were causes of gnawing discontent. This evident lack of frankness in dealing with his companions contrasted strangely with

[1] " . . . Notre Ange tutélaire, le Sieur de la Salle." — Douay.

that keen appreciation of the character of the Indians which had brought him such success in his intercourse with them. The handful of men with whom he set out from Matagorda Bay on the 7th of June, 1687, besides a few whose admiration for their leader knew no bounds, also included others who, like the children of Israel, thirsted for the life of him who had led them out into the wilderness to die.

Week after week the little band of Frenchmen struggled on, now through a sea of prairie grass, now wading through deep savannahs, and presently swimming or fording streams which blocked their progress. Despair invaded the camp, and hostile murmurings arose against La Salle and the little group who remained true to him. A terrible plot was on foot. Presently the blow fell. Moranget, La Salle's nephew, was despatched with an axe ; Nika, the faithful Shawanoe, and Saget, the leader's servant, were murdered as they slept. As for La Salle, a wanton bullet pierced his brain. Thus the man who had braved the poisoned arrows of the Iroquois and the hatchets of Indians without number, against whose iron strength deadly fevers had stormed in vain, whose fortitude had been unbroken by the almost incredible perversities of fortune — this paladin of the wilderness was at last laid low by the hand of a traitor. The New World has no more

piteous tale than that of the unabated sufferings of
La Salle, who knew no fear and acknowledged
no defeat, even at the hands of a relentless
destiny. It has no nobler record than the tale of
his life.

CHAPTER VIII

FIRE, MASSACRE, AND SIEGE

At Quebec, Frontenac did what he could to promote the bold designs of La Salle. Nevertheless, the explorer had been forced to furnish his own men and supplies, getting trading privileges in return — an arrangement by which the King had all the glory without any of the risk. There were those in Quebec, indeed, who suspected the Governor of having a personal interest in La Salle's adventures, and enemies were not slow to credit him further with a share in profits from illegal trade in furs. The Intendant Duchesneau fomented these suspicions, and his letters to the King and the minister were filled with black charges against Frontenac. The latter, in his turn, called the Intendant to account; and Quebec was then ranged into two camps — the Bishop and the Jesuits siding with the Intendant, while the Récollet friars and the merchants supported Frontenac. Every ship carried home to France a budget of letters filled with charges and counter-charges, until it became apparent to the Court that a bitter civil strife was raging in the distant colony; and the King, unable to judge between the antagonists, finally recalled them both.

The new Governor, La Barre, met with ill-omens on arrival. His predecessor had scarce departed when Quebec was visited by the first of those destructive fires which were destined to rage so often through its winding streets. The summer of 1682 had been exceptionally dry, and on the night of the 4th of August a fire began in the house of Étienne Planchon and spread with dreadful speed over the whole of Lower Town. Fifty-five houses were burnt to the ground on this occasion, and Lower Town became a heap of ashes. One house alone escaped, that of the merchant Aubert de la Chesnaye; and more than half the wealth of Canada was destroyed.

If so be that misfortunes ever come singly, the history of Quebec at least has never been able to afford an example; and as if destructive fire were an insufficient visitation of angry fate, other misfortunes, no less cruel, now came upon the city. In these years, indeed, it seemed that Nature herself was leagued with the enemies of Quebec; for in the *Jesuit Relations* we have a circumstantial if highly imaginative account of a violent earthquake which visited the Province in 1663 : —

"Many of the French inhabitants and Indians," says the writer, "who were eye-witnesses to the scene, state that a great way up the river of Trois Rivières, about eighteen miles below Quebec, the hills which bordered the river on either side, and which were of a prodigious height, were torn from their foundations and plunged into the river, causing it to change its course and spread itself over a large tract of land recently cleared; . . . lakes appeared where none ever existed before; mountains were overthrown, swallowed up by the gaping earth, or precipitated into adjacent rivers, leaving in their place frightful chasms or level plains. . . . Rivers in many parts of the country sought other beds, or totally disappeared. The earth and mountains were violently split and rent in innumerable places, creating chasms and precipices whose depths have never yet been ascertained. Such devastation was also occasioned in the woods, that more than a thousand acres in one neighbourhood were completely overturned."

Another account of this event is given by an Ursuline sister : —

"The first shock of earthquake took place on 5th February, 1663, about half-past five in the evening. The weather was calm and serene, when we heard a terrible noise and humming sound like

that of a great number of heavy carriages rolling
over a paved floor swiftly. After this one heard,
both above and below the earth and on all sides, as
it were a confused mingling of waves and billows,
which caused sensations of horror. Sounds were
heard as of stones upon the roof, in the garrets, and
chambers; a thick dust spread around; doors opened
and shut of themselves. The bells of all our churches
and clocks sounded of themselves; and the steeples
as well as the houses swayed to and fro, like trees
in a great wind. And all this in the midst of a
horrible confusion of furniture turned over, stones
falling, boards breaking, walls cracking, and the
cries of domestic animals, of which some entered the
houses and some went out; in a word, it seemed to
be the eve of the Day of Judgment whose signs were
witnessed. Very different impressions were made on
us. Some went forth for fear of being buried in the
ruins of our house, which was seen to jog as if made
of cards; others prostrated themselves at the foot of
the altar, as if to die there. One good lay sister was
so terrified that her body trembled for an hour without ability to stop the agitation. When the second
shock came, at eight o'clock the same evening, we
were all ranged in our stalls at the choir. It was
very violent, and we all expected death every moment,
and to be engulfed in the ruins of the building. . . .
No person was killed. The conversions were extra-

ordinary, and one ecclesiastic assured me that he had taken more than eight hundred confessions."

Such things as these seemed not to dampen the ardour of those whose fortunes were cast in New France. Personal prowess and force of character were the natural result of trouble and disaster. La Barre, however, proved a dire exception to the rule. His hands shook in the hour of trial; he weakly grasped occasion. The magnificent but tragical career of La Salle had annexed a vast domain to the French possessions in North America, while Du Lhut, La Durantaye, Nicolas Perrot, and the rest of the *coureurs de bois* had, by their adventurous trading, given even the remote Sioux and Assiniboins an interest in the fur trade of France. By this rapid expansion of French influence the Five Nation Indians at last saw themselves hemmed in by tribes under the influence of Quebec, their hunting grounds limited to a small and now partly exhausted area. In order to procure guns and ammunition from their English friends they were compelled to take thought for the decreasing peltries. A destructive raid into the Illinois valley was the first step in their new policy, which was the annihilation of all those tribes which traded with the French, and the diversion of the beaver trade to the wealthier merchants of New England.

At all hazards New France was bound to prevent

this dire blow from falling upon her allies, whose adherence to the pact rested upon the ability of French arms to protect them. But French prestige among the Indians so suffered under the weak-kneed administration of La Barre, that the Iroquois became bolder in contravening the treaty of peace, while the Western tribes were on the point of going over to the English. These circumstances prompted the expedition of 1684.

With a hundred regulars, an equal number of Canadians, and a composite band of Indians, La Barre set out from Quebec to destroy the Senecas. News had been sent to the French trading posts of the north, and it was arranged that the main column should be joined at Niagara by a force of Hurons, Ottawas, Ojibwas, Pottawattamies, and Foxes, whom the *coureurs de bois* had rallied for a last supreme effort. But in spite of the strength of this array, it was not expected by those who knew the vacillating Governor that he would be successful. Even the most sceptical, however, were not prepared for the woeful fiasco which followed. Instead of advancing to destroy his enemies, La Barre summoned them to a council, where the Seneca deputies were not slow to perceive the weakness of their foe, and contemptuously dictated terms of peace. Thus the French were degraded in the eyes of their Indian allies, who returned disgusted to their homes. The event being taken seriously in France, La Barre was recalled, and the Marquis de Denonville appointed in his place.

It was now becoming clearer that English intrigue was behind all these troubles with the Iroquois. Dongan, the Catholic Governor of New York at this period, a resourceful and adroit politician, formed the design of absorbing the territory of the Iroquois into the domain of James II. of England; and the Indians, while they resisted his ulterior purpose, were yet glad enough to get English guns for their warfare against the French. Besides this direct official action, Dongan encouraged English traders to go among the Canadian Indians and wean them from their alliance with Quebec.

At first the rivalry was but a diplomatic duel between Denonville and Dongan, England and France being then at peace. Soon, however, the colonies of the two nations were waging a border warfare of their own. While the English were urging the Iroquois against their rivals, the furtive hand of the French was evident in the raids of the Abenakis upon the woods of Acadie; but at this early stage of the dispute the two Powers disclaimed all approval of these savage reprisals.

In 1687 Governor Denonville, mustering a strong force at Quebec, moved quickly up the St. Lawrence upon the Senecas. Like La Barre he invited a number of chiefs to a conference, but when they came he treacherously seized and sent them to the galleys of France. He then crossed from Fort Frontenac, ravaging and burning their villages and towns. Not only the Senecas but the whole Iroquois confederacy burned to avenge the terrible warfare of Denonville. In small bands they ranged the woods round about Quebec and the river settlements, darting to and fro like silent shadows, so that for months the French suffered daily the anguish of battle, murder, and sudden death. Disciplined soldiers were helpless against this stealthy warfare, and a man walked in danger of his life even within the palisades.

Great as was their distress, however, it was but a prelude to one of the cruellest incidents in Canadian history. The night of the 4th of August, 1689, being heavy with thunderclouds, fifteen hundred Iroquois warriors, under cover of the darkness, crept upon the settlement of Lachine, at the western end of the Island of Montreal. They scattered stealthily among the cabins, and at a given signal surprised the victims in their beds. More than two hundred men, women, and children were tomahawked in cold blood or carried off to a lingering death, the lurid flames of the burning seigneury telling their bitter tale to the watchers at Montreal. New France was faint with horror; and once more she sighed for the strong protecting arm of Frontenac.

Meanwhile, the English Revolution of 1688 had driven James II. from the throne, and the French king had taken up the cause of the Stuarts against William of Orange. England and France were face to face in Europe, and in the New World the veiled conflict between the rival colonies now gave place to open war. The King by this time realised that Frontenac, for all his seventy years and his reputation for rashness, was the only man qualified to fill the difficult post of Governor, and accordingly sent him again to New France. He reached Quebec about the middle of October. It was evening, and the citizens had gathered at the quay with torches of welcome, while fireworks and illuminations blazed in his honour over the streets of the Upper Town. Vigorous in spite of his years, the grizzled hero of the siege of Arras stood once more on the soil of New France, and notwithstanding the perfunctory homage of the Jesuits and the studied reserve of the Intendant Champigny, a feeling of relief thrilled Quebec. An enterprise of almost incredible difficulty was to be laid upon the shoulders of the veteran ruler. This was nothing less than an attack upon New York as a preliminary step to the overthrow of all New England. A land force was to descend on Albany, proceeding by way of the Richelieu, Lake Champlain, and the Hudson, while two frigates were to assail

New York from the sea.   The naval project, however, was so feeble and uncertain, so ill-starred, that
adverse winds on the Atlantic brought it to an
untimely end.

Having abandoned for the moment the expedition
against New York, Frontenac turned his attention first
to the ever-present Indian problem.   The defection
of the north-western tribes was becoming more and
more probable notwithstanding the strenuous efforts of
the *coureurs de bois*.   Indians were fast losing faith in
French protection, and before all else it was necessary
to make the Iroquois understand that the great *Onontio*[1]
had returned to chastise them.   Aiming therefore at
the revival of French prestige, the Governor organised
" The three war-parties," a step which may be considered as the initial move in that desperate conflict
which left the flag of England floating over the
citadel of Quebec.

The three war-parties, each consisting of regulars,
coureurs de bois, and Indians, were now despatched
from Montreal, Three Rivers, and Quebec.   The deep
snows of a Canadian winter lay upon the ground as
these forces of destruction sallied forth.   Leaving
Montreal, the first party passed down the frozen St.
Lawrence, and into the wintry ravines of the Richelieu,
and after a march of terrible hardship, now plung-
ing through snow-drifts, now benumbed by frost,

[1] The Indian name for Count Frontenac.

wading knee-deep through the melting swamps, they came at last to the unguarded palisades of the Dutch settlement of Corlaer, or Schenectady.   It was midnight as they stole through the streets of the sleeping village, now suddenly wakened by a hideous war-whoop, the signal for a massacre as terrible as that of Lachine.

With a similarity of grim details the other two war-parties attacked the rival colonies of New England.   Under cover of the night the band from Three Rivers fell upon Salmon Falls, a village on the borders of New Hampshire, and put its inhabitants to the sword.   The victors then joined the column which Portneuf had led from Quebec, and together they moved down Casco Bay to Fort Loyal, where the settlers of the district had assembled for a vigorous defence.   The New Englanders held out for several days against the French and the Abenakis, but at length agreed to surrender with the honours of war. Portneuf's pledge of protection, however, was shame-lessly broken, and the Indian allies fell upon the helpless captives without restraint.

Such success amply fulfilled the expectations of Frontenac, and the wavering tribes of the West now hastened to Quebec to confirm their allegiance.   In New France elation took the place of gloom, and bonfires burned among the settlements along the St. Lawrence.   In New England, however, the threefold atrocity produced an effect that boded ill for Canada. In their eagerness to avenge this outrage, the Atlantic colonies, up to this time disunited and isolated, now pledged themselves to union against a common peril, and planned the conquest of the country. A force of colonial militia set out from Albany against Montreal, while a naval attack was directed against Port Royal and Quebec. Sir William Phipps sailed from Nantasket with a fleet of seven vessels, appearing on the 11th of May before Port Royal, whose commandant surrendered without a blow.

The admiral who won this bloodless victory is one of the most notable figures in New World history. William Phipps was born on the Kennebec in 1650, and spent his early life tending sheep in the rude border settlement of New England. But ambition and love of adventure not being satisfied by a pastoral life, the youth soon adopted the trade of a ship-carpenter and came to Boston. Here fortune in the form of a wealthy widow smiled upon him, and he is next found searching for a wrecked treasure-ship in the Spanish Main. The romantic sailor was, however, at first unsuccessful in his quest; but as he had awakened the interest of the Duke of Albemarle, he obtained from this noble-man a frigate for a similar adventure off the coast of Hispaniola. In the course of this latter voyage his buccaneer crew rebelled, and single-handed the

L

powerful Phipps drove them from the quarter-deck.
Success at length rewarded him, the treasure-ship
was raised, and through the influence of his illustrious patron the bucolic New Englander received a
knighthood.   Sir William Phipps thus returned to
his castle in the Green Lane of North Boston with the
glamour of the court upon him, and was chosen by
the colonists of Massachusetts to carry out their
bold designs against Quebec.

Meanwhile, Frontenac anticipated coming danger
by strengthening the city.   Nature had made the
position impregnable on the river side, but in
the rear it was still open to attack.   All through
the winter gangs of men were employed in cutting
timber in the forest, and dragging hewn palisades
to the city, where Frontenac superintended the
erection of stout barricades.   While the Governor
was thus engaged news reached him that Winthrop
was marching upon Montreal, and thither he hastened
with all speed.   Circumstances, however, had conspired to render futile the expedition from New York
and Connecticut; and intestine quarrels, followed by
Iroquois defection, wrecked the English enterprise
before it had come within striking distance of
Montreal.

In the meantime Sir William Phipps had sailed
for Quebec with a fleet of more than thirty sail, two
thousand men, and four months' supplies.   The

SIR WILLIAM PHIPPS

hope of receiving help from England had somewhat
delayed the expedition, and it was the 9th of August
before the admiral slipped his cables in the harbour
of Nantasket. As this American armada comprised vessels ranging in size from the flag-ship *Six
Friends*, with forty-four guns, down to the fishing
smacks of Gloucester, its progress was slow. The
most serious difficulty, however, was the absence of
a pilot who knew the dangerous navigation of the
St. Lawrence. Nevertheless, Phipps decided to
grope his way up the river. However, news of the
invasion had already reached Quebec, and Prévost, the town Mayor, despatched a messenger
to Frontenac at Montreal, pressing on meanwhile
with the fortifications already so well under
way.

Nature had left the cliffs of Quebec accessible at
only those three points where later stood Prescott,
Hope and Palace Gates, and Prévost secured these by
means of barricades and earthworks. The strand of
the St. Charles, from the Palace of the Intendant to
the Sault-au-Matelot, was protected by a continuous
palisade, and the fortifications begun by Frontenac
in the previous winter having since been completed,
now afforded adequate protection upon the landward
side of the town. Moreover, several batteries were
disposed at salient points. In the garden which
flanks the present Dufferin Terrace was a battery

of eight guns ; while the high cliff of the Sault-au-Matelot and the barricade at Palace Hill were each defended by six guns. The windmill on Mount Carmel was converted into a small battery, a number of light pieces also being collected in the square opposite the Jesuits' College, to serve as a reserve battery for any weak spot in the defences. Six, eighteen, and twenty-four pounders were mounted on the wharves of Lower Town. For several days the men from the surrounding parishes had been flocking into the city, and by the evening of the 15th of October about twenty-seven hundred regulars and militia were gathered within the fortifications. Next day the sun rose upon the New England fleet moored in the expansive basin of Quebec.

All that was possible in the way of defence had been accomplished, but in the face of such imposing naval strength the assault was awaited with anxiety. The women and children repaired to the stone convents for refuge, and the men stood by the guns. The siege, however, was not to open with a cannonade, but a parley. A boat put out from the *Six Friends* with a flag of truce, and soon an English lieutenant landed at the Cul-de-sac, bearing a letter for the commander of the garrison. Before receiving the missive, Frontenac devised a useful and whimsical stratagem to raise the prestige of the beleaguered city. Phipps's messenger was first of all

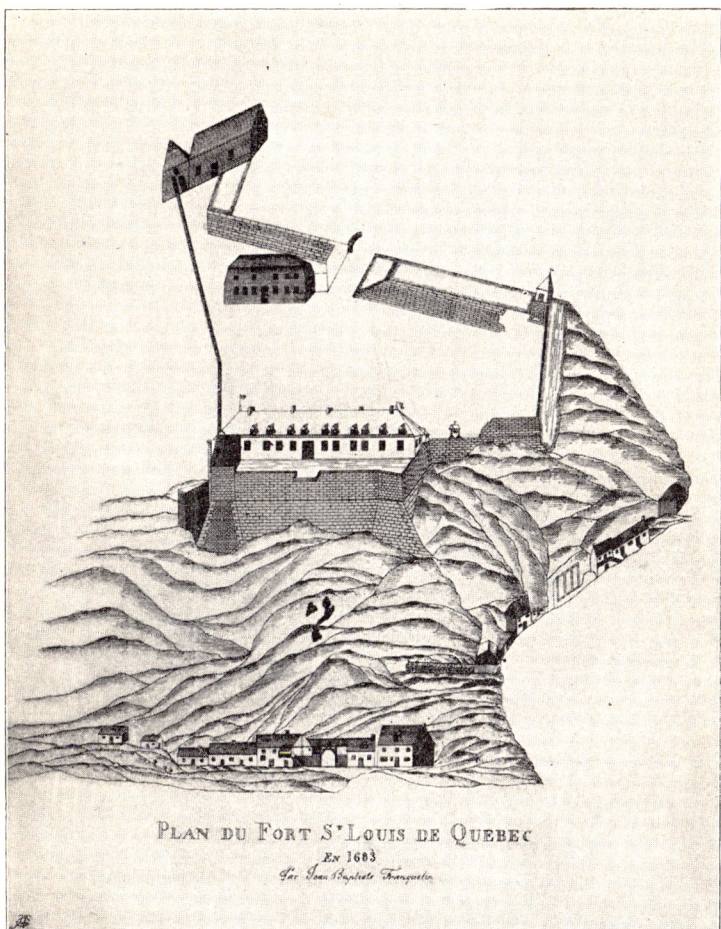

PLAN DU FORT S^T LOUIS DE QUEBEC
EN 1683
Par Jean Baptiste Franquelin

PLAN OF FORT ST. LOUIS, 1683

blindfolded. Then two sergeants led the bewildered
envoy by a devious route from the quay up to Fort
St. Louis, and over the triple barricades of Mountain
Hill, while the noisy soldiers thronged him, and the
din of the streets was designedly increased. Finally
they took the bandage from his eyes. Before him
stood the haughty Frontenac in the brilliant uniform

THE CITADEL TO-DAY (FROM DUFFERIN TERRACE)

of a French marshal, and the council-room of the
Château was crowded with the officers of his staff,
tricked off in laces of gold and silver with ribbons
and plumes, powder and perukes.

Withal, the English envoy was equal to the
occasion. If the strength of Quebec and its garrison
filled him with surprise, he gave no sign of it, but
with a dignity rivalling that of the French Governor
delivered his admiral's summons to surrender.

"Your answer positive in an hour," recited the postscript, "returned by your own trumpet with the return of mine, is required upon the peril that will ensue."

Frontenac and his *aides* were not in the least prepared to accept the brusque demands of Sir William Phipps. Fort Royal, it is true, had been cowed into an immediate surrender, but the blustering sailor of New England had mistaken Quebec and its commandant.

For a moment the fiery Count controlled his temper, then it blazed forth with wonted ardour. "Tell your General," he exclaimed, "that I will answer him only by the mouths of my cannon, that he may learn that the fortress of Quebec is not to be summoned after this fashion. Let him do his best, and I shall do mine."

Blindfolded once more, the bearer of the flag of truce again scrambled over the barricades, and was led down to the river's brink.

To Phipps, the challenge of Frontenac seemed to outdo his own in boldness, and he was filled with doubt by the envoy's accounts of the strength of Quebec. The black rock of Cape Diamond now seemed to tower above him more grimly than ever, and with some misgiving he at length adopted a bold plan of assault. The infantry, under Major Walley, were to land on the flats of

Beauport, cross the St. Charles when the tide was out, and assail the flank of the town on the side of the Côte Ste. Geneviève; while Phipps himself was to cannonade the city from the river, land a storming party, and gain the Upper Town by way of the barricades.

For two more days he delayed putting this plan into operation; and when attempted it was badly managed. Frontenac had despatched Sainte-Hélène[1] with three hundred sharpshooters to oppose any landing on the Beauport shore, a force which was unequal to the task; for Major Walley, though harassed by their fire, succeeded in making his way at the head of 1300 men to the ford on the river St. Charles.

Phipps, however, instead of co-operating with the land force, had made a premature movement, and leaving his moorings had sailed up the channel opposite the city, there to engage in a terrific duel with the guns of Fort St. Louis and the several batteries of Upper Town. Cannon and mortars belched forth their missiles with the rapidity of musketry, making an uproar as of a great battle. The English gunners made poor practice, however, and the projectiles falling within the city did almost no damage. Twenty-six cannon-balls dropped harmlessly in the garden

---

[1] Of the gallant Le Moyne family, of whom also was d'Iberville, the soldier, explorer, and governor.

of the Ursuline convent, and furnished new ammunition for the garrison. On the other hand, the decks of the attacking vessels were swept by fire from the cliffs. One shot carried away the ensign of the flag-ship, and another tore away her rigging and shattered her mizzen, and the rest of the fleet was similarly battered.

This unequal cannonade continued for two days before Phipps realised its futility. On shore, Walley persisted for three days in attempting to force his way across the St. Charles; but his field-pieces were half buried in the mud, sickness had attacked his camp, and the rain and sleet of an early winter completed his discomfiture. Seeing, moreover, that their admiral had now ceased to fight, and that Frontenac was thus able to concentrate defence upon the landward side, the militiamen felt the hopelessness of further assault and returned to the ships. After this rebuff Phipps weighed anchor and dropped down stream with his battered armada.

Quebec had been saved, though not without dire peril and sore straits; for before the withdrawal of the enemy the crowded city had already felt the pinch of famine, and the violence of the batteries had all but emptied her magazines. Throughout the bombardment a picture of the Holy Family had hung inviolate on the spire of the Basilica, defying

the heretical cannonade ; and in cloister and chapel
the beleaguered citizens had ceaselessly invoked their

NOTRE DAME DE LA VICTOIRE

favourite saints.   To one and all the victory was of
Heaven, and in the midst of her rejoicing Quebec
did not forget to redeem her vows.   The little chapel

of Notre Dame de la Victoire, hidden among the quaint windings of the streets below the Terrace, still stands as a monument to that religious fidelity with which the citizens of Quebec had faced another of their many perils.

CHAPTER IX

THE CLOSE OF THE CENTURY

THE great strength of its natural position had enabled the city to withstand the late siege ; but Frontenac saw clearly that the defences would not be sufficient to meet a resolute assault, and it was resolved to reconstruct the fortifications on a larger scale. The great engineer Vauban furnished plans which were carried out under Frontenac's personal direction. For twenty leagues around the *habitants* were pressed into this service, and such was the general anxiety to make the city impregnable, that even the *gentilhommes* gave themselves to pick and spade. A line of solid earthworks soon extended on the flank of the city from Cape Diamond to the St. Charles ; and at the summit of the Cape, now for the first time embraced within the fortifications, a strong redoubt with sixteen cannon was constructed to command both the river and the Upper Town.

A copper plate[1] bearing the following inscription in Latin was deposited in the stone foundation : —

" In the year of Grace, 1693, under the reign of the Most August, Most Invincible, and Most Christian King, Louis the Great, Fourteenth of that name, the Most Excellent and Most Illustrious Lord, Louis de Buade, Count of Frontenac, twice Viceroy of all New France, after having three years before repulsed, routed, and completely conquered the rebellious inhabitants of New England, who besieged this town of Quebec, and who threatened to renew the attack this year, constructed, at the charge of the King, this citadel, with the fortifications therewith connected, for the defence of the country and the safety of the people, and for confounding yet again a people perfidious towards God and towards its lawful king.   And he has laid this first stone."

The repulse of Phipps, while postponing indefinitely any further undertakings of the New England government against Quebec, had conveyed no lesson to the implacable Iroquois.   These fatal hornets of the woods continued to harass the settlements, roving through the forest in small marauding bands. A large force also established a camp on the Ottawa to intercept the furs destined for Quebec, and their blockade was so effective that the city soon

---

[1] Discovered at the demolition of the old wall in 1854.

felt the pinch of want, and the trading ships sailed empty back to France. So bold were the assaults that many settlers fled from their farms to Montreal, Three Rivers, or Quebec; while those who had the hardihood to remain went about in armed groups to reap their harvests. The massacre of La Chesnaye was a typical incident; but perhaps the most characteristic story of these troublous years is the *Récit de Mlle. Magdelaine de Verchères*, well known through a renowned historical narrative.

The seigneury of Verchères lay upon the south shore of the St. Lawrence, seven leagues below Montreal, and from its exposed position as well as from its former tribulation, had earned the name of Castle Dangerous. Its history dated back to the disbandment of the Carignan-Salières regiment, when M. de Verchères, a dashing officer of Savoy, took possession of the fief, building there a fort and blockhouse.

It was already late October, 1692. The seigneur had gone down to Quebec for duty, and the lady of the manor was in Montreal. Their three children, Madeleine aged fourteen, and the two boys aged twelve and ten, had been left behind protected by the feeble garrison of the fort, consisting of two soldiers and an old man of eighty, the servants and *censitaires* being busy with the autumn work of the fields.

M

One morning as Madeleine was playing near the water's edge, she was startled by the sound of firing. A band of Iroquois had fallen upon the field-workers. Commending herself to the Holy Virgin, the girl ran towards the fort. Bullets whistled past her as she flew towards the palisade crying "To arms! To arms!" The two soldiers had already fled in terror to the blockhouse, but by her resolute words she shamed them into a defence of the fort; and picking up a gun, she said to her two young brothers : —

"Let us fight to the death. We are fighting for our country and our religion; remember that our father has taught you that gentlemen are born to shed their blood for God and the King."[1]

Taking their positions at the loopholes, the little company maintained such a vigilant defence that the Iroquois were completely deceived as to the strength of the garrison.

"After sunset," continues the narrative, "a violent north-east wind began to blow, accompanied by snow and hail, which told us that we should have a terrible night. The Iroquois were all this time lurking about us; and I judged by their movements that, instead of being deterred by the storm, they would climb into the fort under cover of the dark-

---

[1] The narrative has been preserved in the heroine's own words, through the care of the Marquis de Beauharnois, sometime Governor of Canada.

ness. I assembled all my troops, that is to say, six persons, and spoke to them thus: 'God has saved us to-day from the hands of our enemies, but we must take care not to fall into their snares to-night. As for me, I want you to see that I am not afraid. I will take charge of the fort with an old man of eighty, and another who never fired a gun; and you, Pierre Fontaine, with La Bonté and Gachet, will go to the blockhouse with the women and children, because that is the strongest place; and if I am taken do not surrender, even if I am cut to pieces and burned before your eyes. The enemy cannot hurt you in the blockhouse if you make the least show of fight.' I placed my young brothers on two of the bastions, the old man on the third, and I took the fourth; and all night, in spite of wind, snow, and hail, the cries of 'All's well' were kept up from the blockhouse to the fort, and from the fort to the blockhouse. One would have thought the place was full of soldiers. The Iroquois thought so, and were completely deceived, as they confessed afterwards to Monsieur de Callières, whom they told that they had held a council to make a plan for capturing the fort in the night, but had done nothing because such a constant watch was kept. . . .

"At last the daylight came again; and as the darkness disappeared our anxieties seemed to dis-

appear with it. Everybody took courage except
Mademoiselle Marguerite, the wife of the Sieur
Fontaine, who, being extremely timid, as all Parisian
women are, asked her husband to carry her to another
fort. . . . He said, 'I shall never abandon this fort
while Mademoiselle Madeleine is here.' I answered
him that I would never abandon it; that I would
rather die than give it up to the enemy; and that
it was of the greatest importance that they should
never get possession of any French fort. . . . I may
say with truth that I did not eat or sleep for twice
twenty-four hours. I did not go once into my
father's house, but kept always on the bastion, or
went to the blockhouse to see how the people there
were behaving. I always kept a cheerful and smiling
face, and encouraged my little company with the
hope of speedy succour.

"We were a week in constant alarm, with the
enemy always about us. At last Monsieur de la
Monnerie, a lieutenant sent by Monsieur de Callières,
arrived in the night with forty men. As he did not
know whether the fort was taken or not, he approached
as silently as possible. One of our sentinels hearing
a slight sound, cried 'Qui vive?' I was dozing at
the time, with my head on the table and my gun
lying across my arms. The sentinel told me that he
heard a voice from the river. I went up at once to
the bastion to see whether it was Indians or French-

men. I asked, ' Who are you ? ' One of them answered, ' We are Frenchmen ; it is La Monnerie, who comes to bring you help.'

" I caused the gate to be opened, placed a sentinel there, and went down to the river to meet them. As soon as I saw Monsieur de la Monnerie, I saluted him, and said, ' Monsieur, I surrender my arms to you.' He answered gallantly, ' Mademoiselle, they are in good hands.' ' Better than you think,' I returned.

" La Monnerie inspected the fort and found everything in good order, and a sentinel on each bastion. ' It is time to relieve them, Monsieur,' I said ; ' we have not been off our bastions for a week.' " [1]

The inner politics of Quebec shared fully the unrest of this critical time. The place had all the intrigue of an Italian republic ; and with its political, religious, and social cleavages, the wonder is that a city so divided against itself was able to stand in the hour of outward adversity. To make clear the underlying causes of such civil strife, it is necessary to go back to the year 1659, when the most notable ecclesiastic in the history of New France arrived in Quebec.

François-Xavier Laval was born in 1622 at Montigny-sur-Avre. Brought up at the College of

[1] Parkman's *Frontenac* c. 14 (quoting from *Collection de l' Abbé Ferland*).

the Jesuits at Laflèche, a prolonged sojourn in the famous Hermitage of Caen set the seal of a militant mysticism upon his life.   While still young the death of an elder brother had made him heir to the title and wealth of one of the most distinguished families in France ; but the ardent student renounced these feudal glories that he might devote himself entirely to the service of God.   To him this service consisted of a perpetual mortification of the flesh, practised chiefly in the hovels of the poor, or by beds of loathsome disease.

Of a mind and temper so austere, he seemed to the Jesuits the heaven-called head for the Canadian Church ; and it was doubtless through their influence, acting upon the Queen Mother, Anne of Austria, and Cardinal Mazarin, that Laval was appointed titular Bishop of Petræa, *in partibus infidelium*, and Vicar-Apostolic of all New France.

The first bishop of Canada was welcomed by pealing bells and general applause ; but the excitement of his advent had scarcely subsided before a sharp ecclesiastical quarrel occurred.   M. l'Abbé de Queylus, a Sulpitian priest, had lately been appointed spiritual head of Quebec by the Archbishop of Rouen, who had been wont to regard Canada as a part of his own diocese ; and the Sulpitian so vigorously refused to be superseded by the new bishop, that Governor D'Argenson, acting upon the King's orders, had him arrested and sent back to France. The quarrel, however, was not so soon decided, and supremacy was not finally conceded to Laval until both contestants had referred the matter to the Pope and the Grand Monarch.

Success in this churchman's conflict, however, had not softened the autocratic temper of the new bishop. In France he had already supported the contention of the Jesuits against the Jansenists that the power of the Pope was above that of the King, and that the Church was superior to the State. Laval insisted that his acolytes should precede the Governor in receiving the consecrated bread, in the distribution of boughs on Palm Sunday, in the adoration of the Cross on Good Friday, and in the presentation of holy water. For a time the gallant old soldier D'Argenson did his best to live in harmony with the Vicar-Apostolic, even under the annoying conditions created by the churchman's imperious temper. But the forbearance of the Governor was not sufficient to save him from his opponent's powerful friends at Court, who finally compassed his recall. His successors, the Baron D'Avaugour and M. de Mézy, however, soon took up the intermitted quarrel on behalf of the State, until the new order of government in 1663.

The institution of royal government in that year had a visible effect upon the ecclesiastical power.

Louis XIV. had declared himself to be the State, and thus acquired a personal and selfish interest in the controversy.   Moreover, Talon, the skilled agent of Colbert, wishing to readjust and balance the disproportionate elements of the body politic, had written in 1670 advising the re-introduction of the Récollet priests, who arrived eight years later to counterbalance the Jesuit forces.

The advent of Frontenac, likewise, had been a severe blow to the priestly autocracy, his strong and reckless character stamping him as a man who required careful handling.   In fact, Laval and the Jesuits preferred a vicarious warfare, and confined themselves to supporting the Intendant Duchesneau in his quarrels with the Governor.

Notwithstanding these rebuffs, however, the great prelate accomplished a lasting work.   To this day a daily procession of schoolboys walks through the streets of Upper Town arresting attention by their singular dress — a battalion similar to that which, two hundred years ago, appeared in the like quaint costume.   These are the boys of the *Seminaire de Laval.* This seminary of Quebec was Laval's most notable foundation ; and though many generations have slipped away since it began, the classic school above the Sault-au-Matelot still remains to recruit and train the ranks of a priesthood whose attainments, piety, and character are honoured throughout the Catholic world.

Late in the afternoon fourscore of these youthful devotees swing out along the Rue St. Jean to the Ste. Foye road for recreation. They go in orderly rows, from the youngest and smallest back to the two priests, in black *soutanes* and broad-brimmed hats, who bring up the rear. *Régimes* have come and gone, but this perennial column still marches out of the past incongruously garbed in peaked caps, black frockcoats faced with green braid, and girt at the waist with a green woollen scarf. This is the daily memorial of the eccentric, despotic, but beneficent bishop, who lived a life of almost abject poverty, devoting the revenues of the most wealthy seigneury in New France[1] to the maintenance of his beloved *Seminaire*. He has left his name also to the splendid university which completes the work so well begun by the *Seminaire*.

For almost forty years Laval had dominated the Church of New France, the whole period of his supremacy being disturbed by the never-ending quarrel between Church and State. The Bishop proposing to alter the ecclesiastical system of the colony by the institution of movable priests, both the King and Colbert objected strongly to a scheme which would have centralized all spiritual power in the

---

[1] Laval was the owner of the Seigneury of Beauport and the Isle d'Orleans, which by royal edict had been freed from feudal burdens. By the census of 1667 it was found to contain more than one-fourth of the entire population of Canada.

hands of one man, and he a spiritual despot, however sincere and high-souled. But the inflexible Laval contrived for a time to evade or disobey the royal instructions that were sent to him, until at length, in 1688, he asked to be relieved of his office, and the King freely granted his request. Thereupon, he handed over the episcopal office to Saint-Vallier, and retired to the seclusion of his cherished school.

The destruction of the college by fire in 1701 almost broke the heart of the venerable prelate; but with invincible energy and spirit he began at once the work of restoration. In four years the new building was completed, and in it he passed the evening of his days, until, at the age of eighty-six, he closed his eyes for ever on the scene of a strenuous, stormy, and holy life.

Time and events meanwhile had been treating Frontenac with equal sternness. The danger from New England had for a time relieved him of domestic troubles; but with the failure of Sir William Phipps, his clerical enemies at Quebec once more began their machinations, in spite of which the versatile old Governor still contrived to hold his way and course. Politically, the city was divided on the question of keeping control of the far west; for while some saw danger in dissipating the strength of the colony, and therefore advised the maintenance of a smaller but more compact territory, Frontenac, the fur traders, and the *coureurs de bois*, on the other hand, were determined to hold the West and to maintain the allegiance of the Indian allies.

Such, up to the last, was the attitude of the martial Governor, who, at the age of seventy-six, was ready once more to undertake the punishment of the Iroquois. He would fain have walked and toiled like the rest of the twenty-two hundred men who composed his column; but the Indian allies, unable to see him endure the hardships of the march, bore him triumphantly on their shoulders. Their faith in the great Onontio was without measure, and French prestige among them was now at its highest point. The Onondagas fled before their advance; the Oneidas begged for peace. The villages of the enemy were given to the flames, and the savages, thus rendered homeless, became a charge upon the friendly English settlements, only to increase the enmity which already marked the relations of the latter with the French colony.

Frontenac returned once more in triumph to Quebec, and a semblance of peace reigned in North America — the ominous calm before a storm which was soon to shake the Continent. The Castle of St. Louis now became a centre of gaiety, despite the grey hairs of its distinguished occupant, whose spirits and buoyancy were still unquenched. Quebec was giving unmistakable signs of a social revolt against the rigorous subjection in which the Church had held her. Exiled from Fontainebleau, the officers of the Governor's suite did their best to improvise a counterpart, and the ladies of the ambitious *noblesse* were not loth to join in the crude but brilliant revels of the castle. The winter carnival, then, as now, afforded merriment to a gay company, the King's representative being as keen a pleasure-seeker as the rest. On Frontenac's suggestion, private theatricals were added to the polite diversions of Quebec. The Marquis de Tracy's ball far back in 1667 had given grievous offence to the Jesuits, and the unholy acting of plays was now declared an open profanity. *Nicomède* and *Mithridate* were condemned as immoral; but when *Tartuffe*, Molière's mordant satire upon religious hypocrisy, was put upon the boards, the limits of endurance were reached and overpassed.

La Motte Cadillac, a staff officer, thus describes the excitement raised by these performances: "The clergy beat their alarm drums, armed *cap-à-pie*, and snatched their bows and arrows. The Sieur Glandelet was the first to begin, and preached two sermons in which he tried to prove that nobody could go to a play without mortal sin. The Bishop issued a mandate, and had it read from the pulpits, in which he speaks of certain impious, impure, and noxious comedies, insinuating

that those which had been acted were such. The
credulous and infatuated people, seduced by the
sermons and the mandate, began already to regard
the count as a corrupter of morals and a destroyer
of religion. The numerous party of the pretended
devotees mustered in the streets and public places,

THE CITADEL IN WINTER

and presently . . . persuaded the Bishop to publish
a mandate in the church whereby the Sieur de
Mareuil, a half-pay lieutenant, was interdicted the
use of the sacraments."

In the midst of it all, death was slowly creeping
upon the central figure of so many stormy scenes.
The treaty concluded at Ryswick in 1697, and proclaimed in Canada, improved the position of the

French in America, encouraging them to new aspirations of conquest. Already on the brink of the grave, the indomitable Frontenac cast his challenge in the teeth of New England, claiming the Iroquois as the recalcitrant subjects of Louis XIV. The gage was duly taken, and although the challenger could not await the issue, his visor remained closed till the end. Even in death Count Frontenac set his face against the Jesuits, for he was buried in the Récollet Chapel. When he was laid to rest the province was stricken with genuine grief, for all men felt that the best bulwark of New France had been laid in mortal ruin.

CHAPTER X

FRONTENAC's best legacy to Quebec and to Canada was the pacification of the Indian tribes. Under his stern rule the prestige of France had been restored, and to the new Governor, De Callières, was left the duty of arranging the formalities of peace with the ancient enemy, the Iroquois. A treaty, however, was only concluded in the face of strenuous opposition from New England, which now beheld with grave concern the changed front of the " Five Nations," who, for the space of a hundred years, had been the sharpest thorn in the side of New France, and whose territory had been as armour-plate about their own settlements.

In opportune time the Treaty of Ryswick had nominally settled all points of contention between France and England in both hemispheres, and it was soon followed by the cessation of hostilities between the whites and Indians. The Governor of New France summoned deputies from all the tribes to a grand council, at which, after many days of debate, he skilfully persuaded them to bury the hatchet and submit their internecine differences to Quebec for arbitration. Belts of wampum were exchanged, and the calumet of peace was passed forthwith between the followers and colleagues of De Callières and the painted chiefs of a dozen tribes.

The conclusion of this treaty was a fortunate stroke of French diplomacy, as not many months were to pass before Europe became once more involved in a war, into which the colonies of the rival powers were naturally drawn. Apart from the recognition of the English Pretender in France, the immediate cause of war in Europe was the question of the Spanish succession; for while Louis XIV. claimed the throne for his grandson, Philip of Anjou, England, on the other hand, recognised that this union of France and Spain would upset the balance of power on both sides of the Atlantic, and that her American possessions would be exposed to a cross fire from both north and south.

The great battles of Blenheim, Ramilies, Oudenarde, and Malplaquet of the European conflict had their counterpart in the *petite guerre* which was waged by the opposing colonies in America. French privateers issuing from Port Royal swept along the coast of New England, the settlements of Acadia suffering reprisals in kind. At last the ruthless destruction of the little village of Haverhill on the Merrimac by a Canadian war-party roused the English colonists to fury, and they loudly demanded the conquest of Canada. The authorities were already predisposed to this large undertaking by the arguments of one Samuel Vetch, whom the Governor of Massachusetts had formerly despatched on a special mission to Canada. Vetch soon perceived that the defences of Quebec and Montreal were not too formidable to be overcome by a well-devised assault; and proceeding to England he made representations to the advisers of Queen Anne, who, in 1709, sent him back to Boston with command to contrive an expedition against the fortress of Canada. A land force from New England was to proceed northward by way of the Richelieu, and to co-operate with an English fleet on the St. Lawrence.

Once more, however, fortune intervened to save Quebec. England long delayed in sending the promised fleet, and it was already late autumn before the colonial forces were ready to set out. While Colonel Nicholson, its leader, perceived the hopelessness of so unseasonable an assault upon the city, he was yet unwilling to remain inactive. Moreover, Acadia lay close by, and the stronghold of Port Royal challenged his arms. He determined on its subjection. The brave high-

N

spirited Subercase[1] was commandant of the town, and although his garrison was ill-provisioned and almost destitute of ammunition, the fort was defended with the utmost boldness against the overwhelming force of the besiegers. Subercase saw the hopelessness of his situation from the first, but in the end his invincible courage secured an honourable capitulation, and, with a pomp and circumstance contrasting strangely with their starved faces and ragged uniforms, the little garrison of Port Royal marched proudly out of the fort. Nicholson took possession of the stronghold and changed its name to Annapolis in honour of the British sovereign. So fell the first of these fortresses, which were the counters in that long game played on the chess-board of a continent.

The capture of Port Royal strengthened the determination of the English colonists to drive the French out of Canada by destroying their grim stronghold upon the St. Lawrence. The home government fell in readily with the project, and despatched seven regiments of the line, fresh from Marlborough's campaigns, together with a fleet of fifteen warships under Admiral Sir Hovenden Walker. This powerful auxiliary to the strength of the colonies arrived duly at Boston, where the details

---

[1] This was the officer who, years before, had striven to rescue the victims of the massacre of Lachine.

of the invasion of Canada were arranged; and when
at length all was ready, the English admiral sailed
from Boston for the St. Lawrence, Nicholson at the
same time setting out overland for Montreal with a
force of twelve thousand men.

In the meanwhile Vaudreuil had succeeded De
Callières as Governor at Quebec, a post which long
military experience in Canada fitted him to hold in
the warfare now enveloping New France. At this
time the total population of the country was not
much more than fifteen thousand souls, and of fighting men — those whose ages ranged from fifteen years
to sixty — Montreal possessed twelve hundred, Three
Rivers four hundred, and the district of Quebec
twenty-two hundred. On the other hand, the population of the New England colonies was something
over one hundred thousand, the colony of New York
alone twice outnumbering New France.

Such disparity in the populations of the warring
colonies was, however, somewhat discounted by
another consideration; for while the power of New
France was well organised and capable of skilful
direction, the English colonists could carry out no
enterprise with the undisciplined soldiery at their
disposal. This explains why the French were able
to survive for more than half a century the attacks
of antagonists richer, more numerous, and not less
valorous than themselves. It further shows why,

throughout their continuous border warfare, the more audacious and better-trained soldiery of New France triumphed so often over the raw levies of Connecticut and New York.

Sir Hovenden Walker's armada set sail from Boston harbour on the 30th of July, 1711, fore-doomed, through the incapacity of its leader, to the most ignominious failure yet befalling any expedition against Quebec. By reason of his former mission to Canada, Colonel Vetch had been commanded to accompany the fleet, and his *Journal of a Voyage Designed to Quebec* furnishes the mournful details of this ill-fated enterprise.

By the Admiral's direction, Vetch was on board the *Sapphire*, the smallest of the frigates, with orders to pick out the safe channel for the rest of the fleet ; and although but a landsman, he did his best to act as a pilot. All went well until they reached the wide mouth of the St. Lawrence. There, instead of depending upon one of the smaller ships to lead the way, the Admiral imprudently sailed with his flag-ship in the van. By a singular want of judgment, moreover, he chose to follow the channel north of the Island of Anticosti.

In the fairest of weathers this reef-strewn passage is full of peril, and a dense fog enveloped the fleet on that disastrous August evening. Although advised

to anchor until the fog should lift, the Admiral
scoffed at fear. Driven by a whistling wind, the
ships of the line leaped forward, shaping a course
north-north-west, until suddenly the sound of
breakers burst upon them ; and as if in relentless
mockery, the rising moon lit up the angry reefs of
Egg Island. Helms were put hard down, and the
Admiral's vessel swung round to the wind ; but eight
of the tall battleships were too late to avoid their
doom. Eight hundred and eighty-four persons were
drowned, thirty-four of these being women.

A council of war was held three days later, but
instead of pressing on up the river with the rest of
the ships, Sir Hovenden Walker and Brigadier Hill,[1]
the commander of the forces, decided to abandon the
expedition. The *Sapphire* was despatched to Boston
to recall the land force ; and on the shores of Lake
Champlain these inglorious orders overtook the
sturdy Nicholson, who regretfully led his column
back to Albany.

Meanwhile, Quebec had awaited this her third
siege in a fever of anxiety. Vaudreuil had disposed
a thousand men, under De Ramézay, at the new stone
fort at Chambly to check the invasion by land, and
strengthened the city with all available forces, regular
and irregular. The *habitants* of the long Côte de

---

[1] Brigadier John Hill was the brother of Mrs. Masham, Queen Anne's favourite,
to whom, and not to his merit, he owed his appointment.

Beaupré had hidden away their goods, and flocked within the walls of the city with all the provisions they could transport. Prayers for deliverance rose unceasingly from the altars of the churches and convents, while the nuns devoted themselves to a nine days' Mass at Notre Dame de Pitié.

Upon this anxiety came the tidings of the wreck at Egg Island. Once more Providence had intervened to save them, and Quebec was delirious with joy. Every belfry in New France pealed forth its hymn of thanksgiving. The little church on the Lower Town market-place changed its name from *Notre Dame de la Victoire* to *Notre Dame des Victoires*, and the citizens added a portico in token of their exultation and gratitude.

The Treaty of Utrecht in 1713, which brought the war of the Spanish succession to a close, deprived France of many of her American possessions. Chief of these were Acadia, Newfoundland, and the Hudson's Bay Territory, all of which were now ceded to England. In the Gulf of St. Lawrence, France retained only the Isle Royale, Isle of St. John,[1] and the two tiny rocks of St. Pierre and Miquelon. New France was, however, unwilling to give up her hold on the Atlantic seaboard, and procured a grant of thirty million francs from the home government

---

[1] Now called Cape Breton and Prince Edward Island respectively.

to build the fortress of Louisbourg at the entrance to
the river St. Lawrence.   Vauban, the great French
engineer, drew the plans of that vast fortification on
the rocky headland of Cape Breton, which was
destined to play so important a part in the final storm
then gathering over the American continent.

In the meantime New France had entered upon a
season of unexpected peace — unexpected because
for at least two generations the conflict with the
English colonists had been so continuous that Quebec
had almost come to regard warfare as her normal
state.   The respite following upon the Treaty of
Utrecht was the more welcome ; and in that breath-
ing space of almost thirty years it seemed as if a
real prosperity had at last visited the St. Lawrence.
The cultivation of flax and hemp and the weaving of
cloth, which had been but a feeble industry since the
days of Talon, now assumed real importance.   Furs
were still the main resource of the colony ; but grain,
fish, oil, and leather also found their way to France
in increasing quantities.   Quebec became the centre
of a considerable shipping trade, and sea-going vessels
were launched from the stocks on the bank of the
little St. Charles.

Moreover, the energies of the people presently
found another and alluring field.   In 1716 a
missionary to the Sault Indians discovered the
gensing root, which, as a medical drug, was quoted

in European markets at its weight in silver. At first its price in Quebec was only forty *sols* per pound, but when the people saw its value rising to almost as many *livres*, the rush of searchers to the woods left all other industries at a standstill. Agriculture furnished a slow road to wealth by comparison with the hunt of the gensing plant, and Quebec passed through the fever of a modern gold-rush. Natural and economic conditions, however, had provided their own remedy; and in time the glut of the market and the extirpation of the gensing plant sent the feverish botanists back to their wonted pursuits. Then ensued a period of peace and quiet progress, of patriotic co-operation of the officials and the people for the good of the land.

In 1725 the long and beneficent rule of the first Vaudreuil came to an end, and the Marquis de Beauharnois succeeded to the governorship of Quebec. The features of this and the succeeding administrations were the further expansion westward of New France and the construction of that chain of forts by which she sought finally to fasten her grip upon the continent. One by one these fortresses rose up in the far wilderness to hem in the English between the sea and the Alleghanies, and one by one they were demolished, as England and her colonies slowly rolled down the curtain on the drama of French dominion in North America.

Nearer home, also, that is to say, nearer to Quebec, French enterprise had taken the form of building and manning forts ; and as the fate of these scattered strongholds closely affects the story of Quebec, a brief outline of their location is here given.

Port Royal had passed for ever out of French hands, and to take its place the giant bastions of Louisbourg had risen on a ridge of rock which made one arm of Gabarus Bay. On the river Missaguash, which the French claimed to mark the northern boundary of English Acadia, stood Fort Beauséjour. Chambly, Sorel, and St. Thérèse, on the Richelieu, were Indian forts of old foundation ; and as a further defence against the English, Beauharnois built Crown Point at the narrows of Lake Champlain. The stronghold of Carillon was situated a few miles beyond. On the Alleghany river, Forts Venango and Le Bœuf barred the westward growth of Pennsylvania ; and Fort Duquesne, begun as an English fort by the Ohio Company, guarded the junction of the Alleghany and the Monongahela. Fort Niagara, near one end of Lake Ontario, and Fort Frontenac at the other, were also to figure in the closing stages of the conflict.

The exploit of the Sieur de la Vérendrye, which marked this period, was perhaps the most picturesque achievement Quebec had witnessed since the days of La Salle. In the spring of 1731, La Vérendrye, with his three sons and a handful of adventurous *coureurs de bois*, set off from the trading post of Michillimackinac to take possession of the West. By a long succession of paddles and portages, La Vérendrye came to the Lake of the Woods. Then, threading his way through its myriad islands, he found and followed a wild stream which bore him down to Lake Winnipeg. From here he passed into the Red River, and at its junction with the Assiniboine built Fort Rouge. From this base the bold explorers made their way as far north as the forks of the Saskatchewan; and by 1743 the distant peaks of the Rocky Mountains had re-warded the vision of a younger La Vérendrye. To no avail: for this wide dominion was destined to pass to hands firmer to hold, if slower to acquire.

P. Hoare. pinx.   J. Brown. sc.

The Earl of Chatham

from the collection in the possession of Lord Bridport.

CHAPTER XI

THE BEGINNING OF THE END

THE growing power of England, on the sea, in America, and in India, was only equalled by the increasing jealousy of the Catholic nations of Europe, and especially of her ancient rival France. The question of the Austrian succession, in which these two conspicuous opposites stood for and against Maria Theresa, supplied a pretext for war; yet it hardly concealed the real purpose of each power to destroy the other; and the battles of Fontenoy, Nollwitz, and Dettingen, though fought in the heart of Europe, were as decisive for an Eastern and a Western empire as was the warfare on the frontiers of India, or the sullen conflict in the Ohio valley.

Across the Atlantic, France, as usual, dealt the first blow. With a thousand soldiers from Louisbourg, Du Vivier assailed Annapolis Royal; but neither by investment nor assault could the French overcome the small but indomitable garrison; and at length, after weeks of useless cannonade, the

besiegers stole back to their stronghold in Cape
Breton. This gallant repulse of a desperate attempt
to regain Acadia prompted New England to an
expedition against the strong fortress of Louisbourg
— the standing menace to peaceful colonial development. Were it but reduced, the English seaboard
would be henceforth free from all danger of French
attack.

Such large considerations fired the English colonists with an enthusiasm which took little thought
for the grave dangers attending such an enterprise.
Excepting the citadel of Quebec itself, there was no
fortress on the American continent to compare in
strength with Louisbourg. Built on a narrow rocky
cape which projected out into the Atlantic, the ocean
girded it on three sides, and on the fourth side a morass
made it difficult of approach. A powerful fortification, known as the Island Battery, protected the
mouth of the harbour, and the guns of Grand Battery frowned over the inner basin. The French
garrison numbered thirteen hundred chosen men.
Such was the fortress which Governor Shirley of
Massachusetts planned to destroy, and against which
the daring Pepperell presently threw the ill-trained
levies of New England.

One night, when the citadel of Louisbourg was
brilliant with festivity, the colonists dancing and
all unconscious of danger, a hundred transports

from New England entered Gabarus Bay. The citizens would have held it a foolish dream that any attempt could be made to capture Louisbourg, but there, in the early morning of April 30th, 1745, Pepperell's army was disembarking before their eyes, and in the offing Commodore Warren, with four British battleships, stood blockading the harbour.

LIEUT.-GENERAL SIR WILLIAM PEPPERELL, BART.

The bells of the martial little town rang madly in alarm, and the booming of cannon at once brought the dismayed citizens to the ramparts.

Without loss of time Pepperell began to make his way across the marshes lying between his camp and Louisbourg, erecting batteries as he went to answer the cannonade of the garrison. Each morning saw the intrepid besiegers closer to the walls, having

advanced their intrenchments under cover of the
darkness.   A daring assault had meanwhile carried
the grand battery, and from a salient post on Lighthouse Point Pepperell's guns were soon able to
silence the island redoubt at the mouth of the
harbour.   The battle swayed from side to side as
the desperate garrison made a sortie, or the besiegers
impetuously rushed to the attack.   But even the
walls of Louisbourg could not for long withstand
that furious and ceaseless cannonade, which shattered
the heaviest bastions ; and when the gallant fort
could hold out no longer, a white flag fluttered from
the broken ramparts, and the brave Duchambon, his
veteran garrison decimated, marched out with the
honours of war.

The loss of Louisbourg was the severest blow yet
sustained by New France, and without delay a
powerful expedition was organised to recapture the
fortress and take revenge upon the enemy.   No such
formidable and menacing armada had ever left the
shores of France as now sailed out of Rochelle,
under command of the Duc d'Anville.   Thirty-nine
ships of the line convoyed transports bearing a
veteran army westward ; and the English colonists
trembled for its coming.   However, the advance
tidings of this terrible flotilla were all that reached
the New World ; for hardly had D'Anville lost sight
of the French coast before two of his ships fell a prey

to British gunboats, and a succession of storms
scattered the rest in all directions.

At length, after weeks of delay, the surviving
vessels struggled one by one into the harbour of
Chedabucto. In deadly dejection, D'Anville had suc-
cumbed to apoplexy; moreover, his successor, the
Admiral D'Estournelle, had committed suicide; and
the new commander was La Jonquière, a distinguished
naval officer, then on his way to Quebec to assume the
office of Governor-General. His sorry fleet notwithstanding, La Jonquière decided to strike a blow at
Annapolis. Thither he shaped his course; but again
a violent storm overtook them on the way, and the
ships, unable to weather the tempest, steered straight
for France once more.

Even in the face of these dark disasters France
was unwilling to abandon Louisbourg, and in 1747
another powerful naval force under La Jonquière set
out for Acadia. Like its magnificent but hapless
predecessor, this fleet had hardly cleared the Bay of
Biscay before it came to grief. Falling in with a
British squadron under Admiral Anson off Cape
Finisterre, it was almost totally destroyed.

In other quarters, however, France had received
amends from fortune, and in the following year
the European powers signed the Treaty of Aix-
la-Chapelle, Louisbourg being restored to France in
exchange for the Indian province of Madras, which

had passed from English hands during the war. To
New England, whose blood and valour had achieved
the demolition of the frowning fortress, this restitution
was a sorrowful blow. But only ten years were to
pass before this menace was removed for ever.

La Jonquière, Governor-designate of Quebec,
had been taken prisoner at the naval battle of
Finisterre; and, pending his release, the Marquis de
la Galissonière presided over the fortunes, or misfortunes, of New France. The indefiniteness of the
western boundary between French and English territory was perhaps the chief source of his perplexity;
and to put an end to persistent English encroachments
in the valley of the Ohio, Galissonière sent Céloron
de Bienville, a colonial captain, to establish a formal
boundary line. This expedition nominally accomplished its purpose; but, judging from the report
submitted to the Governor of Quebec, its chief result
was a painful revelation. It was shown that, in spite
of an expensive chain of fortified posts, the great
West was fast slipping from the martial grasp of New
France, and passing under the stronger influence of
English trade. The huge, unwieldy empire was
clearly falling to pieces, and La Jonquière's arrival
in Quebec brought no improvement to the situation.
Of high merit as a naval officer, the new Governor
had less distinction in morals, and he had frankly come
to Canada to mend his fortune. His administration

BIENVILLE

(Governor of Louisiana, 1732)

marks the advent of that official robbery which dis-
graced Quebec and sapped the remaining vitality of
the country. Though the country had prospered
materially under Vaudreuil, the subsequent war had
stopped all progress, and the people were dreaming
of empire when they needed bread.

To-day, walking down Palace Hill and turning
near the bottom into the Rue St. Vallier, you will find
yourself close to the site of the ancient intendancy,
where the official ruin of New France began. Here
it was that François Bigot, the evil genius of Quebec,
held corrupt sway in the guise of a royal minister.
Here stood, in mordant comment, the Palais de
Justice, so wickedly profaned by the last of the
intendants. Through several fires and two sieges
of later generations parts of this ancient structure
persisted in surviving. Only a few years ago the
heavier timber still hanging together was called
" The King's Wood-yard." But nothing now
remains of it, and imagination only summons the
haunting spirit of this creature of La Pompadour,
whose mischievous influence lost Louis XV. his
colonial empire, and whose infamies sealed the fate
of the Bourbons.

François Bigot arrived at Quebec in 1748, a year
in which the fortunes of New France had reached so
low an ebb that nothing but the most loyal administration might now save her. Even then a strong

honest man might possibly have weathered the storm already lowering over this New World dominion; but, with pitiable perverseness, every trait in Bigot's character helped it on to ruin. In private life vain, selfish, heartless, extravagant to the point of folly; in public life mercenary and venal beyond shame—such were the characteristics of the man whom Louis's favourite chose to be civil administrator at Quebec, where the patriotic faith and labour of a gallant and high-hearted people were rewarded by plunder, misrule, and that neglect which gave them at last into the hands of the conqueror.

On his arrival, the Intendant speedily surrounded himself by sycophants and knaves who joined him in the reckless pursuit of pleasure, and became ready instruments to further his darker designs. A man of ability, adroitness, and culture, Bigot might have won public favour, but his habits instantly estranged the better people of the colony. The *honnêtes gens*, a party which included the great Montcalm, the brave Bougainville, La Corne de St. Luc, M. de Lévis, and M. de Saint-Ours, would have nothing to do with him, and he was left in the hands of servile flatterers, ready enough to serve him. Deschenaux, his *fidus Achates*, was a cobbler's son, whom experience alone had educated and fate and unscrupulousness had advanced. Cadet, his commissary-general, was the gross son of a butcher, and had spent his

DE BOUGAINVILLE

(General under Montcalm, 1759)

dissatisfied youth in the pasture-fields of Charlesbourg.   Hughes Péan was the town major of
Quebec, but his chief hold on Bigot lay in the beauty
of his wife, the charming Angélique des Meloises.
This woman, whose beauty, wit, and *diablerie* are a
subject of popular tradition, possessed a fascination
which gave her an influence at the intendancy analo-
gous to that exerted at Versailles by her notorious
contemporary, La Pompadour.

Ruled by this coterie of dark spirits, Quebec
became the scene of a profligacy unparalleled in her
history.   The Palace, instead of being a hall of justice, was the abode of debauchery and gambling; and
the mad revellers, whom a cynical fate had placed
at the head of affairs, allowed the ship of state to drift
upon the rocks.   Even the fine palace within the
city gave too little scope for the diversion of the
Intendant and his confederates, and, accordingly, a
rustic château was built near the high hill of Charlesbourg.   Here they paused when tired of the chase,
and the revels of the mysterious *Maison de la
Montagne* added sad but vivid colouring to the
closing decade of French rule.   To-day there is an
air of pathetic interest about the picturesque ruin of
Château Bigot.   The high walls are covered with
ivy, and its graded walks and beds of flowers have
disappeared long since.   The immense thickness
of the walls has enabled " Beaumanoir " to elude

destroying Time, but only enough now remains to suggest the hapless revels of a bygone day.

These things, however, are of the private sins of Bigot and his *entourage*. Their public malefactions were more flagrant. The Intendant's salary could by no means meet his appalling extravagances, and he therefore robbed the country and the King by falsifying official accounts as they passed through his hands. As Intendant it was his duty to supply the needs of those chains of forts by which France held her vast dominion ; but while he shamelessly neglected these outposts, he did not fail to debit the royal treasury for supplies which were never forwarded. In this way he and his intriguing friends enriched themselves. They presently adopted another and more contemptible device. Constant hostility towards the British had deprived the farms of their cultivators, and the supply of wheat was greatly reduced throughout the colony. Every day the land grew more distressed, and it was not difficult to foresee a time of famine. Not far from *Le Palais* stood a huge building which went by the name of the King's Storehouse, and the Intendant resolved to fill this with wheat. He had an ancient precedent in Egyptian history, but his motive was not that of provident Joseph. Fixing the price of grain by an edict, and imposing penalties on those who refused to sell, his agents went through the country gathering

up maize and wheat; and when famine came at
length, the starving people flocked to the warehouse
in Lower Town, and were compelled to buy back
their grain at exorbitant prices. They called this
warehouse *La Friponne*—the Cheat—and they cursed
the name of Bigot who had so deceived them.

The interesting legend of *Le Chien d'Or* has its

RUINS OF CHÂTEAU BIGOT

origin in the mercenary practices of this last Intendant
of Quebec. Among the merchants of the city was
one Nicholas Jaquin, *dit* Philibert, whose warehouse
stood at the top of Mountain Hill, on the site of
the present Post-Office. Philibert was one of the
honnêtes gens, and he devoted his wealth and energy
to a commercial battle with *La Friponne*, determined
to supply the people with food at low prices. The
enmity between Philibert and the Intendant was

common talk, and over his doorway the merchant had hung, beneath the figure of a dog in bas-relief, the following whimsical quatrain : —

LE CHIEN D'OR

"Je suis un chien qui ronge l'os,
  En le rongeant je prends mon repos;
  Un jour viendra, qui n'est pas venu,
    Que je mordrai qui m'aura mordu."

The bitter conflict continued until Philibert was murdered in the street. The escape of the assassin was well contrived; but there was no avoiding the vengeance of Philibert's son, who, after years of searching, struck down his father's slayer in far-off Pondicherry.

Meanwhile the walls and bastions of Louisbourg

were rising stronger than ever upon their old foundations, and the French Acadians, relying upon the
Cape Breton stronghold and the nearer fortress of
Beauséjour, grew more and more restless beneath the
English yoke.   By founding Halifax in 1749, England
had taken faster hold upon the peninsula, and through
every possible means she had endeavoured to secure
the true allegiance of her Acadian subjects.   In
spite of all these efforts, however, Acadia was sown
with treason, and when at last disloyalty became
intolerable and dangerous, the innocent as well as the
guilty must reap the harvest of tears and bitterness.
There could only be one end to it all ; and however
hard the fate, the land of Acadia now ceased to be
the home of its makers, who had been goaded and
inveigled into covert rebellion and treason.

" This is the forest primeval ; but where are the hearts that be-
   neath it
   Leaped like the roe, when he hears in the woodland the voice of
      the huntsman ?
   Where is the thatch-roofed village, the home of Acadian
      farmers,
   Men whose lives glided on like rivers that water the woodlands,
   Darkened by shadows of earth, but reflecting an image of
      heaven ?
   Waste are those pleasant farms, and the farmers for ever de-
      parted !
   Scattered like dust and leaves, when the mighty blasts of
      October

Seize them, and whirl them aloft, and sprinkle them far o'er the
ocean —
Nought but tradition remains of the beautiful village of Grand
Pré.''

So sang Longfellow in his sorrowful tale of
Evangeline; and the cold page of history is hardly
less mournful.

The 5th of September, 1755, was a day memorable
alike to the Acadians and to those whose bitter duty
it was to carry out King George's orders for their
expulsion from the peninsula. At three o'clock in
the afternoon the peasants of Grand Pré, Piziquid,
Chipody, and the other parishes assembled in their
chapels to listen to a royal proclamation declaring their lands and houses forfeited to the Crown,
and themselves condemned to exile. The scenes
following this unexpected order wrung the hearts of
the rugged soldiers who were sent to execute the
sentence. Reluctantly and forbearingly they carried
out the royal command, and soon six thousand
Acadians, who had persistently refused allegiance to
the English in the vain belief that New France would
regain the peninsula, found themselves transported
to the English colonies farther south. Those who
swore allegiance were left undisturbed ; while many,
escaping both deportation and the oath of subjection,
fled to Quebec. These were doomed, however, to
misery far greater than that of their comrades who

were set down as strangers among the English colonists. Quebec, which had fomented and abetted their treason, now declined to share the burden of their misfortune.

The years of Bigot's *régime* were the lean years of the city, and this influx of a thousand new starvelings was a most unwelcome addition to the population. Yet even the unfavourable circumstances of the time cannot justify the official neglect and the cruel inhospitality with which the miserable exiles were received in the capital of New France. "In vain," says a chronicler, "they asked that the promises they had received should be kept, and they pleaded the sacrifices they had made for France. All was useless. The former necessity for their services had passed away. They were looked upon as a troublesome people, and if they received assistance they were made to feel that it was only granted out of pity. They were almost reduced to die of famine. The little food they obtained, its bad quality, their natural want of cleanliness, their grief, and their idleness caused the death of many. They were forced to eat boiled leather during the greater part of the winter, and to wait for spring in the hope that their condition would be bettered. On this point they were deceived." [1]

"To supplement a miserable daily ration of four ounces of bread and horseflesh," says another writer,

[1] Archives of Nova Scotia.

" they were obliged to seek scraps in the gutters;
and those who survived starvation were brought low
with a virulent smallpox, which carried off whole
families in its loathsome tumbril."

In the meantime, a series of events had happened
in the Ohio valley which set the New World on fire.
Céloron de Bienville had indeed staked out his boundary line, but the new Governor of Quebec, the Marquis Duquesne, saw clearly that a line of bayonets
was the only limit which English expansionists would
respect. Accordingly, a strong French force marched
into the troublesome valley, and established themselves at a new post called Fort Le Bœuf.

The report of this incursion was evil news for
Governor Dinwiddie of Virginia, the most diligent
and watchful of the thirteen governors of the English colonies. Having never ceased to regard Lake
Erie as a northern boundary of British territory,
this latest invasion on the part of the French was to
him beyond endurance, and he forthwith despatched
the Adjutant-General of the Virginia Militia to deliver England's protest to the French commander.
The messenger was a tall handsome youth of twenty-
one, and the message was the first important commission of George Washington.

In spite of the studied courtesy of his reception
by Legardeur de Saint-Pierre, the English envoy

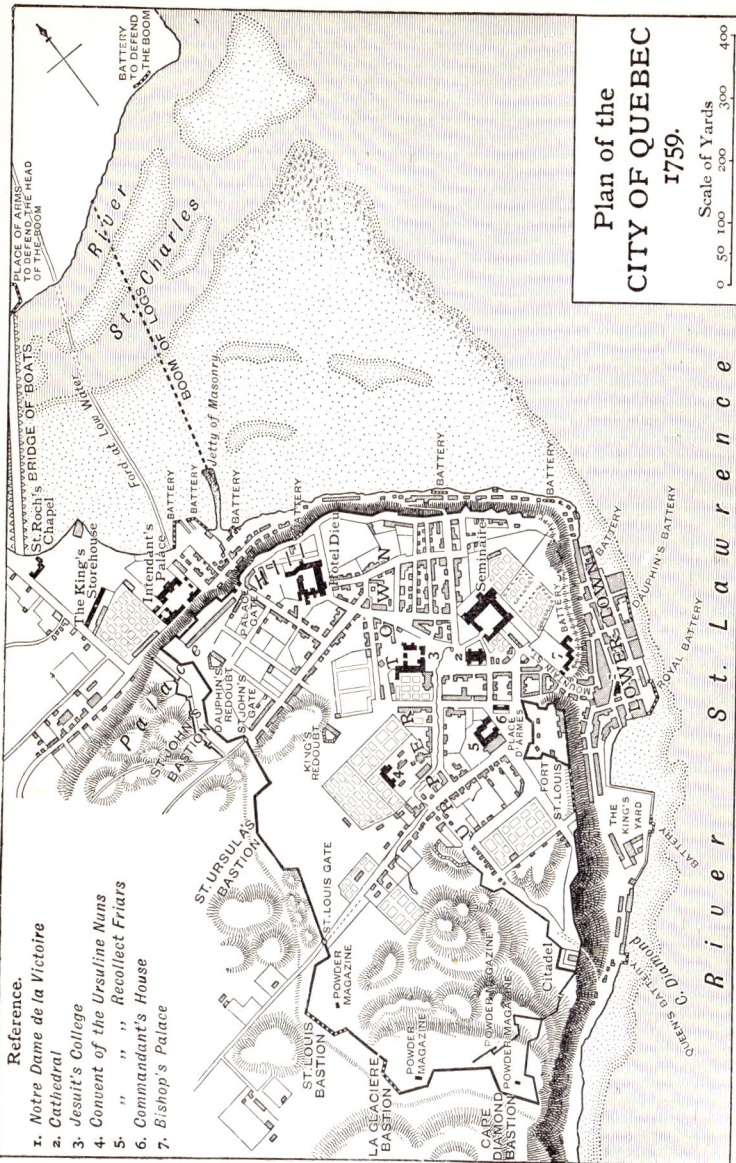

Plan of the
CITY OF QUEBEC
1759.

Scale of Yards
0 50 100 200 300 400

Walker & Cockerell sc.

Reference.
1. Notre Dame de la Victoire
2. Cathedral
3. Jesuit's College
4. Convent of the Ursuline Nuns
5.   "   "   Recollect Friars
6.   "   "   Commandant's House
7. Bishop's Palace

River St. Lawrence

St. Charles River

BOOM OF LOGS

BRIDGE OF BOATS
St. Roch's Chapel

PLACE OF ARMS TO DEFEND THE HEAD OF THE BOOM

BATTERY TO DEFEND THE BOOM

Jetty of Masonry
Ford at Low Water

The King's Storehouse
Intendant's Palace

Hotel Dieu

Seminary

LOWER TOWN
UPPER TOWN

DAUPHIN'S BATTERY
ROYAL BATTERY
QUEEN'S BATTERY
BATTERY

PALACE GATE
ST. JOHN'S GATE
DAUPHIN REDOUBT
ST. JOHN'S BASTION
KING'S REDOUBT

ST. URSULA'S BASTION
ST. LOUIS GATE
ST. LOUIS BASTION
LA GLACIERE BASTION
CAPE DIAMOND BASTION

POWDER MAGAZINE
Citadel
Q.C. DIAMOND BATTERY

PLACE D'ARMES
FORT ST. LOUIS
THE KING'S YARD

saw the hopelessness of his errand, and hastened back
to Williamsburg with his report.   Dinwiddie thereupon resolved to meet force with force.   Although

MAJOR-GENERAL SIR ISAAC BARRE

(Paymaster of Wolfe's Forces)

he scarcely persuaded the disunited colonies to take
a serious view of the French invasion, he was presently able to send George Washington back again
into the Ohio valley at the head of a company of

P

regulars and three hundred soldiers of the Old
Dominion.

Meanwhile the French had seized an English
trading-post at the junction of the Ohio and
Monongahela rivers, and named it Fort Duquesne.
This post was Washington's immediate objective,
and as he approached it his advance-guard met
a French reconnoitring party under Jumonville,
sent, it is alleged, by the commandant of Fort
Duquesne to warn the Virginians off French soil.
The precise purpose served by this handful of
Frenchmen has never, however, been fully determined. Jumonville's movements are certainly hard
to reconcile with the theory of a peaceful mission,
and to Major Washington they certainly appeared
hostile. In the sharp fight which followed, Jumonville and nine others were killed, while of the
remaining twenty-three only one escaped. By the
English, the affair was described as a successful
skirmish, by the French as the "*Assassinat de
Jumonville*"; for all it meant precipitation of the
death-struggle for North America.

Anticipating the French attack, Washington fell
back upon Great Meadows, and the hasty and inad-
equate intrenchments which he there threw up received the name of Fort Necessity. Here he awaited
an assault with a short supply of ammunition and
almost no provisions. Nor was his patience long

tried; for nine hundred Frenchmen under Coulon de
Villiers, brother of the unfortunate Jumonville, were
already marching against him through the woods.
Wishing to entice them to an immediate attack,
Washington had arrayed his men on the open meadow
before the fort; but as his opponent declined to be
drawn from the cover of the surrounding hills, the
Virginians also took shelter in their shallow intrenchments. A blind fusillade now began in torrents
of rain and was maintained for nine hours, punctuated
by the booming of a few light swivel guns upon the
ramparts.

At nightfall, however, the French proposed a
parley, and having weighed the chances of his
little army against such overwhelming numbers,
Washington agreed to capitulate. Next day the
English marched out of Fort Necessity with beating
drums and flying colours; but heart-sick and weary
they toiled back over the mountains to Virginia,
leaving the valley of the Ohio in the full possession
of the enemy. Moreover, the defeat at Fort
Necessity was a double blow, for it threw the fickle
Indians back into the arms of the French, a consideration of great weight in border warfare.

In Europe the rival powers were still maintaining
the semblance of peace, while yet secretly abetting
the open enmity of their American colonies. The
despatch of Major-General Braddock with two

regiments of the line, although accounted for by the lips of diplomacy, was, with equally pacific assurances, promptly checkmated by France. Eighteen ships of war, carrying the six battalions of La Reine, Bourgogne, Languedoc, Guienne, Artois, and Béarn, and convoyed by an auxiliary squadron of nine battleships, were hurried off to New France under the joint command of Baron Dieskau and the Marquis de Vaudreuil, the new Governor of Quebec. As in the case of former expeditions on so large a scale, some of the vessels failed to reach their destination, and two frigates fell into the hands of Admiral Boscawen, who had secret orders to intercept this French flotilla.

Braddock and his thousand regulars were now regarded as the salvation of the English colonies, whose representatives had at last agreed upon a scheme for defending their frontiers. The English general, it was decided, should destroy Fort Duquesne, Governor Shirley attacking the French fort of Niagara; while Colonel William Johnson, a settler of the Upper Hudson, and chiefly remarkable for his influence with the Mohawks, was to proceed against Crown Point. None of these intentions was fulfilled in its entirety, although Johnson, in the course of his operations in the district of Lake Champlain, was able to inflict a crushing defeat upon the French under Dieskau,

and on the scene of his triumph to erect Fort
William Henry.

The feature of the summer campaign of 1755
was, however, the fate of Braddock and his

SIR HUGH PALLISER, BART.
(Raised first English flag over Quebec, 1759)

column. Setting out from Fort Cumberland on the
Potomac, the English General made his way north-
westward at the head of twenty-two hundred
men, four hundred and fifty of these being veteran
Virginians under the command of Colonel George
Washington. But the overweening Braddock con-

sidered these raw colonials to be the least effective of his troops. From the first the progress of this imposing force was painfully slow. " Instead of pushing on with vigour without regarding a little rough road," writes George Washington, " we were halted to level every mole-hill, and compelled to erect bridges over every brook, by which means we were four days in getting twelve miles." Declining colonial advice, Braddock preferred to regulate his motions by the text-book of war ; and as he knew nothing of the country through which he made his way, and still less of the tactics of his foe, the sequel was almost inevitable.

" It was the 10th of June," says Parkman, " before the army was well on its march. Three hundred axemen led the way, to cut and clear the road ; and the long train of pack-horses, waggons, and cannon toiled on behind, over the stumps, roots, and stones of the narrow track, the regulars and provincials marching in the forest close on either side. Squads of men were thrown out on the flanks, and scouts ranged the woods to guard against surprise ; for, with all his scorn of Indians and Canadians, Braddock did not neglect reasonable precautions. Thus, foot by foot, they advanced into the waste of lonely mountains that divided the streams flowing into the Atlantic from those flowing into the Gulf of Mexico — a realm of forests ancient as the world. The road was but twelve feet wide, and the line of march often extended four miles. It was like a thin, long, parti-coloured snake, red, blue, and brown, trailing slowly through the depth of leaves, creeping round in-accessible heights, crawling over ridges, moving always in dampness and shadow, by rivulets and waterfalls, crags and chasms, gorges and shaggy steeps. In glimpses only, through jagged boughs and flickering leaves, did this wild primeval world reveal itself, with its dark green mountains, flecked with the morning mist, and its distant peaks pencilled in dreamy blue. The army passed the main Alleghany, Meadow Mountain, and traversed the funereal pine-forest afterwards called the Shadows of Death." [1]

Meanwhile, French scouts had brought news of the approaching column, and Beaujeu, an officer at Fort Duquesne, conceiving the idea of attacking Braddock as he came up a deep wooded ravine lying about eight miles from the fort, repaired thither with a force of nine hundred men, including French regulars, Canadians, and Indians.

The English troops toiled on, and when the defenceless vanguard was well advanced up the pass, Beaujeu gave the signal which sent down a hail of deadly bullets upon them. Still the redcoats held

[1] Parkman, *Montcalm and Wolfe*, vol. i. chap. vii.

their ground bravely, firing steady volleys against the hidden foe. By this time the main army also had entered the pass, only to be thrown into instant confusion, their solid ranks offering a target to the French sharpshooters. Bewildered by the converging fire, the column huddled together at the bottom of the pass, while the bullets mowed them down pitilessly. The brave but headstrong general exhorted them to preserve the order of their ranks, and when they would have fled in terror, he beat them back into line with his own sword. The Virginians alone knew how to avert a massacre, and spreading out quickly into skirmish order, they took cover behind the trees and rocks to meet their wily foe on even terms. But the brave and stubborn Braddock was blind to so obvious an expedient, and with oaths he ordered the irregulars back into the death-line.

All the long July afternoon the carnage continued. Four horses fell dead beneath the indomitable General, and two were killed under the gallant Washington who, with his Virginian rangers, covered the retreat of Braddock's miserable remnant when at last they resolved on flight. Only six hundred escaped out of that fatal valley, while the General himself, in spite of his command that they should leave him where he fell, was borne away fatally wounded in the lungs.

So ended the summer campaign of 1755; and even Johnson's brilliant success at Fort William Henry could not offset the terrible disaster which had befallen British arms in the valley of the Ohio.

CHAPTER XII

FOR all its sombre background bright threads run through the warp and woof of the *ancien régime*. From Normandy, Brittany, and Perche they came, these simple folk of the St. Lawrence, to brave the dangers of an unknown world and wrestle with primeval nature for a livelihood. If their hands were empty their hearts were full, Gallic optimism and child-like faith in their patron saints bringing them through untold misfortunes with a prayer or a song upon their lips. The savage Indian with his reeking tomahawk might break through and steal, the moth and rust of evil administration might wear away the fortunes of New France, yet the *habitant* ever found joy in labour and made light of hard circumstance.

In every language there is a pensive attraction in the words " the good old days " ; and even to-day the phrase brings a tear to the eye of the French Canadian as his mind dwells on the time before the Conquest ;

THE CITY OF QUEBEC IN 1759

for while conscious of his growth in freedom and
wealth, the sentiment for past days and vanished
glory obscures in his mind the thought of these
material blessings.   Spirits of the *ancien régime* still
haunt the dreamy firesides of the Province, yet their

BARON GRANT

(Whose family represents the Barony of Longueil, the only existing French Canadian
Barony of the old *régime*)

presence does not impair the loyalty of these
adopted sons of Britain.

When Wolfe came to Quebec, the flight of a
century and a half had transformed Champlain's
" Habitation " and its clustering huts into the
strongest and fairest city of the New World.
Churches, convents, and schools huddled together,

and composed a varied picture upon the uneven
summit of .a towering rock; cannon thrust their
black muzzles through the girdling walls of stone;
and the bastioned citadel rose over all, commanding the river, the city, and the graceful country
rolling inland from high Cape Diamond.

Sunshine reflected from the spires and towers of
the town made a beacon of hope to the peasant as he
laboured on the seigneuries leagues and leagues away.
Far down the Côte de Beaupré, beyond the Mont
Ste. Anne, from the rich farms of Orleans, and
across on the Lévi shore, the glistening light on the
city roofs by day, and at night the twinkling candles
in the windows, were as guiding stars to these
children in the wilderness. Twice in the early days,
so their folklore told them, miraculous intervention
had saved their city from the invader; and was
she not impregnable still? And as he gazed happily
across the uplands towards his Mecca, the *habitant*
could conceive of no power which might prevail
against her stony ramparts. To this day the
emblems of their faith abound, scattered along the
wayside; and here and there a little wooden cross,
set on with two or three rough steps, invites the
wayfarer to pause and pray. Bareheaded, the
pilgrim waits before the holy symbol to whisper an
Ave or to tell his beads. Rough bushmen cease
from riot and laughter, and touch their caps as they

pass. All down the côtes, these casual shrines
exhort the simple peasant to his twofold duty — to
God and to his neighbour.   Throughout the river

BARONESS DE LONGUEIL
(Of the sole remaining Barony of the old *régime*)

parishes the size and richness of the churches con-
trasts strangely with the poverty of the rough-cast
cottages, revealing the devout spirit of the villagers,
to whom the church stands before all else.

Seven leagues below the city of Quebec is the

greatest of all these shrines, *L'Église de la bonne Ste. Anne.* In the foreground, the wide bosom of the St. Lawrence stretches across to the Isle of Orleans, while Mont Ste. Anne rises in graceful lines upon the flank, making a green background for the stone Basilica, which draws nearly two hundred thousand pilgrims every year to its healing altars. Perhaps, as you enter the village, the rich chimes of Ste. Anne are ringing a processional, and the cripples are thronging through the pillared vestibule. Some of these pious sufferers have come a thousand miles to wait, like those in days of old, for the moving of the waters. Inside the church, the pillars are covered with cast-off crutches, which faithful pilgrims leave behind when they go forth healed.

The history of the shrine of Ste. Anne de Beaupré goes back almost to the time of Champlain. A traditional account of its foundation relates that some Breton mariners, being overtaken by a violent storm on the St. Lawrence, vowed a sanctuary to Ste. Anne if she would but bring them safe to shore. Their prayers were heard, and forthwith they raised a little wooden chapel at Petit-Cap, seven leagues below Quebec. History, however, gives 1658 as the date of the first chapel of Ste. Anne; and it was while engaged in its construction that Louis Guimont became the subject of the first miraculous cure. Other cures rapidly followed, and soon the shrine

became renowned for its miracles.   The Marquis de
Tracy made two pilgrimages; and Anne of Austria,
the mother of Louis XIV., accorded her patronage,
sending to the little chapel a vestment embroidered
by herself.

During two and a half centuries the church of

UPPER TOWN MARKET TO-DAY

Ste. Anne has been several times rebuilt.   The
present imposing structure dates from 1886, and has
been raised by the Pope to the rank of a Basilica
Minor.   Beaupré has become the Lourdes of the
New World, where the halt, the maimed, the sick,
and the blind piously contend together in effort to
reach the healing shrine.

In the old days once or twice a week, according
to the season and the distance of the city, the peas-

ant made his way to Quebec, to take up his stand on the market-place, and sell his produce to the townspeople. The practice still survives, and on a Saturday half the women of Upper Town busily drive their bargains outside St. John's Gate, while at the river's brink Champlain Market is equally alive.

When the ancient Seigneur came to town his sword was upon his thigh, and he wore his smartest toilet of peruke, velvet, and lace. The Château upon the cliff was his Versailles, and hither came the quality of the district to pay their court and attend the receptions of the Governor. The Seigneur's wife was gowned according to the latest intelligence from Paris, with *coiffe poudre*, court-plaster, ribbons, and fan. She could curtsey with fine grace and dance the stately minuet; and her sprightly conversation was the amazement of those visitors who have recorded their impressions of Quebec. La Potherie, in 1698, and Charlevoix, in 1720, both remarked upon the purity of the French language as spoken in these *salons* of the far-distant West.

In spite of clerical anathema, the first ball in Canada was given at Fort St. Louis as early as 1646, and from that time forward social life at Quebec steadily progressed. The Marquis de Tracy with his suite of nobles and the regiment of Carignan-Salières brought unwonted lustre to the remote court; and when a native order of noblesse was founded a few

years later, the Château on the St. Lawrence reflected
the elegance and gaiety of France itself.

The account of Madame de Vaudreuil's reception
at Versailles in 1709, or the Duc de Saint-Simon's
comment upon that lady's wit and deportment,
affords a high certificate of the *savoir vivre* of the
old fortress town ; and the letters of the Marquis de

NEW ST. JOHN'S GATE

Montcalm, keen connoisseur of social arts, show
that the drawing-rooms of the Rue du Parloir were
far from uncongenial. Moreover, the fascinating
Angélique des Meloises was something more in the
history of New France than the prototype of the
heroine in *Le Chien d'Or*.

Towards the close of the French period Quebec
had a population of about seven thousand, of whom
more than half lived in the Lower Town.   Here,

on the narrow strand beneath the cliff, the tenements stood in irregular groups, parted by winding streets. Up the hill, too, these tortuous pathways ran, changing, now and then, to breakneck stairs where the declivity was specially steep. The graded slope of Mountain Street zigzagged from the harbour up to the Castle, while on the St. Charles side the ascent was commonly made by way of Palace Hill. The Upper Town was chiefly occupied by public buildings, which comprised the Château, the Cathedral, churches, schools, and convents. Here also the streets followed no definite plan, but ambled hither and thither along the uneven summit. Out through the city gates ran the roads of St. Louis and St. John, highways to the straggling suburbs, which yet hung close to the protecting ramparts.

The houses were built of wood or of grey stone, usually to the height of one story, being also surmounted by a tall, steep roof, through which the tiny dormer windows peeped in picturesque disorder. Inside, a slight partition divided the dwelling into two chambers. In the end of the living-room stood a large open fireplace, the household cooking-pots swinging from an iron crane. A sturdy table occupied the centre of the floor, and benches or blocks of wood were ranged as chairs around the walls. The inevitable cradle, consecrated to the service of two, three, or four generations, pounded

PETIT CHAMPLAIN STREET TO-DAY

monotonously to and fro upon the uneven floor,
and by the low-set window the thrifty housewife
wove her flaxen homespun in a venerable loom.
Saints, in pictures of fervid tints, looked down
serenely from low, unplastered walls, while from the
rafters of the ceiling were hung the weapons of the
family arsenal — flint-lock muskets and hilted hunt-

OLD PRESCOTT GATE

ing-knives, and sometimes too an ancestral sword or
silver-handled pistol.

In the matter of dress, social distinctions were
punctiliously regarded. The *gentilhomme* was as
careful as his wife to follow the latest vogue at
Versailles. His hair was curled, powdered, and tied
in a *queue*, his headgear was the ceremonious three-
cornered hat. A stately, coloured frockcoat, an embroidered waistcoat, knee-breeches, silk stockings,

and high-heeled buckled shoes completed the toi-
lette of the Canadian seigneur.

"The dress of the *Habitants*," says an observer
of a much later date than Saint-Simon or Montcalm,[1]
"is simple and homely; it consists of a long-skirted
cloth or frock, of a dark grey colour, with a hood
attached to it, which in winter time or wet weather
he puts over his head. His coat is tied round the
waist by a worsted sash of various colours, ornamented
with beads. His waistcoat and trousers are of the
same cloth. A pair of moccasins, or swamp boots,
complete the lower part of his dress. His hair is
tied in a thick long *queue* behind, with an eelskin;
and on each side of his face a few straight locks
hang down like what are vulgarly called 'rat's tails.'
Upon his head is a *bonnet rouge*, or in other words, a
red night-cap. The *tout ensemble* of his figure is
completed by a short pipe, which he has in his
mouth from morning till night. A Dutchman is
not a greater smoker than a French Canadian.

"The visage of the *Habitant* is long and thin, his
complexion sunburnt and swarthy, and not unfre-
quently of a darker hue than that of the Indian.
His eyes, though rather small, are dark and lively;
his nose prominent, and inclined to the aquiline or
Roman form; his cheeks lank and meagre; his lips
small and thin; his chin sharp and projecting."

[1] Lambert, *Travels*, vol i. p. 158.

In winter, rich and poor alike were wrapped in homespun blanket *paletots*, whose vivid colours made a charming picture, as the wayfarers trudged over the deep white snow-fields on their buoyant snow-shoes, or coasted through the clear and bracing air on swift toboggans. In the evening they flocked to a chosen *rendezvous*, where a home-bred violinist tuned them through gay quadrilles; and anon the lonely violin would be drowned in the lusty voices of the dancers, who suited a folk-song to their steps —

> " Malbrouck s'en va-t-en guerre,
> Mironton, mironton, mirontaine ;
> Malbrouck s'en va-t-en guerre,
> Ne sait quand reviendra.
> Il reviendra z-à Pâques
> Ou à la Trinité.
> La Trinité se passe,
> Malbrouck ne revient pas."

Moreover, winter, the idle half of the year, was the season of social visits; and in these courtesies the *habitants* were assiduous. Between Christmas and Ash Wednesday they strove, it would seem, to fill themselves with gaiety against the coming grey season of Lent. An unbidden throng of visitors would drive to a selected house, and sheer bankruptcy would indeed have been the housewife's portion if this welcome invasion had been wholly unexpected; but to meet such an emergency cooked meats and pies stood ready upon her pantry shelves, while *croquignoles* and sweet pasties needed only a few moments in the oven before a meal was ready. Thus during the days of snow they went gaily from homestead to homestead, all being victimised in turn by these "surprise parties." For *la haute no-*

A CARRIOLE

blesse also, the winter season was the gayest of the year. Their quaint carrioles sped jingling over the snow from one manor-house to another; here a dinner-party, there a dance, and everywhere a frugal happiness.

In *Les Anciens Canadiens* De Gaspé portrays the life of this seigneurial class to which he himself belonged. The manor-house was usually a long, low, stone-built structure, surmounted by overhanging gables and a lofty roof. A wing was sometimes added at right angles, and always a group of strongly-built outhouses, stables, and sheds clustered near by; among them standing a stone mill which had perhaps served as a tower of refuge in the troublous times

VILLAGE OF BEAUPORT

of the Iroquois raids, but which the *censitaires* now used merely to grind their grain. If the Seigneur was possessed of power to execute high, middle, and low justice, a gallows and a pillory might be found within the precincts; but towards the close of the *ancien régime* these crude implements of punishment had happily fallen into disuse. The parish church was never far away, the Seigneur being at all times the patron of the *presbytère,* as well as the potent bulwark of the feudal village springing up within sight of his manor-house.

These country mansions were much the same as those of Quebec, and there was little difference in the manner of living within and without the city walls. At eight o'clock the *gentilhomme* and his family breakfasted on rolls, white wine, and coffee; while dinner was served at noon, and supper at seven in the evening. The dining-room of a fashionable house-hold was tastefully arranged. One end of the room was completely occupied by the massive side-board, filled with ancestral silver and china. Upon a shelf apart stood cut-glass decanters for the table service, and as a *coup d'appétit* cordials were handed round in the drawing-room. On coming into the dining-room the guest might, if he chose, rinse his hands in a blue and white porcelain water-basin, which stood upon a pedestal in one corner of the room. Arrived at the table, he found his *couvert* to consist of a napkin, plate, silver goblet, fork and spoon, being expected to supply his own knife. For these occasions men usually carried knives in their pockets, the ladies wearing them in a leathern, silken, or birch-bark sheath. This peculiar custom caused some embar-rassment to those English officers who were billeted in French houses after the capture of the city.[1]

The maple sugar season brought to the *habitants*

[1] Captain Knox's *Journal of the Siege.*

their first relaxation from the severities of Lent.
Huge caldrons of sap hung on poles over the roaring
fires, and the children gathered round to taste the
syrup, and salute with songs of welcome the coming
of jocund spring.   May-day soon followed, " the
maddest merriest day " in all the calendar.   In the
early morning the *habitant* repaired to the seigneury
to assist in erecting the May-pole.   Almost every one
he knew — man, woman, or child — was there with
similar intent.   Presently the tall fir-tree, stripped of
its bark, was firmly planted in the farmyard, and a
deputation waited upon the Seigneur to beg his acceptance of this homage.   A fusillade of blank musket
shots was now kept up until the May-pole was
thoroughly blackened.   This done, the doors of the
manor-house were thrown wide open in welcome;
and the rest of the day was one long banquet.   The
Seigneur's tables groaned beneath burdens of roasted
veal, mutton, and pork, huge bowls of stew, pies, and
cakes, to which was added white whiskey and tobacco.
Songs, stories, and homely wit sped the day until the
banqueters were weak in flesh and spirit.   Baptisms,
betrothals, and weddings also were occasions of feast-
ing; and the long-suffering Seigneur hardly escaped
standing godfather to every child born within seven
leagues of the manor.

   Even the holy sisters came under the spell of the
joyous life in which they moved; and one of the

Ursuline nuns who came to Quebec with Madame de la Peltrie, thus writes in 1640 : —

"Although confined in a small hole, with insufficient air, yet we continue in good health. If in France one eat only bacon and salt fish, as we do here, one might be ill without a word said; but we are well, and sing better than in France. The air is excellent, and this is a terrestrial paradise, where the difficulties and troubles of life come so lovingly, that the more one is piqued, the more one's heart is filled with amiability."

Behind all this gaiety, however, brooded the Church; for even in her lightest moments Quebec never strained far on her sacred leash. From its foundation as a mission trading-post to its consecration as an episcopal see, the rock city remained a fortress of the faith. Its early governors, Champlain, D'Ailleboust, and Montmagny, were monks military, dividing their services equally between faith and fatherland. First the Récollets, then the Jesuits, came into spiritual possession; and later on, episcopal rule succeeded to the influence of Loyola's disciples. The relative estimation in which these various orders of the Church were held being illustrated by a Canadian proverb: "Pour faire un Récollet, il faut une hachette, pour un Prêtre un ciseau, mais pour un Jesuit, il faut un pinceau."

Thus, and in spite of resistance from D'Argenson,

D'Avaugour, and Frontenac, Quebec had been held
fast under a firm ecclesiastical control. Alternating
penance with persuasion, the priests imposed their
will upon the people. Absence from church and
confession brought its sufficient penalty; and the
calendar was filled with special days for prayer

THE BASILICA

and purification. Priests, monks, and nuns crowded
the city, in numbers disproportionate to the
lay population. The place was heavy with the
incense of a constant worship — the very atmosphere redolent of piety. From the unrestrained
hands of the early governors, the administration of
justice passed to the *Conseil Supérieur*, a body com-
prising the governor, the bishop, the intendant, and
a varying number of councillors. Their code took

special account of offences against religion, sins for
which the bishop was careful to exact proper expia-
tion.   The pillory, the stocks, and a certain wooden
horse with a sharp spine were the ready instruments
of correction.   Proclamations were made either from
the pulpit or read at the church-door after Mass.
Royal edicts and ordinances of the *Conseil Supérieur*
prescribed the duties of citizens, and stated without
vagueness the penalties which would overtake breakers of the law.   Yet in spite of this apparent harsh-
ness, the laws were administered in so patriarchal a
spirit as to justify the observation : " It requires
great interest for a man to be hung in Canada."

   The peasants, moreover, were far from rebelling
against the impositions of their seigneurs, which they
took as part of the order of nature ; and General
Murray, writing after the Conquest, thus bears testimony to the feeling of good-fellowship prevailing
between the two classes : " The tenants, who pay
only an annual quit-rent of about a dollar a year
for about a hundred acres, are at their ease and
comfortable.   They have been accustomed to respect
and obey their noblesse ; their tenures being military
in the feudal manner, they have shared with them
the dangers of the field, and natural affection has
been increased in proportion to the calamities which
have been common to both, from the conquest of
the country.   As they have been taught to respect

their superiors, and are not yet intoxicated with the
abuse of liberty, they are shocked at the insults
which their noblesse and the King's officers have
received from the English traders and lawyers since
the civil government took place."

JESUITS' BARRACKS

Each householder was responsible for the street
before his property, being compelled to keep it clean
of snow and refuse. Innkeepers required a license,
and had to conform to rigid laws. Cattle, pigs, and
sheep were impounded if found straying in the
streets, and the Intendant strictly regulated the
possession of live-stock.

The first horse seen in New France had been

R

brought out by the Governor Montmagny about 1636; but before the end of the century many more were shipped from Havre, and it was not long before the law began to regulate this new feature of social life. An ordinance forbade any *habitant* to possess more than two mares and one colt. In riding away from service on Sunday the horseman was forbidden to break into a canter until he had travelled ten arpents from the church. Private baptism of children was refused except in cases of absolute necessity. The order in which the personages of Quebec should receive the sacrament was precisely established. Roads, bridges, and churches were built by forced labour. The construction of houses, both as to material and design, was regulated by law. Builders were required to conform to a line and face their houses on the highway. Certain personages, however, claimed exemption from this rule, and to these was accorded the right — *d'avoir pignon sur rue* — to have the gable on the street, the purpose being to secure a certain degree of privacy by means of an entrance away from the public highway.

As to the law of inheritance, the testator was bound to divide his estate fairly among all his children, the title and the largest share going to the eldest son. This legislation, which affected seigneur and *censitaire* alike, subdivided the country into

ribbon-like farms, with narrow frontages on the river
and running back long distances inland. This
attenuated appearance of the rural holdings strikes
the stranger forcibly as he travels through the
province of Quebec even at this day, and denotes a
condition which prevailed in England also in the
most primitive days of agriculture. The system had

MODERN CALÈCHES

some justification, however, in the necessity which
each peasant felt of having access to the St. Lawrence,
the most convenient, and, for nearly a hundred years,
the only highway to the city of Quebec. Moreover,
it enabled the settlers to build their houses close
together, thus protecting themselves against the ever-
present danger of Indian raids. Even now the river

St. Lawrence looks like a gigantic road bordered by homely white-washed cottages.

Examples of the quaint laws and customs of the *ancien régime* might be multiplied indefinitely; but perhaps enough has already been said to show the paternalism of the legal system and the medievalism of the social life which prevailed. Before the Conquest the French Canadian had nothing whatever to do with the making of his own laws; and so far from struggling to obtain this right, he preferred to be without it. The Curé knew all about the laws, and the *habitant* was willing to leave the matter to him!

On the whole, if we except the wicked exactions of the Intendant Bigot and his confederates, Quebec was happily governed. From generation to generation the light-hearted *habitant* cheerfully paid his *dîme* to the Church, his *cens et rente* to the Seigneur, his military service to the Governor. If the call came for a raid upon New England, he took down his musket and his powder-horn, and set out blithely upon his snow-shoes for the rendezvous of war; if to rally to the defence of Quebec, he was equally ready to bury his chattels and take his place upon the city ramparts, or to withstand a landing on the Beauport shore.

Such were the people who drew from the first British Governor a generous testimony: " I glory,"

says General Murray, " in having been accused of
warmth and firmness in protecting the King's
Canadian subjects, and of doing the utmost in my
power to gain to my royal master the affections of
that brave, hardy people, whose emigration, if it

QUEBEC (FROM LÉVI)

should ever happen, would be an irreparable loss to
this empire."

So sped life beside the broad St. Lawrence, within
and around Quebec. So flew the days of the *ancien
régime ;* some sunshine, some shadow, and always an
honest fearless people who served God, honoured the
King, and stood ready to die for New France and
the golden lilies.

CHAPTER XIII

DURING THE SEVEN YEARS' WAR

REALISING that even a nominal peace could no longer be maintained, England threw down the gauntlet in the spring of 1756 by formally declaring war. Three weeks later France responded to the challenge, and presently the four corners of the earth were shaken by the most terrible conflict of the century. England's alliance with Prussia drew Austria and Russia into the war on the other side; and notwithstanding the smallness of his kingdom, the military genius of Frederick the Great was able to hold the three proudest powers of Europe at bay, while Clive and Wolfe smote off the heads of the triple alliance in India and North America. The history of Quebec is concerned with only the latter campaign.

The Marquis de Montcalm, the newly appointed commander of the forces in Canada, arrived about the middle of May, bringing with him the Chevalier de Lévis, Bourlamaque, and Bougainville, all of them

better generals than those to whom the fatuous
Duke of Newcastle entrusted the leadership of the
English army.   Montcalm himself is indeed one
of the most heroic and gallant figures in French
Canadian history — the personage, *par excellence*, of
the closing chapter of French dominion.

Born at his father's château in Candiac in 1712,
he inherited all the martial impetuosity of the
southern noblesse.   At fifteen he was an ensign in
the regiment of Hainaut, at seventeen a captain ;
and, in the campaigns of Bohemia and Italy, his
conspicuous valour won him quick promotion.   At
forty-four he was a General, commanding the troops
of Louis XV. in New France.   In appearance he
was under middle height, slender, and graceful in
movement.   Keen clear eyes lighted up a handsome
face, and wit sparkled upon his lips.

The Governor, Vaudreuil, son of a former ruler,
was a Canadian by birth, and accordingly prejudiced
against officers who came from France.   A veiled
antagonism springing up between himself and Montcalm was a source of weakness to the French cause
in America, and darkened the closing struggle of
the devoted French Canadians to keep the land
for their mother-country.

Montcalm on his arrival at once took stock, so to
speak, of his command.   His two battalions of La
Sarre and Royal Roussillon added about twelve

hundred men to the troops of the line already in New France. These, it will be remembered, consisted of the battalions of Artois and Bourgogne, — now the garrison at Louisbourg, — and the battalions of La Reine, Languedoc, Guienne, and Béarn, numbering in all about three thousand men. Besides these, about two thousand *troupes de la marine* constituted the permanent military establishment. Last of all came the militia, nominally made up of all the male inhabitants of Canada between the ages of sixteen and sixty, but rarely mustering more than two thousand men. Such was the soldiery in New France under Montcalm; and to them were added the Indian allies, whose numbers rose or fell with the fortune of war.

Against a Canadian population of less than seventy thousand, the English colonies could count more than a million souls; and although they lacked cohesion, and, indeed, regular military establishment of any kind, their greater wealth and numbers foretold the inevitable result of the struggle. At first the tide of war set against the English : an event to be expected with Newcastle guiding the ship of state, and believing in his generals, Loudon, Webb, and Abercrombie, vain and obtuse military martinets, who fumbled their opportunities, mismanaged their campaigns, and learned no lessons from their failures.

From Oswego, on the south-east corner of Lake

Ontario, the English had planned to attack Fort
Frontenac and Fort Niagara, so cutting off New
France from her western outposts. But Montcalm,
with the speed and energy that marked his character,
determined to act upon the offensive. With three
thousand men he hurried to Fort Frontenac, and
crossed the lake under cover of the night In the
morning the garrison of Oswego found themselves
besieged. The cannonade on both sides was brief
but vigorous ; but the French fought with greater
spirit, their dash and resource were disconcerting, and
presently this, the most important English stronghold
of the west, was compelled to capitulate. Sixteen
hundred prisoners, a hundred pieces of artillery, and
a vast quantity of stores and ammunition fell into
the hands of the triumphant French. Having thus
secured the west, Montcalm hurried back to Lake
Champlain, and intrenched himself at Carillon, by
this means to prevent an invasion of Canada by way
of the Richelieu. Owing to the lateness of the
season, however, his opponents undertook no new
expedition that year, and waited for the spring.

In 1757 Loudon conceived the idea of attacking Louisbourg, and accordingly he withdrew his
troops to Halifax in order to co-operate with
an English squadron under Admiral Holbourne.
Loudon's incompetency alone would have fore-
doomed so hazardous an undertaking ; but once

more the elements fought on the side of France, and Holbourne's fleet was shattered by a storm.

So far Montcalm had maintained a defensive attitude in the Richelieu valley, but taking advantage of Loudon's diversion towards Louisbourg, he now resolved upon attacking Fort William Henry, strongly held by over two thousand English troops. Moving out of his intrenchments at Carillon, therefore, and supported by Lévis and Bougainville, he advanced up the valley with six thousand soldiers and over a thousand Indians. Monro, the British commandant, sharply rejected the summons to surrender, and Montcalm began the investment of the fort.

Fourteen miles away, General Webb lay encamped at Fort Edward with twenty-six hundred men, and to him Monro sent for assistance. But the timorous Webb had no stomach for a fight. Huddling behind his breastworks, he listened to the booming of the fierce cannonade across the hills, but made no move to save Fort William Henry. Monro, seeing himself thus abandoned, his powder gone, his ramparts and bastions shattered by Montcalm's heavy artillery, at length asked for terms. Surrendering their arms, the garrison marched out with the honours of war, drums beating; but they also marched into one of the most shameful disasters recorded in American history.

Frenzied by the protracted siege, and burning

with vengeance for their slain in the trenches, the savage allies of the French burst all restraint and fell upon the disarmed garrison. In vain Montcalm,

DE LÉVIS

Lévis, and Bourlamaque begged, threatened, and even interposed their own bodies to prevent a massacre. Defenceless men, women, and children were toma- hawked in cold blood, or reserved for more leisurely torment. Some of the poor fugitives, fleeing at the first war-whoop, reached Fort Edward through the woods. Four hundred of the captives were eventually rescued by the French, while the Indians, decamping after their carnival of blood, carried two hundred wretched victims back to their lodges. Then followed the work of demolishing Fort William Henry, and soon its blazing ruins, a funeral pyre for the slaughtered garrison, lit up the summer night, and cast a lurid flame soon to kindle the avenging wrath of England.

To these ill-boding events, moreover, the loss of Minorca was now added, until England at last refused to endure longer the incapacity of Newcastle, and clamoured for the appointment of Pitt. "England has long been in labour," commented Frederick of Prussia, "and at last she has brought forth a man." From that moment the fortune of war was changed. Corruption and divided counsels no longer paralysed the government, and the Great Commoner, healthy minded, rugged, and enthusiastic, now stood to middle-class England as an embodiment of strength and purpose, which sent new blood coursing through her veins and braced her for the gathering storm.

To America, where the clouds were darkest, Pitt first turned his attention. Louisbourg, Carillon, Duquesne, and Quebec must be brought low, if, as was his purpose, French power was not only to be crushed but absolutely destroyed.   And towards this goal Pitt moved swiftly at the head of a nation as resolute as himself.   Loudon and Webb were instantly recalled, and Amherst, Wolfe, and Howe were appointed in their places, the last being ordered to second Abercrombie, whom Pitt had reluctantly retained in his command.

The years since 1745 had been years of growing strength for Louisbourg, and in 1758 it almost equalled Quebec itself in importance.   Its capable commandant, the Chevalier de Drucour, counted four thousand citizens and three thousand men-at-arms for his garrison; while twelve battleships, mounting five hundred and forty-four guns, and manned by three thousand sailors and marines, rode at anchor in the rock-girt harbour, the fortress itself, with its formidable outworks, containing two hundred and nineteen cannon and seventeen mortars.   Bold men only could essay the capture of such a fortress, but such were Wolfe, Amherst, and Admiral Boscawen, whose work it was to do.

The fleet and transports sailed from Halifax, bearing eleven thousand six hundred men full of spirit and faith in their commanders.   All accessible landing-places at Louisbourg had been fortified by the French; but in spite of this precaution and a heavy surf, Wolfe's division gained the beach and carried

the redoubts at Freshwater Cove.   A general landing
having been thus effected, Wolfe marched round the
flank of the fortress to establish a battery at Lighthouse Point.   The story may only be outlined here.
First the French were forced to abandon Grand
Battery, which frowned over the harbour, then the
Island Battery was silenced.   On the forty-third day
of the siege, a frigate in the harbour was fired by
shells, and drifting from her moorings, destroyed two
sister ships.   Four vessels which had been sunk at the
mouth of the harbour warded Boscawen's fleet from
the assault, but did not prevent six hundred daring
blue-jackets from seizing the *Prudent* and *Bienfaisant*,
the two remaining ships of the French squadron.

Meanwhile, zigzag trenches crept closer and closer
to the walls, upon which the heavy artillery now
played at short range with deadly effect.   Bombs
and grenades hissed over the shattering ramparts and
burst in the crowded streets ; roundshot and grape
tore their way through the wooden barracks ; while
mortars and musketry poured a hail of shell and
bullet upon the brave defenders.   Nothing could save
Louisbourg now that Pitt's policy of Thorough had
got headway.   On the 26th of July a white flag
fluttered over the Dauphin's Bastion ; and by midnight of that date Drucour had signed Amherst's
terms enjoining unconditional surrender.

Then the work of demolition commenced.   The

mighty fortress, which had cast a dark shadow over
New England for almost half a century, "the
Dunkirk of America," must stand no longer as a
menace. An army of workmen laboured for months
with pick and spade and blasting-powder upon those
vast fortifications ; yet nothing but an upheaval of
nature itself could obliterate all traces of earthwork,
ditch, *glacis*, and casemate, which together made up
the frowning fortress of Louisbourg. To-day grass
grows on the Grand Parade, and daisies blow upon
the turf-grown bastions ; but who may pick his way
over those historic mounds of earth without a sigh
for the buried valour of bygone years !

In the Richelieu valley, meanwhile, the armies of
England and France had met in even fiercer conflict.
Montcalm lay intrenched at Carillon at the head of
the battalions of La Sarre, Languedoc, Berry, Royal
Roussillon, La Reine, Béarn, and Guienne, three
thousand six hundred men in all. To this high
rocky battlement overlooking Lake Champlain, the
French had hastily added a rugged outwork of felled
trees on the crest of a flanking hill. The ridge thus
fortified now looked down upon a valley stripped of
its timber, but covered with rugged stumps and a
maze of stakes and branches, which, while afford-
ing no cover for an enemy, presented insuperable
obstacles to his advance.

On came Abercrombie at the head of fifteen

thousand men, offering the most imposing military spectacle yet seen in the New World. They advanced in three divisions — the regulars in the centre, commanded by the gallant Lord Howe, and a blue column of provincials on either flank. To the martial music of their bands or the shrill notes of the bagpipe they gaily marched through the midsummer woods, the Forty-Second Highlanders in the van.

As the army drew near to the French position, Lord Howe pressed forward to reconnoitre the approaches. This young nobleman, although but thirty-four years of age, had already reached the top of his profession. Keen and daring, with a hand of steel in a glove of velvet, and a magnetism that charmed the regular and the provincial alike, Lord Howe had become the soul of Abercrombie's army; and as he fell in this engagement, shot through the breast by a skirmisher's bullet, that army at once declined to its ruin.

Notwithstanding this loss, Abercrombie swept on along the Indian trail; and when Montcalm looked down from the rough ramparts of Carillon upon that splendid pageant, all hope of saving his stronghold was banished. All hope save one. The indiscretion of the English General might lead him to decide upon assault instead of siege. The inept Abercrombie did not disappoint him — Carillon was to be taken at the point of the bayonet!

All day long the fearless battalions of Old and New England hurled themselves against the fatal breastwork; all day long those steady columns of British infantry, headed by Campbell's Highlanders, brilliantly valiant, pressed up the rough *glacis* under a cross-fire which swept them front and flank. At night two thousand of Abercrombie's stubborn soldiery lay dead upon the field. Their splendid valour had been all in vain against the invisible musketeers of Montcalm, Lévis, and Bourlamaque.

Among the slain was the brave Duncan Campbell of Inverawe, of whom Parkman relates the following legend : —

" The ancient castle of Inverawe stands by the banks of the Awe, in the midst of the wild and picturesque scenery of the Western Highlands. Late one evening, before the middle of the eighteenth century, as the laird, Duncan Campbell, sat alone in the hall, there was a loud knocking at the gate; and opening it, he saw a stranger, with torn clothing and kilt besmeared with blood, who, in a breathless voice, begged for asylum. He went on to say that he had killed a man in a fray, and that the pursuers were at his heels. Campbell promised to shelter him. ' Swear on your dirk ! ' said the stranger ; and Campbell swore. He then led him to a secret recess in the depths of the castle.

s

" Scarcely was he hidden when again there was a loud knocking at the gate, and two armed men appeared. ' Your cousin Donald has been murdered, and we are looking for the murderer ! '

" Campbell, remembering his oath, professed to have no knowledge of the fugitive ; and the men went on their way.

" The laird, in great agitation, lay down to rest in a large dark room, when at length he fell asleep. Waking suddenly in bewilderment and terror, he saw the ghost of the murdered Donald standing by his bedside, and heard a hollow voice pronounce the words : ' *Inverawe ! Inverawe ! blood has been shed. Shield not the murderer !* '

" In the morning, Campbell went to the hiding-place of the guilty man, and told him that he could harbour him no longer. ' You have sworn on your dirk ! ' he replied ; and the laird of Inverawe, greatly perplexed and troubled, made a compromise between conflicting duties, promised not to betray his guest, led him to the neighbouring mountain, and hid him in a cave.

" In the next night, as he lay tossing in feverish slumbers, the same stern voice awoke him, the ghost of his cousin Donald stood again at his bedside, and again he heard the same appalling words : ' *Inverawe ! Inverawe ! blood has been shed. Shield not the murderer !* ' At the break of day he hastened, in strange agitation, to the cave; but it was empty, the stranger was gone.   At night, as he strove in vain to sleep, the vision appeared once more, ghastly pale, but less stern of aspect than before. '*Farewell, Inverawe!*' it said; '*farewell, till we meet at Ticonderoga!*'[1]

"The strange man dwelt in Campbell's memory. He had joined the Black Watch, or Forty-Second Regiment, then employed in keeping order in the turbulent Highlands.   In time he became its major; and a year or two after the war broke out he went with it to America.   Here, to his horror, he learned that it was ordered to the attack of Ticonderoga. His story was well known among his brother officers. They combined among themselves to disarm his fears; and when they reached the fatal spot they told him on the eve of the battle, 'This is not Ticonderoga; we are not there yet; this is Fort George.'   But in the morning he came to them with haggard looks.   'I have seen him!   You have deceived me!   He came to my tent last night! This is Ticonderoga!   I shall die to-day!'

"And his prediction was fulfilled."[2]

However magnificent was the triumph of the French arms at Carillon, it could not balance the loss of Louisbourg; and before the summer of 1758

---

[1] Ticonderoga, the Indian name for the fort of Carillon.
[2] Parkman, *Montcalm and Wolfe*, vol. ii., Appendix.

had ended, the heart of Quebec was wrung with news of further disasters. Crossing Lake Ontario with a force of three thousand colonials, Colonel Bradstreet appeared suddenly before Fort Frontenac. In spite of the abundant store of furs, ammunition, and implements of war which the lake fort contained, its garrison had been hopelessly weakened to supply troops for the Richelieu district, and when surprised by Bradstreet it consisted of but one hundred and ten soldiers. Without firing a shot, the commandant, De Noyan, surrendered the position.

This blow cut New France into halves, severing the western forts from their base of supplies, and effectually destroying what remained of French influence over the wavering Indian tribes. Meanwhile, General Forbes, with six thousand men, was marching from Philadelphia to attack Fort Duquesne. After three months of hardship he arrived at the junction of the Ohio and Monongahela; but the commandant De Ligneris had not awaited his coming, and the fort now lay in ashes, having been destroyed by its own garrison when it became clear that succour could no longer be expected from Quebec.

Quebec itself, though up to this time beyond the range of actual war, was in the usual throes of civil discord. If Vaudreuil, the Governor, had previously been jealous of Montcalm, the recent success achieved

by the latter at Carillon now doubled his resentment.
Casting about for any conceivable point of criticism,
Vaudreuil blamed the General for not turning
Abercrombie's retreat into a rout.   Regarding this
inspiration, Montcalm writes to Bourlamaque : " I
ended by saying quietly ' that when I went to war I
did the best I could ; and that when one is not
pleased with one's lieutenants, one had better take
the field in person.' He was very much moved, and
muttered between his teeth that perhaps he would ;
at which I said that I should be delighted to serve
under him.   Madame de Vaudreuil wanted to put
in her word.   I said : ' Madame, saving due respect,
permit me to have the honour to say that ladies
ought not to talk war.'   She kept on.   I said :
' Madame, saving due respect, permit me to have the
honour to say that if Madame de Montcalm were
here, and heard me talking war with Monsieur le
Marquis de Vaudreuil, she would remain silent.' "

Thus the cloaked strife between the General and
the so-called Canadian party proceeded.   Vaudreuil
wrote earnestly to the Court to have Montcalm recalled ; while Montcalm, who was not blind to the
malversations of Bigot and his clique, made this
matter the burden of some of his official letters.
The result was a rebuke administered to Vaudreuil
and the Intendant, which further heated their feeling
against Montcalm.   Bougainville was despatched to

France to lay an account of the dire distress of
Canada before the Court. Montcalm's letters highly
commended the envoy, but Vaudreuil as promptly
described him as a creature of the General, and
their quarrel did not help New France at the Royal
Court. Berryer, the Colonial Minister, received
Bougainville coldly, and to his appeal for help
replied : " Eh, Monsieur, when the house is on fire
one cannot concern one's self with the stable." But
the Canadian envoy responded, with caustic wit,
" At least, Monsieur, nobody will say that you talk
like a *horse*."

Berryer's remark, however, exactly described the
state of affairs. Worsted by Clive at Plassey, and
by Frederick the Great at Leuthen and Rossbach,
even the loss of Louisbourg, the Forts Duquesne and
Frontenac, could hardly add to France's cup of
bitterness, and to save herself in Europe she was
prepared for sacrifice in America. Within the
single twelvemonth during which Pitt had been at
the helm of England, France had altered her pretentious claim upon almost the whole of North
America to the extremely reasonable demand for a
foothold on the river St. Lawrence. Even this last
claim was now assailed ; and as she fell back into
her last intrenchments, the armies of England
advanced to the final encounter.

The general hopelessness of the situation in

Sᴿ GEORGE BRIDGES RODNEY Bart.
Admiral of the White.

GOVERNOR OF NEWFOUNDLAND, 1759

Canada is reflected in a letter written by the Minister of War, M. de Belleisle, to Montcalm, under the date 19th February, 1759 : " Besides increasing the dearth of provisions, it is to be feared that reinforcements, if despatched, would fall into the power of the English. The King is unable to send succours proportional to the force the English can place in the field to oppose you. . . . You must confine yourself to the defensive, and concentrate all your forces within as narrow limits as possible. It is of the last importance to preserve some footing in Canada. However small the territory preserved may be, it is indispensable that *un pied* should be retained in North America, for if all be once lost it would become impossible to recover it."

And Montcalm wrote in reply : " For my part, and that of the troops under me, we are ready to fall with the colony, and to be buried in its ruins." And later : " If we are left without a fleet at Quebec, the enemy can come there ; and Quebec taken, the colony is lost. . . . If the war continues, Canada will belong to the English in course of this campaign or the next. If peace be made, the colony is lost unless there be a total change of management." Lévis bore similar testimony to the discouragement caused to the colonials by the indifferent attitude of the Government of France. " I see," he wrote, " that it is necessary to defend ourselves foot by foot, fighting to the death ; for it will be better for the King's service that we should die with arms in our hands than for us to accept disgraceful terms of surrender like those permitted at the capitulation of Cape Breton."

The plan of the campaign of 1759 embraced simultaneous attacks upon Quebec and Montreal. The former was entrusted to Wolfe and Admiral Saunders, and the latter to Amherst. The French, on their part, disposed their troops entirely upon the defensive, Montcalm and Vaudreuil, commanders of the regulars and the militia, concentrating their soldiers round Quebec ; while Bourlamaque, with less than four thousand men, was despatched to hold the gateway of the Richelieu against Amherst.

Bourlamaque first took up his position at Carillon, but on the approach of the English he blew up the walls of his fortress and retired to Crown Point. Meanwhile the deliberate Amherst marched slowly forward, building forts as he went, in this mistaken zeal for military efficiency defeating the purpose of Pitt, which was, to make a strong diversion for covering Wolfe's movement upon the St. Lawrence. It was August before he arrived at Crown Point. This fortress, however, the wily Bourlamaque had previously abandoned for the stronger position of Isle-aux-Noix, at the outlet of Lake Champlain.

Even then Amherst refrained from hurrying forward to overwhelm the French with his superior numbers; and when at length autumn came, he was still advancing cautiously from Crown Point. But Wolfe no longer needed his help.

CHAPTER XIV

" HERE DIED WOLFE VICTORIOUS "

IN spite of her strong position, Quebec did not await the arrival of the enemy with folded hands. Since 1720 walls and bastions of grey stone had completely girded the city, but within that time no invasion had tested its strength. Even now, in the midst of the most desperate war the New World had ever known, Vaudreuil loudly proclaimed that the fortress was impregnable; and his letters, promising annihilation to his foolhardy foes, are painful gasconade. Yet with all this show of assurance, he was careful to send through the parishes, calling out to service every available man, and in some cases boys of thirteen and fourteen years of age; while the women and children, hiding the household valuables, withdrew from the river to places of safety.

A council of war had in the meantime decided to place the city under cover of an intrenched camp, which Montcalm was at first in favour of locating on the Plains of Abraham; but in view of the fact that

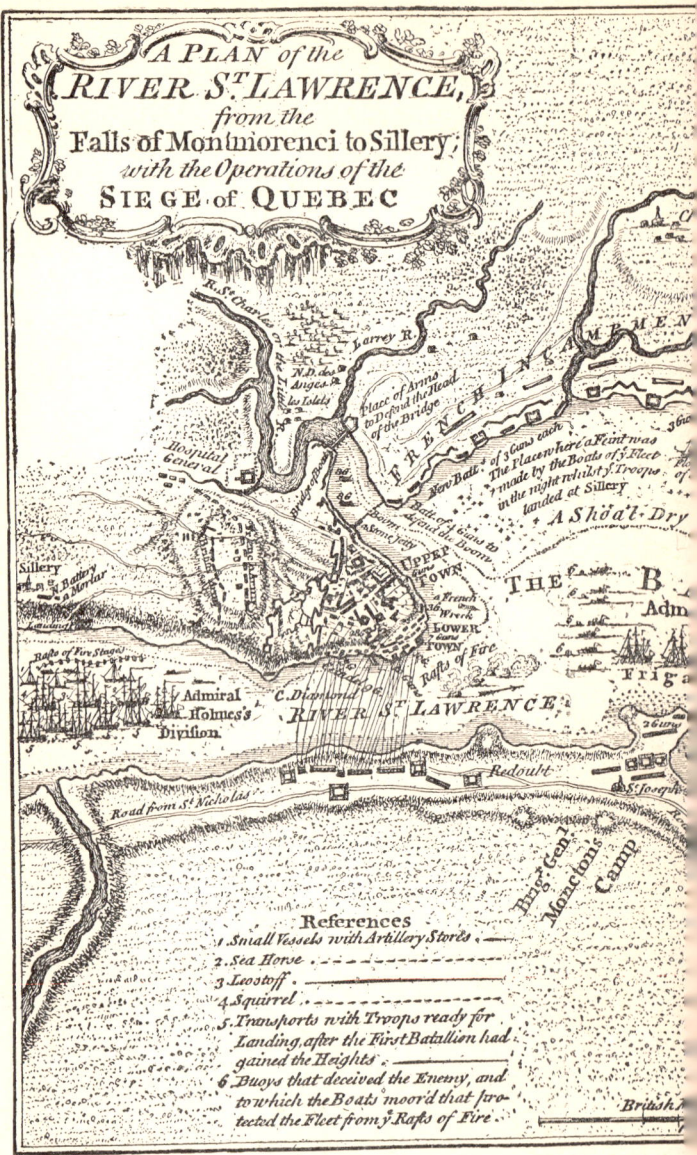

A PLAN of the
RIVER St. LAWRENCE,
from the
Falls of Montmorenci to Sillery;
with the Operations of the
SIEGE of QUEBEC

R. St Charles

Larrey R.

N.D. des Anges les Islets

Place of Arms to Defend the Head of the Bridge

FRENCHMEN

Hospital General

New Batt.

of 3 Guns each The Place where a Feint was made by the Boats of y. Fleet in the night whilst y. Troops landed at Sillery

A Shoal Dry

Battery of 8 Guns to defend the Boom

Boom

Sillery

Battery & Mortar

Upper Town

A French Work

THE
B.
Adm

LOWER TOWN

Rafts of Fire Stage

Admiral Holmes's Division

C. Diamond
RIVER St. LAWRENCE

Rafts of Fire

Friga

26 Guns

Redoubt

St. Joseph

Road from St Nicholas

Brigd. Genl. Moncton's Camp

References

1. Small Vessels with Artillery Stores ————
2. Sea Horse ————————————
3. Leostoff —————————————
4. Squirrel ————————————
5. Transports with Troops ready for
   Landing, after the First Batallion had
   gained the Heights ——————————
6. Buoys that deceived the Enemy, and
   to which the Boats moor'd that protected the Fleet from y. Rafts of Fire

British

A PLAN OF THE
ACTION gained by the ENGLISH
near QUEBEC, Sep. 13, 1759.

British   French
Army.   Army.
a. Anstruthers, d. M. de
b. Lascelle's,   Senezergue
c. Louisburg   Royal
   Granad.   e. Roussillon

Hospital
General

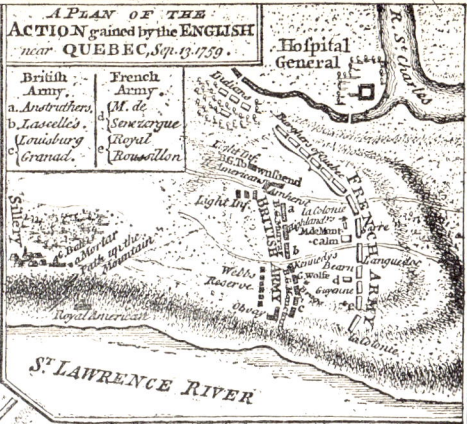

R. St. Charles

FRENCH ARMY

Light Inf.

Sillery

Mortar
Falls in the
Mountain

BRITISH ARMY

a la Colonie
b MacMont.
c calm.

Knuidys Bragg
d Wolfe
e Gwatne

Langudec

la Colonie

Webb's
Reserve.

Royal American

ST. LAWRENCE RIVER

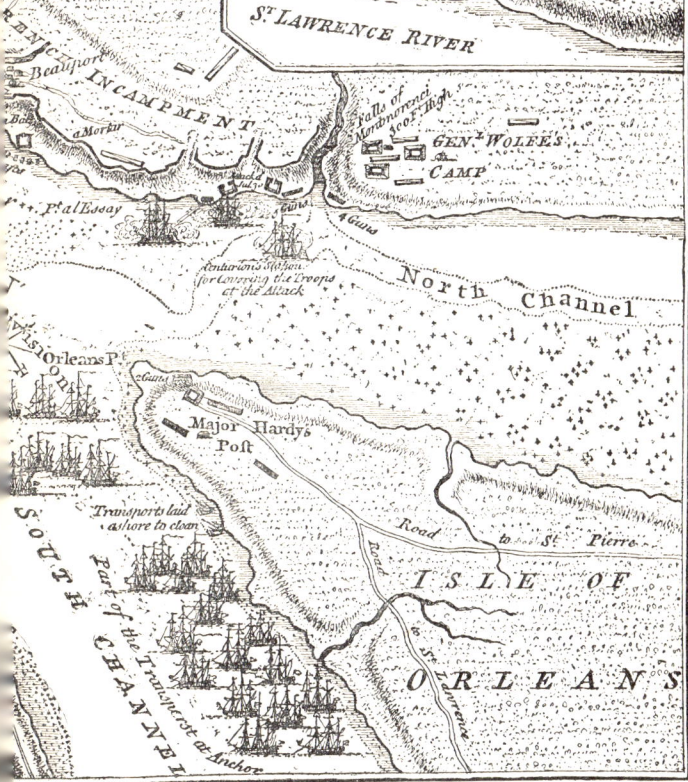

FRENCH
Beauport

INCAMPMENT

a Morky

Ft. al Essay

Falls of
Montmorenci
140 ft. high

GENL. WOLFE'S
CAMP

4 Guns

Centarions Station
for Covering the Troops
of the Attack

North   Channel

Orleans P.

2 Guns

Major Hardy's
Post

Road
to St. Pierre

Transports laid
ashore to clean

ISLE   OF
Road

SOUTH   CHANNEL

Part of the Transports

ORLEANS

Part of the Transports at Anchor

the bastions of the citadel and the batteries erected on the quays of Lower Town were already in full command of the river, another site was finally selected.   Assuming that the enemy could never force his way up the river past the city batteries, he concluded that the enemy must land by way of the lowlands below the town; and Wolfe himself had a like opinion until long after the investment had begun.

Since spring, when the proclamation of Vaudreuil had been read at the doors of the country churches, a constant stream of men and boys had been flowing towards Quebec; and by the middle of June Montcalm found himself in command of more than sixteen thousand men, including regulars, militia, and Indians.   The mouth of the St. Charles had been closed with a heavy boom of logs, in front of which was moored a floating battery mounting five cannon; and behind it two stranded hulks, armed with heavy ordnance, were able to sweep the Bay.   From this point to the height where, seven miles away, the Montmorency leaped foaming over its dizzy precipice, the lowlands of Beauport had been strongly fortified and intrenched.   Redoubts had been erected at all possible landing-places ; and behind these vast earthworks which followed the curving shore, the Canadian forces lay securely encamped.   The right wing, composed of the militia regiments of Quebec

and Three Rivers, under M. de Saint-Ours and M.
de Bonne, took up its position facing the city on
the flats known as La Canardière; the centre,
stretching from the St. Charles to the Beauport
river, consisted of two thousand regulars under
Brigadier Sénézergues; and the left, including the
Montreal militia, held the road from the Beauport

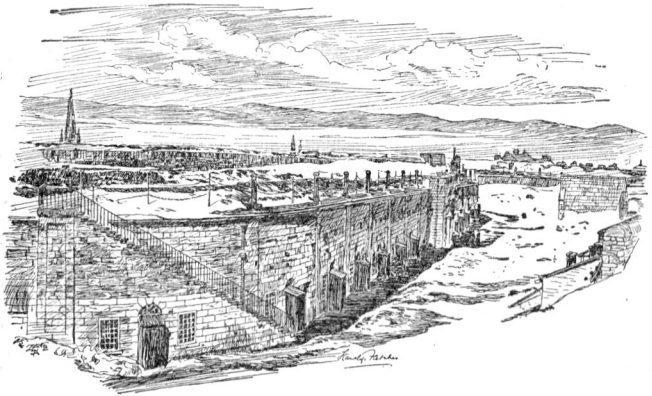

ENTRANCE TO THE CITADEL TO-DAY

to the Montmorency.   Montcalm established his
headquarters in the centre, wisely entrusting the
left wing to the capable De Lévis, the right being
assigned to Bougainville.

Within the walls, the Chevalier de Ramézay
commanded a garrison of above a thousand men.
Every gate but one had been closed and barricaded,
the Porte du Palais being left open to afford com-
munication between the city and the camp by way of

a bridge of boats across the St. Charles. Vaudreuil
transferred the seat of government to Beauport,
taking up his quarters at the centre with Montcalm;
and those of the citizens who were not required to
man the ramparts removed themselves and their
valuables for safety to the country. Quebec was
armed to the teeth. Three hundred feet above the
river rose the battery of the citadel; on a lower
level the Castle Battery frowned over towards Point
Lévi, the Grand Battery commanding the harbour;
while, on the wharves of Lower Town, the Queen's,
Dauphin's, and Royal batteries were able to sweep
the narrows. Even though the English fleet might
run this gauntlet of heavy ordnance, the high cliffs
for miles above the city remained practically inacces-
ible, and at almost any point a hundred resolute
men would suffice to beat back an army. In the
face of these preparations, it seemed an act of
madness to attempt the reduction of Quebec. But
within defences so secure the ardent spirts of the
Canadian troops were chafing at enforced inaction;
for although diligently exercised by their commanders, they still had leisure to think of the homes
they loved, where the corn would never be garnerèd.

On the English side Captain Cook, as his biographer relates, " was employed to procure accurate
soundings of the channel between the Island of
Orleans and the shore of Beauport — a service of

great danger, which could only be performed in the night-time. He had scarcely finished when he was discovered, and a number of Indians in canoes started to cut him off. The pursuit was so close that they jumped in at the boat's stern as Cook leaped out to gain the protection of the English sentinel. The

HOPE GATE

boat was carried off by the Indians. Cook, however, furnished the admiral with as correct a draft of the channel and soundings as could afterwards have been made when the English were in peaceable possession of Quebec."

At length, towards the end of June, the invading ships sailed up the channel south of the Isle of Orleans; twenty ships of the line, twenty frigates,

and a swarm of transports, bearing in all about nine
thousand men.   But Quebec, so often threatened in
the past, and ever fortunate in resistance, gazed com-
placently down upon this imposing fleet.   Montcalm feared but one contingency, the co-operation
of Amherst with Wolfe from the west; and this, as
we have seen, was a needless anxiety.   Disembarking, Wolfe pitched his camp at the western end
of the Isle of Orleans, four miles from Quebec.
Before him rose the portentous batteries of the city,
and, on his right, the long battle-line of Montcalm
flaunted a desperate challenge.   Remembering, however, that defences stronger still had been carried at
Louisbourg, the English General confidently drew
up his plans.

The only vantage-ground left unoccupied by the
French was the Heights of Lévi, opposite the city,
Montcalm having thought it unwise to isolate there
any portion of his force.   Thither, accordingly,
Monckton's brigade was now despatched; and
English batteries, rising darkly on the high cliffs,
were soon directing across the narrow channel of the
river that hail of shot which, within a month, had left
the Lower Town a heap of ashes, and dropped destruction upon the crowded summit of the citadel.
So galling grew this fire, that at last a force was
sent to destroy the English camp; and on the
night of July the 12th, fifteen hundred soldiers and

T

Indians stole silently from Sillery across the river. But as they picked their way through the dark

ADMIRAL SIR CHARLES SAUNDERS
(Under Wolfe before Quebec)

woods, trembling with the excitement of a dangerous adventure, a sudden panic seized them, and in the confusion, the students of the Seminary, who formed

part of the column, opened fire upon their own men.
Discipline and order were at once discarded, and the
whole party rushed back in terror to the boats.   At
dawn they returned from this unhappy and futile
expedition, bringing new terrors to their fellow-
citizens, who nicknamed this bloodless effort the
"Scholars' Battle"; and Quebec again endured the
misery of ceaseless bombardment.

With strange fatuity the French employed another
device to destroy the fleet of the invaders and carry
terror into their ranks.   A flotilla of fireships was
loaded to the gunwale with pitch, tar, powder bombs,
grenades, and scrap-iron; and towards midnight
these floating hell-boats slipped their moorings and
drifted with the tide towards the English fleet riding
at the Point of Orleans.   Tide and stream bore them
swiftly through the gloom; and at a given signal,
fuses were ignited and the crews escaped in boats.
Sharp tongues of flame ran along the bulwarks,
and the loose powder sputtered and hissed.   Then,
suddenly, the night was rent by explosion after
explosion, reverberating through the cañons of the
distant Laurentides, and echoing along the river
walls beyond Cap Tourmente.   A lurid glare lit up
the broad harbour, the towers and minarets of the
beleaguered city, revealing in red light the full tents
of the French army along the Beauport lowlands.

To the English it was "the grandest fireworks

that can possibly be conceived"; but the French were in no mood to enjoy its harmless effulgence. The fuses had been lighted half an hour too soon, and before the tide of the north channel carried them to the English fleet, the magnificent flotilla, upon which Quebec had squandered a million *livres*, had become a squadron of blazing hulks which the British sailors grappled and towed to shore. All night long their impotent fires lit up the Bay, and by sunrise another hope of New France had turned to ashes.

Although the unquenchable batteries of Point Lévi continued to pour destruction upon Quebec, Wolfe saw that the defeat of Montcalm must precede the capture of the city; and to this end he now directed his attention. Beyond the rocky gorge of the Montmorency, a high open land seemed to offer a possible avenue of attack upon the French camp across the river, and thither the English General resolved to transfer his main camp. On the night of the 8th of July he embarked with three thousand men — the brigades of Townshend and Murray, a body of grenadiers, light infantry, and the Sixtieth Regiment, or Royal Americans. Before dawn they made a landing at the village of L'Ange Gardien, and gained the heights after a slight skirmish with an irregular body of native militia. Earthworks were hastily thrown up, fascine batteries were erected, and Mont-

THE MANOR-HOUSE AT BEAUPORT, MONTCALM'S HEADQUARTERS

calm's reveille next morning was a heavy cannonade
from this new quarter.

Wolfe had now divided his army into three
camps, each so far removed from the other that little
or no help could be expected in case of separate
attack. Yet it was in vain that he tempted Montcalm to battle. For weeks his guns roared challenge
across the Montmorency ; but the cautious French
General only shrugged his shoulders and remarked:
" Let him amuse himself where he is. If we drive
him off he may go to some place where he can
do us harm." To discover this vulnerable spot
Wolfe would have risked much, as appears from his
daring instructions of the 18th of July. On this
day the *Sutherland* and several small frigates ran the
gauntlet of the city batteries, and racing through
the hail of lead and iron falling from a hundred
guns upon the ramparts, they reached Cap Rouge
above Quebec.

To the French the impossible had happened.
Montcalm, therefore, hastily detailed a small force to
defend the cliffs ; and the right wing of the army
under Bougainville was charged with the protection
of the city upon its flank, or landward side. To
Wolfe, however, who himself made the hazardous
voyage in the *Sutherland*, the result of the recon-
naissance was not cheering. No point upon those
rugged cliffs seemed to offer a favourable landing ;

and he came back to his camp on the Montmorency more than ever convinced that Montcalm's army could be defeated only by a direct assault upon its strong intrenchments. This desperate enterprise he essayed on the last day of July.

When the tide runs out past the Isle of Orleans, it leaves a wide sandy beach at the foot of the cliffs between Beauport and Montmorency, the mouth of the latter river also being hardly more than knee-deep at ebb-tide. Aware of these conditions, the French had erected a strong redoubt at the edge of the strand, and posted a large force of musketeers in the intrenchments capping the heights above it. This was the point which Wolfe selected for attack.

In the morning at high tide the *Centurion*, of sixty-four guns, took up a position near the Mont-morency ford and opened fire upon the French redoubt. During this movement two armed trans-ports detailed to second her cannonade, running too close upon the shore, were stranded with the receding tide. At the same time, the batteries of Wolfe's camp across the river were pounding the enemy's flank. Towards noon five thousand British soldiers pressed towards the point of attack; some in boats from Point Lévi and Orleans, some crossing the ford from Townshend's camp. The first to reach the spot were thirteen companies of grenadiers and a detachment of Royal Americans, who having landed from the boats, instead of waiting for Monckton's brigade which was close behind, dashed boldly forward across the strand.   The French gave way before their impetuous rush, and abandoned the redoubt at the foot of the hill.   Then, suddenly, the crest of the ridge above them blazed with musketry, and the cross-fire from the trenches poured a hail of death upon their panting ranks.   Up the terrible *glacis* they still strove to climb in the face of a splashing downpour of bullets.   At that moment the sky became overcast, and from the pall of cloud hanging over Beauport a wild storm of rain broke over the battlefield.   It was impossible to scale the slippery rocks, the powder was drenched and useless.   Seeing the madness of further attack, Wolfe now sounded a retreat.   A force of less than a thousand men had attempted to storm a bristling cliff whose double line of defence consisted of the muskets of Canadian sharpshooters and the bayonets of Béarn, Guienne, and Royal Roussillon; and before the order to retire was given, nearly half their number had fallen in this bootless conflict on the Beauport Flats.

It was now August, and the hopes of Quebec rose higher with the advancing season.   So far the English had scored no perceptible success; and although the batteries of Point Lévi had laid the Lower Town in ruins, and were still pounding at

the high ramparts, the defences of the city remained
practically as strong as ever.   The steady bombardment, however, was causing much suffering and
anxiety to those inhabitants who had been unable to
flee from the city ; and for two full days the Lower
Town was in flames, the large company of sappers
and miners, detailed as a fire brigade, being powerless against the conflagration.   The walls of Notre
Dame des Victoires kept guard upon the poor wreck
of its venerated altars, while in the Upper Town
the Cathedral tower had been shot away, and the
Basilica itself was half a ruin.   Some of the rampart
batteries were buried beneath the *débris* of demolished
houses, and bursting shells ploughed up the streets ;
moreover, the wooden palisade, hastily erected in the
Quartier du Palais to provide against a possible
assault by way of the St. Charles, had been destroyed
by fire.   At last forsaking the dangerous walls
of their exposed convents, the Ursulines and the
nuns of Hôtel-Dieu sought shelter further afield.
The Hospital Général, established by Bishop St.
Vallier, Laval's successor, on a bend of the St.
Charles, being beyond the range of the English
artillery, the homeless poor flocked thither for refuge,
until the convent and all its *dépendances* were filled
to overflowing with miserable refugees.   The chapel
was pressed into service as a ward for the wounded ;
and holy Masses were said by special permission in

General Sir Jeffery Amherst.

To whom Montreal surrendered 1760.

the *chœur*. During this time of trial Bishop Pont-briand remained in the city, exhorting its defenders to be of good courage and cheering the wounded by his ministrations; while, as if to counteract his influence for good, the more heartless spirits were tempted to robbery and pillage — a shameless addition to the general suffering promptly checked by a gallows in the Place d'Armes.

Provisions had been plentiful enough up to mid-summer; but as the siege was prolonged beyond harvest time, and as Wolfe's soldiers were laying the country waste in every direction as far as eye could see, it was no wonder that Montcalm felt some anxiety for the feeding of fifteen thousand troops. Moreover, an unexpected consequence of Wolfe's repulse at Beauport now brought a new anxiety to the French; for British operations were presently begun at a point above the city, to the great peril of its food-supply. Admiral Holmes's division had forced a passage up the river, soon to be joined by twelve hundred men under Brigadier Murray, who had instructions to menace the city upon its flank. Up and down the river this composite squadron cruised, making feints now here, now there, ex-hausting the energies of Bougainville and his column of fifteen hundred men, who were thus forced to cover an exposed shore for a distance of fifty miles. Murray attempted a landing at Pointe-aux-Trembles,

but was beaten back; at La Muletière he was also
unsuccessful; but at Deschambault, forty-one miles
above the city, he was able to destroy a large
quantity of French stores without the loss of a man.
Up to this time the French had conveyed their
supplies from Batiscan to St. Augustin by water, and

GENERAL HOSPITAL

thence overland to Quebec, a distance of thirteen
miles. But the presence of Admiral Holmes's
squadron rendered this method of transport pre-
carious, and an attempt was made to drive supplies
overland from Batiscan; but as this place was
sixty-seven miles distant from Quebec, famine
laid its hand upon the city before they could arrive.
French transports were therefore compelled to

run the perilous blockade of the vigilant English fleet.

Meanwhile, upon the report of the slow but successful advance of Amherst in the Richelieu Valley, news had come of the fall of Fort Niagara. New France now retained no vestige of her Western empire. Except for Bourlamaque at Isle-aux-Noix, Montreal had no defence against British attack; and thither, on the ninth of August, Montcalm despatched Lévis with eight hundred men. Even though Wolfe had failed to carry the city by assault, the garrison were now thoroughly alarmed at the protracted siege, and prayed for an early winter which must drive the English out of the river. The militia of Montcalm's army were deserting by hundreds, their fortitude breaking down as they saw the sky reddened with the flames of the river parishes, and languished under the strain of short rations.

Montcalm himself felt the pinch of a failing commissariat, but with good-humour he made the best of the position. An example of his whimsical mood and gay fortitude may be found in a menu he presents in a letter to Lévis —

> " Petits pâtés de cheval, à l'Espagnole.
> Cheval à la mode.
> Escalopes de cheval.
> Filet de cheval à la brochu avec une poivarde bien liée.
> Semelles de cheval au gratin."

On the other hand, the English army had its own discouragements. Night after night, Canadian irregulars and Indians crept up to Wolfe's lines to murder and scalp the outposts and sentries. Fever invaded the camp, and, more than all else, the serious illness of the General himself depressed the spirits of his men. Ceaseless anxiety over a hitherto ineffective campaign had played sad havoc with the nervous, high-strung temperament of the English commander; and the grey, inaccessible city still rose grimly to mock his schemes. Only the most invincible spirit could have borne so frail a body through those weeks of hope deferred. A vague melancholy marked the line of his tall ungainly figure; but resolution, courage, endurance, deep design, clear vision, dogged will, and heroism shone forth from those searching eyes, making of no account the incongruities of the sallow features. Straight red hair, a nose thrust out like a wedge, and a chin falling back from an affectionate sort of mouth, made, by an antic of nature, the almost grotesque setting of those twin furnaces of daring resolve, which, in the end, fulfilled the yearning hopes of England.

August had nearly gone, and the gallant General, only thirty-two years of age and already touched by the finger of death, lay sick in a farmhouse at Montmorency. Success seemed even further away than it had been in the early summer. Yet, in consultation with his three brigadiers — Monckton, Townshend, and Murray — Wolfe had decided upon a new and desperate plan.

"I know perfectly well you cannot cure me," he said to the surgeon ; "but pray make me up so that I may be without pain for a few days, and able to do my duty ; that is all I want." To Pitt he wrote — and this was his last despatch : "The obstacles we have met with in the operations of the campaign are much greater than we had reason to expect, or could foresee ; not so much from the number of the enemy (though superior to us), as from the natural strength of the country, which the Marquis de Montcalm seems wisely to depend upon. When I learned that succours of all kinds had been thrown into Quebec — that five battalions of regular troops, completed from the best inhabitants of the country, some of the troops of the colony, and every Canadian that was able to bear arms, besides several nations of savages, had taken the field in a very advantageous situation, — I could not flatter myself that I should be able to reduce the place. I sought, however, an occasion to attack their army, knowing well that with these troops I was able to fight, and hoping that a victory might disperse them. . . . I found myself so ill, and am still so weak, that I begged the general officers to consult together for the general utility. They are

all of opinion that, as more ships and provisions are
now got above the town, they should try, by conveying up a corps of four or five thousand men (which
is nearly the whole strength of the army after the
Points of Lévi and Orleans are left in a proper state
of defence), to draw the enemy from their present
situation and bring them to an action. I have
acquiesced in the proposal, and we are preparing to
put it into execution."

Carrying out this new plan, Wolfe first abandoned
his camp at Montmorency, and for the moment con-
centrated his strength at Lévi and Orleans. Then
Admiral Holmes's division in the river above the city
was strengthened, and on the night of the 4th of
September ships and transports, carrying five months'
provisions, silently and successfully ran the blockade
of the citadel's guns and anchored off Cap Rouge.
On the 5th, Murray, Monckton, and Townshend
marched seven battalions overland from Point Lévi
to the mouth of the river Etechemin opposite Sillery
Cove ; and on the 6th, Wolfe found himself cruising
above the town with twenty-two ships and thirty-six
hundred men.

Meanwhile, Montcalm and Vaudreuil were greatly
perplexed and all unconscious of the new designs
and movements of the enemy. The position at the
Point of Orleans still seemed to be strongly occupied,
for every day Colonel Carleton paraded his men up

and down in full view of the camp at Beauport; the
batteries at Point Lévi thundered with their accustomed vehemence, and Admiral Saunders's division
still lay threateningly in the basin below the city.
Thus the weakening of these camps by twelve
hundred men, who marched up the south shore to
join Wolfe, was not perceived by Montcalm. Above
Quebec, Bourlamaque was not less perplexed by the
mysterious movements of Holmes's squadron and the
army transports. Up and down the river they sailed,
now threatening to land at Pointe-aux-Trembles, now
at Sillery, and greatly confusing the right wing of
the French army by their complex movements.

At last the great night came, starlit and serene.
The camp-fires of two armies spotted the shores of
the wide river, and the ships lay like wild-fowl in
coveys above the town. At Beauport, an untiring
General of France, who, booted and spurred, through
a hundred days had snatched but a broken sleep, in
the ebb of a losing game, now longed for his adored
Candiac, grieved for a beloved daughter's death, sent
cheerful messages to his aged mother and to his wife,
and by the deeper protests of his love, foreshadowed
his own doom. At Cap Rouge, a dying soldier of
England, unperturbed and valiant, reached out a
finger to trace the last movement in the desperate
campaign of a life that had opened in Flanders at
the age of sixteen, now closing as he took from

U

his bosom the portrait of his affianced wife, and said to his old schoolfellow, " Give this to her, Jervis, for we shall meet no more." Then, passing from the deck, silent and steady, no signs of pain upon his face — so had the calm come to him as to nature, and to this beleaguered city, before the

CAPTAIN JAMES COOK
(Piloted Wolfe's Army up the Harbour of Quebec)

whirlwind — he viewed the clustered groups of boats filled with the flower of his army, settled down into a menacing tranquillity. There lay the Light Infantry, Bragg's, Kennedy's, Lascelles', Anstruther's Regiments, Fraser's Highlanders, and the much-loved, much-blamed Louisbourg Grenadiers. Steady, indomitable, silent as cats, precise as mathematicians,

he could trust them, as they loved his awkward, pain-
twisted body and ugly red hair. " Damme, Jack,
didst ever take hell in tow before?" said a sailor
to his comrades as the marines, some days before,
had grappled with a second flotilla of French
fire-ships. " Nay, but I've been in tow of Jimmy
Wolfe's red head; that's hell-fire, lad!" was the reply.

From boat to boat the General's eye passed,
then shifted to the ships — the *Squirrel*, the *Leostaff*,
the *Seahorse*, and the rest — and lastly, to the spot
where lay the army of Bougainville. Now an officer
came towards him, who said, quietly, " The tide has
turned, sir. " For reply, he made a swift motion
towards the *Sutherland's* maintop shrouds, and almost
instantly lanterns showed in them. In response, the
crowded boats began to cast away. Immediately
descending the General passed into his boat, drew to
the front, and drifted in the current ahead of his
gallant forces.

It was two hours after midnight when the boats
began to move, and slowly they ranged down the
stream, silently steered and carried by the ebbing tide.
No paddle, no creaking oarlock broke the stillness;
but ever and anon the booming of a thirty-two
pounder from the Point Lévi battery echoed up the
river walls.

To a young midshipman beside him, the General
turned and said, " How old are you, sir? "

"Seventeen, sir," was the reply.

"It is the most lasting passion," he said, musing. Then, after a few moments' silence, he repeated aloud these verses from Gray's *Elegy* —

> "The curfew tolls the knell of parting day ;
> The lowing herds wind slowly o'er the lea ;
> The ploughman homeward plods his weary way,
> And leaves the world to darkness and to me.
>
> *   *   *   *   *   *
>
> "The boast of heraldry, the pomp of power,
> And all that beauty, all that wealth e'er gave,
> Await alike the inevitable hour —
> The paths of glory lead but to the grave."

"Gentlemen," he said, "I would rather have written those lines than take Quebec."

Meanwhile, the tide had swept the foremost boats round the headland above the *Anse du Foulon*,[1] a tiny bay where Wolfe had determined to land. Suddenly, down from the dark heights there came a challenge : "*Qui vive?*"

"*La France*," answered an officer of Fraser's Highlanders, who had learned French in Flanders.

"*À quel Régiment ?*"

"*De la Reine*," responded the Highlander ; and to disarm suspicion he added, "*Ne faites pas de bruit, ce sont les vivres.*" From a deserter, the English had learned that a convoy of provisions was

---

[1] Now known as Wolfe's Cove.

expected down the river that night; and the officer's response deceived the sentry.

The boats of the Light Infantry swung in to the shore. The twenty-four volunteers, who had been given the hazardous task of scaling the cliff and overpowering Vergor's guard at the top of the path, now commenced the ascent. On the strand below, the van of Wolfe's army breathlessly waited the signal to dash up the cliff to support their daring scouts. Presently quick ringing shots told the anxious General that his men had begun their work, and in a few moments a thin British cheer claimed possession of the rocky pathway up which Wolfe's battalions now swarmed in the misty grey of early morning.

While this army climbed up the steep way to the Heights of Abraham, Admiral Saunders was bombarding Montcalm's intrenchments, and boats filled with marines and soldiers made a feint of landing on the Beauport flats, while shots, bombs, shells, and carcasses burst from Point Lévi upon the town. At last, however, the French General grew suspicious of the naval manœuvres, and in great agitation he rode towards the city. It was six in the morning as he galloped up the slope of the St. Charles, and in utter amazement gazed upon the scarlet ranks of Britain spread across the plain between himself and Bougainville, and nearer to him, on the crest, the

white-coated battalion of Guienne which, the day
before, he had ordered to occupy the very heights
where Wolfe now stood.

Montcalm summoned his army from the trenches
at Beauport. In hot haste they crossed the St.
Charles, passed under the northern rampart of the
city, and in another hour the gates of St. Jean and
St. Louis had emptied out upon the battlefield a
flood of defenders. It was a gallant sight. The
white uniforms of the brave regiments of the line —
Royal Roussillon, La Sarre, Guienne, Languedoc,
Béarn — mixed with the dark, excitable militia, the
sturdy burghers of the town, a band of *coureurs
de bois* in their picturesque hunters' costume, and
whooping Indians, painted and raging for battle.
Bougainville had not yet arrived from Cap Rouge,
and for some mysterious reason Vaudreuil lagged
behind at Beauport. Nevertheless, Montcalm determined to attack the English before they had time
to intrench themselves. As for Wolfe, he desired
nothing better, for while the two forces were numeri-
cally not unequal, yet every man among the invaders
could be depended upon, while even Montcalm had
yet to test fully the undisciplined valour of his
Canadian militia.

Outside the city gates, the French at first took up
their position on a rising ground in three divisions,
having an irregular surface towards the St. Lawrence

Admiral Earl St Vincent

from a portrait by Hoppner.

on their left, and extending across the St. Louis and
Ste. Foye roads towards the St. Charles on their
right. Indian and Canadian marksmen were posted
among the trees and bushes which skirted the plains.
Montcalm himself took command of the centre, at
the head of the regiment of Languedoc, supported
by the battalion of Béarn. M. de Sénézergues led
the left wing, composed of the regiments of Guienne
and Royal Roussillon, supported by the militia of
Three Rivers. The right, under M. de Saint-Ours,
consisted of the battalion of La Sarre and the militia
of Quebec and Montreal.

Wolfe had first drawn up his army with its front
towards the St. Louis road, and its right towards
the city, but afterwards he altered his position. Con-
fronting the French formation Brigadier Townshend,
with Amherst's and the Light Infantry, and Colonel
Burton, with a battalion of the Royal Americans,
made up the British left, holding a position near
the Ste. Foye road, to meet the advance of
Bougainville from the west. The centre, under
Murray, was composed of Lascelles', Anstruther's,
and Fraser's Highlanders; while Monckton commanded the right, which included Bragg's, Otway's,
Kennedy's, and the Louisbourg Grenadiers, at whose
head, after he had passed along the line, Wolfe
placed himself for the charge.

At eight o'clock the French sharpshooters opened

fire upon the British left, and skirmishers were thrown out to hold them in check, or drive them from the houses where they sheltered themselves and galled Townshend's men. Three field-pieces, brought from the city, opened on the British brigades with roundshot and canister. The invaders, however, made no return, and were ordered to lie down. No restlessness, no anxiety marked those scarlet columns, whose patience and restraint had been for two months in the crucible of a waiting game. There was no man in all Wolfe's army but knew that final victory or ruin hung upon the issue of that 13th of September.

From bushes, trees, coverts, and fields of grain came a ceaseless hail of fire, and there fell upon the ranks a doggedness, a quiet anger, which settled into grisly patience. These men had seen the stars go down, the cold mottled light of dawn break over the battered city and the heights of Charlesbourg; they had watched the sun come up, and then steal away behind slow-travelling clouds and hanging mist; they had looked over the unreaped cornfields, and the dull slovenly St. Charles, knowing full well that endless leagues of country, north and south, east and west, now lay for the last time in the balance. The rocky precipice of the St. Lawrence cut off all possibility of retreat, and their only help was in themselves. Yet no one faltered.

At ten o'clock Montcalm's three columns moved
forward briskly, making a wild rattle — two columns
moving towards the left and one towards the right,
firing obliquely and constantly as they advanced.
Then came Wolfe's command to rise, and his army
stood up and waited, their muskets loaded with an
extra ball.   Suppressed rage filled the ranks as they
stood there and took that damnable fire without
being able to return a shot.   Minute after minute
passed.   Then came the sharp command to advance.
Again the line was halted, and still the withering discharge of musketry fell upon the long silent palisade
of red.

At last, when the French were within forty yards,
Wolfe raised his sword, a command rang down the
long line of battle, and with a crash as of one terrible
cannon-shot, the British muskets sang out together.
After the smoke had cleared a little, another volley
followed with almost the same precision.   A light
breeze lifted the smoke and mist, and a wayward sun-
light showed Montcalm's army retreating like a long
white wave from a rocky shore.

Thus checked and confounded, the French army
trembled and fell back in broken order.   Then, with
the order to charge, an exultant British cheer arose,
the skirling challenge of the bagpipes and the wild
slogan of the Highlanders sounding high over all.
Like sickles of death, the flashing broadswords of the

clansmen clove through and broke the battalions of La Sarre, and the bayonets of the Forty-Seventh scattered the soldiers of Languedoc into flying companies.

Early in the action Wolfe had been hit in the wrist by a bullet, but he concealed this wound with his handkerchief. A few minutes later, however, as he pressed forward, sword in hand, at the head of the charging Louisbourg Grenadiers, a musket ball struck him in the breast. They bore him, mortally wounded, to the rear.

" It's all over with me," he murmured. The mist of death was already gathering in his eyes.

" They run ; see how they run ! " exclaimed Lieutenant Brown of the Grenadiers, who supported him. " Who run ? " demanded the General like one roused from sleep. " The enemy, sir," responded the subaltern. " Go, one of you, to Colonel Burton," returned Wolfe, with an earnestness that detained the spirit in his almost lifeless body ; " tell him to march Webb's regiment down to the St. Charles to cut off their retreat from the bridge."

Then, overcome at last, he turned on his side and whispered, " Now, God be praised, I will die in peace ! "

CHAPTER XV

WITHIN the beleaguered city the sights and sounds of battle caused sickening excitement. An enemy who had gained the heights by such determined valour was destined for victory; and the weary garrison and townsfolk, as they watched and waited anxiously on the ramparts, were more than half prepared for the view presently to meet their eyes. A fresh wind lifting the thick clouds of smoke from the battlefield revealed the scattered legions of France in flight before a conquering army, wildly dashing towards the city gates or the bridge of boats crossing the St. Charles. Montcalm sought in vain to rally his stricken battalions, and was borne backward in the confusion of their mad retreat, until suddenly, pierced by a bullet, he sank in the saddle. Bravely keeping his seat with support from a soldier on either side, he succeeded in entering the city by the St. Louis Gate. Here the excited crowd, which had gathered to hear the latest news from the field, raised a troubled cry at sight of their vanquished chief pale and streaming with blood. "*Mon Dieu, O mon Dieu! le Marquis est tué!*" they wailed. "It is nothing, it is nothing, do not distress yourselves for me, my good friends," responded the broken hero.

His black charger slowly bore him down the *Grande Allée* and along the Rue St. Louis, leading a sad procession to the house of Arnoux the surgeon. Being carried inside, he was told that his wound was mortal. "How long have I to live?" he asked. "Twelve hours perhaps," responded the surgeon. "So much the better," said Montcalm; "I am happy that I shall not live to see the surrender of Quebec." Then, turning to Commandant de Ramézay and the colonel of the Regiment of Royal Roussillon, who stood by, he said: "Gentlemen, to your keeping I commend the honour of France. Endeavour to secure the retreat of my army to-night beyond Cap Rouge. As for myself, I shall pass the night with God, and prepare for death."

Yet ever mindful of the wretched people who hung upon him, he addressed this note to the commander of the English army —

"Monsieur, the humanity of the English sets my mind at peace concerning the fate of the French prisoners and the Canadians. Feel towards them as they have caused me to feel. Do not let them per-

General Gage.

1.ᵗ *Military Governor of Montreal.*

ceive that they have changed masters.   Be their
protector as I have been their father.''

By dawn the next morning his gallant soul had
fled.   And when another day had gone, and night
came again, a silent funeral passed, by the light of
a flambeau, to the chapel of the Ursulines for the

NEW KENT GATE

lonely obsequies.   A bursting shell had ploughed a
deep trench along the wall of the convent, and there
they sadly laid him — fitting rest for one whose life
had been spent amid the din and doom of war.   In
1833 his skull was exhumed; and to-day it is reverently exposed in the almoners' room of the Ursuline
convent — all that remains of as fine a figure, as
noble a son of his race as the years have seen.

Here also an interesting tablet, erected by Lord
Aylmer in 1835, bears the sympathetic inscription —

HONNEUR

A

MONTCALM

LE DESTIN EN LUI DEROBANT

LA VICTOIRE

L'A RÉCOMPENSÉ PAR

UNE MORTE GLORIEUSE.

Besides Montcalm, the French army lost its second and third in command, De Sénézergues having expired on one of the English ships, while M. de Saint-Ours was killed in the same bloody charge in which Wolfe also met his death. The French losses in killed and wounded numbered almost fifteen hundred officers and men, the British record being fifty-eight killed, and five hundred and ninety-seven wounded.

When Wolfe was slain the chief command of the British army in Canada had passed to Brigadier Townshend.[1] Expecting every moment to be attacked by Bougainville, Townshend called back his battalions from the charge, and drew them up anew, a movement scarcely accomplished before Bougainville's army was seen advancing from Cap Rouge. Bougainville, however, soon perceived signs of Montcalm's defeat, and unwilling to risk an engagement with a wholly victorious enemy, he retreated without a blow.

Meanwhile, Governor Vaudreuil had held a council of war in the hornwork which protected the St. Charles bridge. Roused now to intelligent action, he was for

---

[1] Afterwards Marquis of Townshend.

making an immediate junction with Bougainville and attacking Townshend before the English position could be strengthened. Bigot recommended the same course; but all the other officers were against it, and the brave but vacillating Vaudreuil was overborne by their counsel. A despairing note was despatched to the little garrison at Quebec; and an army that still outnumbered the British forces began a march thus described by one of the participants: "It was not a retreat, but an abominable flight, with such disorder and confusion that, had the English known it, three hundred men sent after us would have been sufficient to cut all our army to pieces. The soldiers were all mixed, scattered, dispersed, and running as hard as they could, as if the English army were at their heels." Their tents were left standing at the Beauport camp, where in their inglorious haste they had even abandoned their heavy baggage. Passing through Charlesbourg, Lorette, and St. Augustin, by the evening of the 15th they had covered the thirty miles intervening between Quebec and the Jacques-Cartier river.

This desertion by the army was a cruel blow to those who still manned the ramparts of the city. For more than two months they had mended the breaches and fought the fires kindled by the guns of Point Lévi; they had stood by their feeble batteries for weary weeks, toiling night and day on half-rations.

And now ignominious abandonment was their reward! Of the total population within the walls,
twenty-six hundred were women and children, ten
hundred were invalids, while the able-bodied defenders, all told, numbered less than a thousand, and
even these were worn out by privations.

De Ramézay, the commandant, called a council
of war which fourteen officers attended, and all of
these but one were in favour of capitulation. The
citizens assembled at the house of M. Daine the
Mayor, and drew up a petition praying that De
Ramézay would not expose the city and its inhabitants to the further horrors of assault. The citizens'
memorial recited the tribulations they had already
undergone, and pointed out that neither a bombardment continued for sixty-three days, nor ceaseless
fatigue and anxiety had sufficed to kill their spirit;
that though exhausted by famine, yet in the constant
hope of final victory they had forgotten the gnawings
of their hunger. But now, deserted by the army, they
were not justified in making further sacrifices. Even
with the most careful distribution, only eight days'
rations remained in the city. Moreover, a conquering
army was encamped between Quebec and its source
of supply. While there was yet time, they pleaded,
honourable terms of capitulation should be demanded.

All this time the *milice de la ville*, naturally brave,
but unwisely led, were fleeing to their neglected home-

steads. Some even crossed over to the enemy's camp;
and a sergeant actually deserted with the keys of the
city gates in his pockets. Meantime Townshend,
fully aware of the danger of his position, determined
to force the city without delay if the enemy should
show a resolute face. In a few weeks at the most,
the approach of winter would compel the fleet to
leave the river, and should the English army then
find itself outside the walls, the fruits of the Battle
of the Plains would be entirely lost. Accordingly, he
was ready to grant almost any terms of capitulation.

The English trenches drew closer and closer to
the walls, and on the evening of the 17th the fleet
made a movement as if to bombard the Lower
Town, while a column of troops threatened Palace
Gate. The drums of the garrison beat the alarm ;
but the citizens failed to rally, and in despair De
Ramézay at last resolved to surrender. A white flag
showed upon the ramparts, and as the stars came
out, an envoy appeared in the English camp to ask
for terms. At eight o'clock the next morning,
September 18th, the articles of capitulation had been
signed by De Ramézay, Townshend, and Admiral
Saunders. Their provisions were, in brief: That
the garrison should be accorded the honours of war,
and march out bearing their arms and baggage, with
flying colours and beating drums ; that the troops
should be conveyed to France ; that the inhabitants,

x

on laying down their arms, should retain their houses, property, and privileges, at least until the treaty of peace should be signed by the sovereigns of England and France. Artillery and military stores were to be surrendered; the sick were to be cared for, and guards were to be posted to protect the convents and churches against possible outrage.

The general orders for the 18th of September describe, prospectively, the formal cession of the fortress town —

"The gates to be taken possession of by Colonel Murray and three companies of Grenadiers, after which the hour will be appointed when the army should march in. Fifty of the Royal Artillery, officers in proportion, one field-piece with a lighted match following them, will march to the Grand Parade, followed by the Commanding Officer and his party, sent to take possession of the town, to whom all the keys of the forts will be delivered, from which party officers' guards will immediately be sent to take possession of all ports and outlets from the town. . . . During this time the Commanding Officer of Artillery will hoist the Union flag of Great Britain at the most conspicuous place of the garrison; the flag-gun will be left on the Grand Parade, fronting the main guard."

Thus passed Quebec into British hands. And the surrender was made none too soon; for even as the garrison yielded, horsemen dashed up to the city gates to announce the return of the French army. M. de Lévis, hurrying from Montreal, when the danger of

The Hon. Robert Monckton. Major General

Sometime Governor of New York – under Wolfe at Quebec 1759

Amherst's advance no longer threatened, had come
upon the retreating army of Vaudreuil soon after
its arrival at Jacques-Cartier.   Notwithstanding their
appalling want of discipline, he soon made his
presence felt among the fugitives, and despatching
courtiers to De Ramézay to admonish him against
surrender, this worthy successor of Montcalm
marched on to the relief of Quebec.   But it was
now too late; for when, having made a junction
with Bougainville at Cap Rouge, De Lévis drew
near the city, he saw the red flag of Britain floating
from the bastion of Cape Diamond.

On the 19th of September, the day after the capitulation, a fast frigate left for England, bearing the news
of victory, together with the embalmed body of the
gallant general to whom it was due.   Though the
event was celebrated there with bonfires and shouts
of triumph, yet the nation's tears could not be
restrained.   " The incidents of dramatic fiction,"
writes Walpole in his *Memoirs of George II.,* "could
not be conducted with more address to lead an
audience from despondency to sudden exultation,
than accident prepared to excite the passions of a
whole people.   They despaired, they triumphed, and
they wept; for Wolfe had fallen in the hour of
conquest.   Joy, curiosity, astonishment was painted
on every countenance.   The more they inquired,
the more their admiration rose.   Not an incident

but was heroic and affecting." Wolfe's body was laid beside that of his father in Greenwich church; and Parliament erected a monument to his honour in Westminster Abbey. On the Plains of Abraham, also, a large stone was set up to mark the spot where he had fallen; but in 1835 this primitive memorial was superseded by a beautiful pillar, upon which Lord Aylmer, then Governor-General, caused to be inscribed the simple legend —

> "HERE DIED
> WOLFE
> VICTORIOUS."

Eight years before, in 1827, Lord Dalhousie laid the first stone of the beautiful obelisk overlooking what is now known as Dufferin Terrace, to commemorate the heroism of Wolfe and Montcalm, and bearing this impartial inscription —

> WOLFE   MONTCALM
> MORTEM VIRTUS COMMUNEM
> FAMAM HISTORIA
> MONUMENTUM POSTERITAS
> DEDIT
> A.D. 1827.

But to return to the newly conquered city. It was indeed a scene of desolation. The Lower Town was a heap of ruins, and the streets were all but impassable. In the Upper Town, the Bishop's Palace

was in ruins, and of the Cathedral only the shattered
walls remained. The Church of the Récollets, which
faced upon the Place d'Armes, was a wreck of
masonry, while that of the Jesuits was battered
beyond repair. The three convents, Ursuline, Hôtel-
Dieu, and Hospital Général, although further removed, had not escaped the terrific cannonade. The

CHURCH OF THE RÉCOLLETS AND LA GRANDE PLACE

Jesuit College, situated in the midst of the town,
seemed to have suffered least. As for the inhabitants, they had seen their possessions dissolve in
smoke, and were now for the most part dependent
upon the English garrison for provisions; in truth,
it is difficult to exaggerate the misery and ruin which
became the care of the new garrison.

Nor were the French the only sufferers. At the
first sign of winter the English fleet departed for

home, Admiral Saunders and General Townshend sailing away on the 22nd of October, followed four days later by the wounded Brigadier Monckton with the remaining ships. All available stores had been landed, but General Murray was compelled to limit the number of his garrison owing to the scarcity of supplies; and now, with about seven thousand men on short rations, he must hold Quebec until English ships could return to his relief in spring. Such was the doubtful situation in which Murray stood in November; and to add to his danger, De Lévis and Bougainville lay encamped only a few leagues away, with a force far more numerous than his own, and untroubled by anxiety as to supplies.

The hardships of that winter are detailed in the journals of General Murray and Captain Knox. The first distress was a famine of firewood, to meet which detachments of soldiers were detailed to fell trees in the woods of Ste. Foye. They harnessed themselves to the timber like horses, and dragged it thence over the snow to the city. The storms and keen frosts of a Canadian winter were a painful experience for the ill-clothed soldiery, who adopted the most eccentric devices to keep themselves from freezing. "Our guards at the grand parade," writes Knox, "make a most grotesque appearance in their different dresses; and our inventions to guard us against the extreme rigours of this climate are various beyond imagina-

tion. The uniformity, as well as the nicety, of the
clean, methodical soldiers is buried in the rough,
fur-wrought garb of the frozen Laplander; and we
rather resemble a masquerade than a body of regular
troops, insomuch that I have frequently been accosted
by my acquaintances, whom, though their voices were
familiar to me, I could not discover, or conceive who
they were." So long as the troops relied upon their
regimental uniforms, the Highlanders necessarily
suffered most of all from cold, until the nuns of the
Hospital took pity upon them and fell to knitting
long woollen hose.

By the first week in December it became necessary
to relieve the guard every hour instead of every two
hours; but even then frozen ears and fingers and
toes were common casualties. Discipline relaxed,
and the soldiers began to solace themselves by
debauch. Drunkenness became so frequent that
Murray cancelled the tavern licenses; and any man
convicted of that offence received twenty lashes every
morning until he divulged the name of the liquor-
seller. Theft and pillage were strenuously dealt with,
one man expiating his offence upon the citadel gibbet.
Finding that many of his soldiers were deserting, the
General banished from the city certain priests whom
he suspected of intrigue. On the other hand, he
proved a generous friend to those well-disposed
Canadians who had laid down their arms and main-

tained their neutrality, allowing them all the liberty and freedom consistent with the dangers of his own predicament. No French inhabitants, however, were allowed to work upon the batteries or fortifications, to walk upon the ramparts, or to frequent the streets after dark without a lantern; and if found abroad after tattoo-beating they were arrested.

So great was the fear of treason and surprise that a strong force constantly held the gates, the guard-houses always containing about a thousand men, who permitted none to pass without a permit from the General. To protect the approaches of the town, strong outposts were maintained at Ste. Foye and Lorette; and on the other side of the river, at Point Lévi, a detachment of two hundred men held the south shore against surprises. As the winter wore away, it became increasingly evident that an attempt to recapture Quebec would not long be delayed. But although more than a thousand of the garrison were on the sick list, owing mainly to the tainted water of the wells, the laborious commandant kept good heart for the struggle, being in temperament cheerful, generous, and full of resource. Events proved, moreover, that he was daring even to the point of indiscretion.

It was now March, and the campaign opened with a series of skirmishes round the newly-fortified English outposts. Sharp fights took place at Point Lévi

and at Lorette; and Captain M'Donald, with five
hundred men, even ventured as far up the river
as St. Augustin to attack the strong post which
Bougainville had established at Le Calvaire.   Within
the walls of Quebec, fever, dysentery, and scurvy
grew so malignant that by the middle of April hardly
more than three thousand men were fit for duty; and
all the while evidence of the concentration of the
French forces grew more apparent.   So long before
as the 26th of January, Lieutenant Montresor had
been despatched over the snow with twelve rangers
to apprise General Amherst of the plight of the
city; and on the 21st of April the battered
schooner *Lawrence*, the only craft upon which Murray
could lay hands, was sent eastward to hasten Lord
Colville's fleet when it should arrive in the river.

Still, the vigilant defenders of Quebec were only
half aware of the threatening danger; and even as
the *Lawrence* raced down the stream to bring help,
the French army was advancing upon the city.
Starting at Montreal in a fleet of bateaux, the forces
of De Lévis and Vaudreuil had picked up the river
garrisons as they advanced; and by the time they
arrived at Pointe-aux-Trembles, their numbers had
swelled to nine thousand men, while no word of their
approach had as yet reached Quebec.   On the night
of the 26th of April, however, a remarkable incident
brought timely warning.

Darkness lay upon the river, and as they saw the creaking ice-floes sweeping up and down with stream or tide — a condition of the river known in Quebec as " the chariot," — the watchmen shivered, and thanked the fates which kept them on dry land on such a night. Suddenly a cry of distress blew up from the river — the moaning of the wind, thought the guard who paced the quay of the Cul-de-sac. But again the plaint fell upon his ears; and as he peered through the darkness, holding his breath to listen, he knew it was a human voice. A boat put out amid the drifting ice, and guided by the cries, the sailors found a man half dead upon a tiny floe. With difficulty he was rescued and carried ashore; and when cordials had revived him he told his story. He was a sergeant of artillery in the army come to retake Quebec. In attempting to land at Cap Rouge his boat had come to grief; all his companions had been drowned before his eyes; but he had contrived to drag himself upon the drifting ice.[1]

It was three o'clock in the morning when General Murray was awakened to receive this disturbing news. At once the reveille was sounded, and while it was yet dark the troops stood under arms. At

---

[1] This romantic story is not fully established. Parkman cites it as historical, but Kingsford considers it disproved by General Murray's *Journal*. Its original source is the diary of the Chevalier de Lévis, but it also appears in *The Campaign of* 1760, attributed to the Chevalier Johnstone, Montcalm's Scotch *aide-de-camp*.

dawn a strong detachment marched out through the
St. John and St. Louis gates, skirted along the plains,
and came to the declivity in which, at Ste. Foye,
the plateau of Quebec falls away to the lowlands.
Here, in a strong position, they awaited the enemy.

OLD FRENCH HOUSE, ST. JOHN STREET

On swept De Lévis to the city he had sworn to
recapture; and as his army emerged from the
wood, the strengthened outpost of Ste. Foye opened
its guns upon them. Discouraged by the brisk
cannonade and musketry fire, De Lévis, who was
ignorant of the comparative weakness of the English

force, made no attempt to storm the heights, but
ordered his men to fall back, his new plan being to
outflank the enemy by a night march. As for the
English, seeing how impossible it was to hold the
outpost against so large an army, they spiked their
guns, destroyed their works, and finally withdrew to
the city.

Once again Quebec was on the eve of invasion,
and as Murray contemplated his serious position, it
is hardly a matter of wonder that his plan of defence
savoured more of boldness than of prudence. The
breached ramparts offered but a feeble defence; the
frost-bound earth made it impossible to protect the
city by an intrenched camp; and the commissariat
department could not sustain a long investment.
The situation is well summarised in the General's
letter to Pitt: "The enemy was greatly superior in
number, it is true; but when I considered that our
little army was in the habit of beating the enemy,
and had a very fine train of field artillery; that
shutting ourselves at once within the walls was
putting all upon the single chance of holding out for
a considerable time in a wretched fortification, I
resolved to give them battle; and half an hour after
six in the morning we marched with all the force I
could muster, namely, three thousand men."

It was the 28th of April, and the snow still lay
upon the ground. Murray's army marched out

General Sir A. P. Irving.

2nd Governor of Canada 1766.

through the gates in two columns, and took up a strong position on that rolling mound upon the Plains which was known as *Les Buttes-à-Neveu*. The force was disposed as follows : The right wing, consisting of the divisions of Amherst, Anstruther, and Webb, with the second battalion Royal Americans, was commanded by Colonel Burton ; Colonel Fraser was in charge of the left, which comprised Kennedy's and Bragg's divisions, and Lascelles' Highlanders ; while Otway's and the third battalion Royal Americans, commanded by Colonel Young, formed a corps of reserve. Major Dalling, with the Light Infantry, covered the right ; and Hazen's Rangers and a company of volunteers, under Captain Donald M'Donald, were on the left. Each battalion had two field-pieces.

As the English troops were thus forming, Murray rode ahead to reconnoitre the enemy's position. Their vanguard had already reached the brink of the cliff above the *Anse du Foulon*, where they were hastily engaged in throwing up redoubts ; and further away, the main body was moving along the road from Ste. Foye. Even as he looked, the two foremost brigades swung across the plateau towards Sillery woods. Now, thought Murray, was the most favourable moment for attack, De Lévis being still on the march ; and hurrying back, he ordered his columns to the attack. With a cheer the red lines swept forward, dragging their howitzers and field-pieces through the heavy slush of mud and snow ; and when at length they halted and opened fire at short range, their artillery caused such disorder in the forming French lines, that De Lévis was forced to withdraw the brigades composing the left wing to the cover of the woods upon their flank.   The English mistook this movement for a retreat, and pressing forward Murray soon found himself on less advantageous ground. His right division stood knee-deep in a meadow of melting snow, where the guns could only be served with the greatest difficulty, and upon this disabled wing the French left once more swept out of the woods.   Before their impetuous rush the Light Infantry gave way, and so great was the disorder of this brigade that it could take no further part in the action.   The English left was meeting a similar repulse, and from Sillery wood, where the French had taken temporary cover, there issued such a storm of musketry, that Fraser's column recoiled before it. Murray was outnumbered all along the line, and when De Lévis overlapped both left and right and threatened his enemy's flank, the English General gave the order to retire.   The guns, however, being immovably fixed in the snow and mud, had to be spiked and abandoned.   With muttered curses the grisly veterans retreated unwillingly towards the city walls ; but they had inflicted on De Lévis so

decided a check that he judged it prudent to refrain
from pursuit.

Such was the battle of Ste. Foye, without doubt the
most severe of the campaign.   The English lost more
than a thousand, or more than a third of the whole
army ; the losses of the French have been variously
estimated, but they were probably as heavy as those

MANOR HOUSE, SILLERY

of their foe.   Officially reported by De Lévis, they
numbered eight hundred and thirty-three.

It is a pretty walk to-day, out through St. John's
Gate and along the Ste. Foye road.   For a mile or
two the leafy avenue is lined with villas till the picturesque heights are reached, overlooking the valley of
the St. Charles, where Murray and De Lévis met
in fateful conflict.   Here, where the April snow

was dyed by the blood of two valorous armies, is set up a tall pillar of iron, surmounted by a statue of Bellona, the gift of Prince Napoleon Bonaparte in 1855.

Aux Braves [1]

This is its simple inscription — to the brave of both nations whose sons contended for the mastery of a wide dominion. The heroes of Quebec, French and English, have shared more than one common monument, and this community of interest and tradition, nursed from wise beginnings, and accepted as a matter of course for a century and a half of good understanding, has with a subtle and gracious alchemy helped to solve a national problem.

The defeat of Murray at Ste. Foye is sometimes called the Second Battle of the Plains. Its issue was so far from decisive that De Lévis no longer thought of redeeming Quebec by assault, believing that if the city was again to fall into the hands of France, it could only be through regular investment and siege. Accordingly, moving his lines forward to the high ground of *Les Buttes-à-Neveu*, he there began his intrenchments. Meanwhile, the soldiers in the city were working night and day to better its defences. Barricades were erected in the streets, fascines

---

[1] Aux braves de 1760, érigé par la Société St. Jean Baptiste de Québec.

strengthened the ramparts, the St. Jean and St. Louis gates were closed, the latter being placed under the protection of an outwork. Men and officers alike toiled ceaselessly, harnessing themselves to the guns, and working on the batteries with pickaxe and spade. Even the wounded demanded employment, the convalescent filling sand-bags for the fortifications, while those in the hospitals made wadding for the cannon which night and day belched shot and shell upon the besiegers' trenches. When, however, the enemy's field-pieces were in position, the city once more tasted the horror of bombardment. But within the walls, in spite of scurvy, fever, and short rations, the most resolute spirit prevailed. Murray's energy and resource fired the enthusiasm of his men, who saw that only the failure of food and ammunition could bring them to defeat. Both besiegers and besieged dwelt in hourly expectation of ships from Europe — De Lévis, because he had sent to France for help at once upon Montcalm's defeat, and Murray because the return of the English fleet was part of the first plan of campaign. Both knew that the fate of Quebec belonged to the fleet arriving first.

At last, on the 9th of May, a ship of war was descried in the river. The gaunt and toil-worn garrison were almost prostrate with excitement. Slowly the frigate beat up into the basin before the town, not yet displaying her ensign. Through a mishap to the

Y

halyards, no flag floated over the high bastion of Cape Diamond; but to make the stranger declare herself, Murray ordered a sailor to climb up the citadel flag-staff with the colours. Immediately the Union Jack ran up to the frigate's masthead, and the pent-up feelings of the garrison found relief. It was the *Leostaff*, no stranger, indeed, to Quebec; and she brought news that Colville's fleet was already in the river. "The gladness of the troops," writes Captain Knox, "is not to be expressed. Both officers and soldiers mounted the parapets in the face of the enemy, and huzzaed with their hats in the air for almost an hour. The garrison, the enemy's camp, the bay, and circumjacent country resounded with our shouts and the thunder of our artillery, for the gunners were so elated that they did nothing but fire and load for a considerable time."

The French commander, however, was not the man to abandon the siege on account of a single warship, for as yet he did not know that the *Leostaff* was but the herald of further arrivals; and his guns continued to hurl grenades and roundshot into the city. The English batteries returned their fire with so much violence that De Lévis again determined to try and carry the place by direct assault. Scaling-ladders and battering-rams were made ready, but no opportunity came to use them. Another week of vigorous siege passed; and at nightfall, on the 15th of May, to the unspeakable joy of the harassed garrison, the *Vanguard* and the *Diana*, British ships of war, came to anchor in the basin. Next morning the three vessels made their way up the river past Quebec, and attacked the French squadron which had brought the army of De Lévis from Montreal. These were the ships, it will be remembered, which withdrew up the river on the approach of Holmes's fleet in the summer of 1759. The naval engagement was fierce but decisive, the French commander Vauquelin behaving with the utmost gallantry, and refusing to strike his flag even when his powder was spent and his ship a wreck. "Our ships," says Knox, in describing the battle, "forced *La Pomone* ashore and burned her, then pursued the others; drove *l'Atalanta* ashore near Pointe-aux-Trembles, and set her on fire; took and destroyed all the rest, except a small sloop of war which escaped to Lake St. Peter." On the English side, the *Leostaff* was wrecked on the rocks.

To De Lévis the destruction of the French squadron was the greatest possible catastrophe, for the ships carried his supplies. No alternative but retreat remained; and next morning, when Murray marched out for a sortie, he found the French camp deserted by all save the sick and wounded, whom in a letter left behind De Lévis had commended to his care. Their tents still stood upon the Plains, and their guns and mortars gaped silently in the trenches; but the French army had already passed over the Cap Rouge, and the fourth siege of Quebec had come to an end.

So, too, had the *ancien régime:* for although Bougainville still held his strong position at Isle-aux-Noix, and Montreal, whither Vaudreuil had transferred his government, was not subdued till the 8th of September, 1760, when three British columns under Amherst, Murray, and Haviland compelled Vaudreuil to make a formal surrender of that city and of the whole of Canada; still, the key of New France had passed into English hands. Quebec, the Gibraltar of America, was never more to salute the Bourbon lilies, and French empire in the Western world had ceased to be.

CHAPTER XVI

THE FIRST YEARS OF BRITISH RULE

THE period which immediately succeeded the capitulation of Canada is known as the *règne militaire*; but the administration so sternly named was remarkable for the most careful equity. Allowing for circumstances which made military rule a necessity, it was in fact an era of almost unexampled tenderness; for though still on the threshold of her colonial empire, England already realised that the lightest yoke is the longest borne. She had annexed the vast domain of Canada, and the sentiment of its seventy thousand French inhabitants was her first concern. These must be won to a new loyalty and schooled in the free institutions of a progressive nation.

The note of the new administration was struck in the general orders issued by General Amherst, September 9th, 1760: "The General is confident that when the troops are informed that the country is the King's, they will not disgrace themselves by the least appearance of inhumanity, or by unsoldierlike behaviour in taking any plunder, more especially as the Canadians become now good subjects, and will feel the good effects of His Majesty's protection." This confidence in a policy of conciliation was fully justified by the event.

Ever since the Battle of the Plains, the *habitants* and the citizens of Quebec had been slowly but steadily settling to allegiance, and now, when the fall of Montreal had destroyed the last vestige of French dominion, the people generally came forward to enroll themselves. And that they were received into the British fold with something more than a perfunctory welcome is proved by an extract from Amherst's instructions: " These newly acquired subjects," he writes to General Gage, " when they have taken the oath, are as much His Majesty's subjects as any of us, and are, so long as they remain deserving of it, entitled to the same protection. I would have you particularly give it in charge to the troops to live in good harmony and brotherhood with them, and avoid all differences soever."

Naturally enough, the recent belligerents were deprived of their weapons ; and commissioners went through the different parishes administering the oath and collecting arms. A firelock was left to each native militia officer, and, under certain conditions, the rank and file also could retain guns for hunting.

General Townshend.

(afterwards 1st Marquess of Townshend)

The Canadians were allowed the free exercise of their religion; and although nothing was said about the retention of the French language, its employment followed as a matter of course, since only the soldiers of the garrison knew English. The adjustment of civil disputes was placed in the hands of the officers of militia, who met for that purpose every Tuesday; and from their tribunal an appeal to the Governor was also allowed.

Criminal cases were submitted to a court of military officers, civil misdemeanours being defined in the police regulations. To secure the city as far as possible from her ancient scourge of fire, and to lessen the chances of incendiarism, it was ordered that chimneys were to be swept at least once a month under penalty of six *livres*. The fire-brigade of the capital consisted, *ex officio*, of all the carpenters, who were required to attend with axes, the citizens being compelled to assemble with buckets. The *habitants*, while forbidden to harbour English deserters, received due recompense for any of the garrison billeted upon them. For the better regulation of prices, they were forbidden to sell their produce to strangers—"*coureurs de côte*"—but were required to bring it to market. Through representations made by the English Government, France at length consented to redeem the *billets d'ordonnance* with which her moribund administration had hopelessly flooded the country. The hand of the

new government was light, the civic burden easy.
The days of the *corvée* were now passed, and harsh
impressment no longer compelled the *habitant* to fight
on short rations and without pay.   Very soon the
French Canadian, as he felt the improvement in his
condition, ceased to feel resentment against his English conqueror.

That the military rule succeeding to the conquest
of the country was benevolent, that its quality of
mercy was not strained, is shown by the citizens
of Montreal, who at the death of George II.
"placed themselves in mourning," and presented the
following robust address to the Governor : —

"To His Excellency General Gage the Governor
of Montreal and its dependencies.

"The address of the Officers of Militia and
Merchants of the City of Montreal.

"Cruel Destiny has thus Cutt short the Glorious
Days of so Great & so Magnanimous a Monarch!
We are come to pour out our Grief into the paternal
Bosom of Your Excellency, the sole Tribute of
Gratitude of a People who never Cease to Exhalt
the mildness and Moderation of their New Masters.
The General who has conquered Us has rather
treated Us as a Father than a Vanquisher, & has
left us a precious Pledge (*gage*) by Name & Deed
of his Goodness to Us ; What acknowledgments are
we not beholden to make for so many Favours?

A Perspective View of MONTREAL in Canada, 1760

MONTREAL IN 1760

They shall be for ever Engraven in our Hearts in Indelible Character. We Entreat Your Excellency to continue Us the Honour of Your Protection. We will endeavour to Deserve it by our Zeal & by the Earnest Prayers We shall ever offer up to the Immortal Being for Your Health and Preservation."

On the other hand, there were those whose temperaments were opposed to acceptance of the new order of things — those to whom conquest by the hereditary enemy was intolerable. These irreconcilable spirits were mainly civil and military officers, seigneurial families, and *émigrés* of the first generation. To them estates in the New World meant much, but the motherland and the Bourbon lilies meant yet more; and as for the more recent arrivals, not having yet struck deep root in the land of their adoption, they were content to return to France. Accordingly, many of these availed themselves of the transportation provided for in the terms of capitulation, and their departure robbed Canada of much of her best blood. The new government was hard pressed to find ships to accommodate these distinguished passengers, as well as the two thousand disarmed soldiers of De Lévis. At last, however, they were all embarked, and the crowded vessels set sail, only to be attacked by furious gales. De Lévis narrowly escaped a watery grave off the rocks of Newfoundland, while the ship carrying Vaudreuil and his suite fared little better.

But the most distressing disaster of all befell the *Auguste,* a frigate bearing the French officer La Corne, his family, his friends, and a large number of soldiers. Scarcely had the ill-fated ship passed the island of Anticosti when a dreadful storm overtook her from the west and drove her into the Gulf. A few days later, a fire broke out in the cook's galley, which was extinguished only by the most desperate energy of passengers and crew, and not before most of the provisions had been destroyed. Off Isle Royale another storm arose, in which they helplessly tossed for several days, being finally driven upon the coast. The *Auguste* went to pieces on the reefs. La Corne and six companions gained the shore, and unable to render assistance, saw their families drown in the surf. De Gaspé, in his work *Les Anciens Canadiens,* recounts the tragic story in the words of La Corne himself.

" From the 13th to the 15th [of November] we were driven at the mercy of a violent storm, without knowing where we were. We were obliged as best we could to replace the crew, for the men, worn out with fatigue, had taken refuge in their hammocks and would not leave them ; threats, promises, even blows, had been tried in vain. Our mizzen-mast being broken, our sails torn to shreds, and incapable of being clewed up or lowered, the first mate proposed as a last resource in this extremity to run into shore. It was a desperate act. The fatal moment arrived! The captain and mate looked sadly at me with clasped hands. I but too well understood this mute language of men who from their profession were accustomed to brave death. We made the land to starboard, where we perceived the mouth of a river, which might prove to be navigable. Without concealing anything, I informed the passengers of both sexes of this manœuvre, which was for life or death. . . . Who could describe the fury of the waves! The storm had burst upon us in all its violence; our masts seemed to reach up to the clouds, and then to plunge into the abyss. A terrible shock told us that the ship had touched the bottom. We then cut away the cordage and masts to lighten her and try to float her again; this came to pass, but the force of the waves turned her over on her side. . . . As the ship was already leaking in every part, the passengers all rushed on deck; and some . . . threw themselves into the sea and perished. . . . The passengers and crew had lashed themselves to the shrouds and spars in order to resist the waves which, breaking over the ship, were snatching fresh victims every moment. . . . Our only remaining resource was the two boats, the larger of which was carried away by a wave and dashed to pieces. The other was lowered into the water. . . . I hastily seized a rope, and by means of a tremendous leap fell into the boat; the same wave which saved my life carried away my two children. . . . It would be difficult to describe the horror of this terrible disaster, the cries of those still on board the ship, and the harrowing spectacle of those who, having thrown themselves into the waves, were making useless efforts to gain the beach. . . . Seven living men at last found themselves on the shore of that unknown land . . . and (in the evening) it was a heartrending sight which presented itself when a hundred and fourteen corpses were stretched on the sand, many of them with arms and legs broken, or bearing other marks of the fury of the elements."

For weeks the fugitives wandered about the woods, and at last were rescued by a party of Indians thirty leagues from Louisbourg. The indefatigible La Corne crossed in a birch-bark canoe from Cape Breton to the mainland, and, travelling five hundred and fifty leagues on snow-shoes, came again to Quebec. Here, in spite of his own dire predictions, he found a gaiety and contentment which fairly startled him. Within the walls of the grim old river-fortress the ancient foes were making peace in the re-construction of industry. The wise forbearance of the conquerors, and the facile temper of the conquered, provided, far beyond hope, a solution for what was, *prima facie*, a difficult situation. "It is very surprising," writes an officer of the Highlanders, "with what ease the gaiety of their tempers enables them to bear misfortunes which to us would be insupportable. Families, whom the calamities of war have reduced from the height of luxury to the want of common necessaries, laugh, dance, and sing, comforting themselves with this reflection — *Fortune de guerre*. Their young ladies take the utmost pains to teach our officers French ; with what views I know not, if it is not that they may hear themselves praised, flattered, and courted without loss of time." Those who remained behind, sacrificing allegiance to their old flag for the sake of allegiance to the soil, were indeed far happier than the irreconcilables who had elected to return to the motherland, bereft of all but their movable property. And among these homing Frenchmen were some whose reception caused them a very reasonable anxiety. Vaudreuil, Bigot, Péan, Cadet, Varin, Penisseault, and several others who had held offices in Canada, were cast into the Bastille, charged with the corruptions which had sapped the life-blood of New France. For months they contemplated their misdeeds in the sombre silence of the dungeon, and the next year were brought forth for trial. Vaudreuil, for lack of evidence, was acquitted —

properly acquitted, so far as can be known, his chief fault having been a fatal ill-judgment; but a just fate overtook Bigot, Cadet, and their knavish parasites. The Intendant was banished from France for life, and all his property confiscated; Cadet was banished for nine years and fined six million *livres;* the others received sentences in keeping with the measure of their guilt.

Meanwhile, in Quebec, a decade of English rule slipped uneventfully by, marked chiefly by new perceptions of citizenship on the part of the French. The *ancien régime* had been conducted on the principle of centralised authority, allowing no place to personal liberty. Neither on its civil nor its military side were any rights extended to the individual. Up to the Conquest, the citizens of Quebec had been no more than cogs in the wheel of State, driven fast or slow according to the spasmodic interest felt by the Home government in her always troublesome colony — a land which had first claimed consideration as the gateway to Cathay, and presently appeared to be nothing better than a "thousand leagues of snow and ice." This decline from the equator of enthusiasm to the north pole of neglect indicated the unstable fortunes of the colony. National spirit was left to fill up the ranks of her army when danger threatened the frontiers;

and to the simple *habitant*, who had no interest to keep alive the memory of France, Quebec and Louisbourg were the ends of the earth, and the annals of his parish the Alpha and Omega of knowledge.

With British rule all this was changed. In Quebec the *Tiers État* awoke to its latent destiny thirty years before the same realisation came to Paris; and it was the new principles of government which achieved this bloodless revolution. The rights of man were no longer confined to the Governor, Intendant, and the Sovereign Council; and the plainest citizen felt a new pulse within him as soon as he saw the trend of the English system. Instead of being kept in the dark as to what was taking place in the outside world, he found a strange solicitude in high quarters to keep him informed on every subject of public importance. Under General Murray a newspaper was established, the *Quebec Gazette*, which began as a weekly in 1764.[1] The first issue of this pioneer of Canadian journalism consisted of four folio pages, two columns to a page, one French, one English; and the outline of its policy is given in the *Printer's Address to the Public*, promising: —

" A view of foreign affairs and political transactions from which a judgment may be formed of the interests and connections of the several powers of

---

[1] It was changed into a bi-weekly in 1818, and in 1874 was merged into the *Chronicle* as a daily paper.

z

Europe; to collect the transactions and occurrences of our mother-country; and to introduce every remarkable event, uncommon debates, extraordinary performances, and interesting turn of affairs that shall be thought to merit the notice of the reader as matter of entertainment, or that can be of service to the public as inhabitants of an English colony. . . . And here we beg leave to observe that we shall have nothing so much at heart as the support of virtue and morality and the noble cause of liberty. The refined amusements of literature and the pleasing veins of well-pointed wit shall also be considered as necessary to the collection — interspersed with other chosen pieces and curious essays extracted from the most celebrated authors — so that, blending philosophy with politics, history, etc., the youth of both sexes will be improved, and persons of all ranks agreeably and usefully entertained." [1] With such a high conception of its functions, the *Quebec Gazette* launched itself twenty-four years in advance of the London *Times*, and fourteen years before Benjamin Franklin founded the *Montreal Gazette*.

Since the Conquest, Quebec had been governed under the terms of a royal proclamation which, remarkable to relate, prescribed no definite forms of administration; and by the articles of capitulation almost everything was left to the discretion of the

[1] Article by John S. Reade in the Centenary number, *Quebec Gazette*, 1864.

Governor. General Murray proved himself a discreet ruler; but friction of some sort was almost inevitable in a situation presenting such conflicting interests and delicate problems; and it now came from those few hundred British settlers who wrongly supposed that their nationality gave them privileges over ten times their number of French fellow-subjects. Governor Murray, fortunately, held no partisan views; and his policy was followed with equal firmness and greater success by Sir Guy Carleton, who next assumed the administration in 1766.

The new Governor had, indeed, a remarkable connection with the history of Quebec. In 1759 he had accompanied his friend James Wolfe to the siege of the city, and like his General, was wounded on the Plains of Abraham. He remained with Murray in Quebec during the trying winter of 1760, and fought in the battle of Ste. Foye. And now, after a brilliant campaign in the West Indies, the gallant soldier was returning to the fortress on the St. Lawrence at another critical moment in its history.

Events were rapidly moving to a crisis in the English colonies to the south. In spite of Burke and Pitt, England was blindly imperilling her possessions in America by the imposition of the Stamp Act, and a failure to realise that the Thirteen Colonies had long outgrown a state of tutelage, and were not prepared to accept legislation from the motherland.

But as a preliminary measure of offence, the newly
assembled congress determined to detach Canada from
the·British crown, and, naturally, they counted most
of all upon disaffection among the French Canadian
population. It is not possible to give in full the
letter which George Washington despatched on this
occasion to "The Inhabitants of Canada"; but the
following is part of it : —

"FRIENDS AND BRETHREN — The unnatural contest between the English colonies and Great Britain has now risen
to such a height that arms alone must decide it. The
colonies, confiding in the justice of their cause, and the
purity of their intention, have reluctantly appealed to that
Being in whose hands are all human events. . . . Above
all, we rejoice that our enemies have been deceived with
regard to you. They have persuaded themselves, they have
even dared to say, that the Canadians were not capable of
distinguishing between the blessings of liberty and the
wretchedness of slavery ; . . . but they have been deceived ;
instead of finding in you a poverty of soul and baseness of
spirit, they see with a chagrin, equal to our joy, that you
are enlightened, generous, and virtuous ; that you will not
renounce your own rights, or serve as instruments to deprive
your fellow-subjects of theirs. Come then, my brethren,
unite with us in an indissoluble union, let us run together
to the same goal. . . . Come then, ye generous citizens,
range yourselves under the standard of general liberty, against
which all the force and artifices of tyranny will never be able
to prevail.   GEORGE WASHINGTON."

The blandishments of the Thirteen Colonies, or

"The Provincials," as they were called, found almost no response in Canada. Sir Guy Carleton had left nothing undone to foster loyalty in the hearts of the French Canadians; and the passing of the Quebec Act in 1774, which secured to them freedom of worship and confirmed their own system of jurisprudence, held the French fast to their allegiance at a time when disaffection would have been ruinous to the Empire.

Controversies still rage over the propriety of legalising the French language in a British dominion; but any one who examines well the circumstances which induced it must see that not only justice but military expediency required liberal treatment and wide consideration for seventy thousand subjects speaking an alien tongue, if the fruits of the Seven Years' War were not to be heedlessly thrown away. The solution of the language problem lies in the peaceful assimilation which time and growing population alone can bring. Almost a thousand years ago a Norman race was grafted upon a Saxon stock, and the blending of these elements has produced Great Britain, the strongest nation of the modern world. In Canada religious, industrial, and social conditions have as yet prevented definite fusion of the two races; but the march of events and the pressure of common interests must secure it in good time.

CHAPTER XVII

THE FIFTH SIEGE

BESIDES Sir Guy Carleton, Wolfe's army of 1759 contained other officers who were destined to re-appear in the history of the city. One of these was Richard Montgomery, then a lieutenant in the Seventeenth Foot, but now, after a lapse of sixteen years, a brigadier-general, and charged with a far different commission. Moses Hazen and Donald Campbell, two officers who figured prominently in the battle of Ste. Foye, were likewise returning in different guise to the scene of their former exploits; and Benedict Arnold, no stranger in Quebec, came there once more. All of these had made merry at Freemasons' Hall, the festive hostelry at the top of Mountain Hill, which had been a jovial rendezvous in the days of military rule. Here they had toasted and sung, little dreaming that one day they would assail that fort they had so dearly won, and face in battle their former messmates. Yet fate had so ordained; and when the thirteen revolting colonies determined to

342

General Sir James Henry Craig, K.C.B.

Governor General of Canada 1807-1811.

strike the mother-country by an attack on Canada, it was to Richard Montgomery and Benedict Arnold that Congress gave the command of the two invading armies. The former was despatched against Montreal, the latter was sent to take Quebec.

Down the Richelieu came Montgomery, and the forts of Ticonderoga, Crown Point, St. John, and Chambly fell before him. Sir Guy Carleton hurried to Montreal, but as he was unable to rally the citizens to their own defence, the town soon fell into the hands of the impetuous invader. General Carleton escaped in the guise of a peasant through the provincial lines, and paddled to Quebec in a canoe. There his first step was to purge of treason the city upon which the hope of all Canada now rested. Citizens suspected of disaffection were banished beyond the walls; and though the garrison numbered only eighteen hundred men, French and English, the loyalty of all was secure, begetting confidence in their power to meet the attack. A contemporary diary, that of James Thompson, refers thus to the defences: " I received order from General Carleton to put the extensive fortifications of Quebec in a state of repair at a time when there was not a single article of material in store with which to perform such an undertaking. . . . My first object was to secure stout spar timber for palisading a great extent of open ground between the gates called Palace and

Hope, and again from half-bastion of Cape Diamond along the brow of the cliff towards Castle St. Lewis. I began at Palace Gate, palisading with loopholes for musketry, and made a projection in the form of a bastion, as a defence for a line of pickets, in the gorge of which I erected a blockhouse, which made a good defence. . . . Also a blockhouse on the Cape under Cape Diamond bastion. . . . I also had a party of the carpenters barricading the extremities of the Lower Town by blockading up all the windows of the houses next to the riverside and those facing the water, leaving only loopholes for musketry, as a defence in case the St. Lawrence should freeze across. . . . At this time, the nights being dark, I strongly recommended the use of lanterns extended on poles from the salient angles of all the bastions. By means of these lights even a dog could be distinguished if in the great ditch in the darkest night. This we continued in the absence of the moon, with the exception of a composition burned in iron pots, substituted for candles."

It was November, and up to this time General Carleton had feared only the arrival of Montgomery's army from Montreal. Suddenly, however, a new enemy appeared at Point Lévi. Benedict Arnold, at the head of seven hundred men, had accomplished an amazing journey. Through the tangled forests of New Hampshire and Maine, beset by

GENERAL RICHARD MONTGOMERY
(Fell at Quebec 1775)

the driving storms of an early winter, this intrepid
army toiled overland from Boston to Point Lévi.
On the night of the 14th of November, Arnold's
force crossed the river, and gained the Plains
of Abraham without opposition.   Three weeks later
Montgomery's army arrived from Montreal, and the
united forces established themselves at Ste. Foye.
Both Montgomery and Arnold had counted upon
the co-operation of the French Canadians; and
owing to the success of the army against Montreal,
some of the fickle *habitants* were persuaded to join
the invaders.   In general, however, the French
population were not forgetful of the just treatment
they had met at the hands of the British, and if they
were not to be depended upon for a powerful defence, they at least rendered no assistance to the
besiegers.   About half of those whom Carleton had
kept within the walls were French, but these, as has
been said, were wholly trustworthy.

The Governor paid no heed to Montgomery's call
to surrender.   His envoys were turned away from
the gates, and the resolute equanimity of the town
disturbed him.   That his temper hardly stood the
strain is evident from the following letter to the
Governor: —

" SIR — Notwithstanding the personal ill-treatment
I have received at your hands, and notwithstanding

your cruelty to the unhappy prisoners you have taken, the feelings of humanity induce me to have recourse to this expedient to save you from the destruction which hangs over you.   Give me leave, sir, to assure you, I am well acquainted with your situation.   A great extent of works, in their nature incapable of defence, manned with a motley crew of sailors, the greatest part our friends, of citizens who wish to see us within their walls, and a few of the worst troops who ever styled themselves soldiers.   The impossibility of relief, and the certain prospect of wanting every necessary of life, should your opponents confine their operations to a simple blockade, point out the absurdity of resistance. . . .   I am at the head of troops accustomed to success . . . and so highly incensed at your inhumanity, illiberal abuse, and the ungenerous means employed to prejudice them in the minds of the Canadians, that it is with difficulty I restrain them till my batteries are ready. . . .   Beware of destroying stores of any kind, public or private. . . .   If you do, by Heavens, there will be no mercy shown !

" Richard Montgomery,
" Continental Army, G.C."

If there was one man who knew the impracticability of a " simple blockade," it was the General in command of the Continental army.   No one stood in greater need of " stores of any kind, public or private." The spirit of his army was doubtless as he described it; but he had wholly mistaken the temper of the garrison.

Kirke, Phipps, Wolfe, and Lévis had all left their mark upon Quebec, and now the battered walls were once more threatened by Montgomery. The Provincial army had taken posession of every point of vantage outside the gates, the General having established his headquarters at Holland House, by the Ste. Foye road, while Arnold occupied the suburb of St. Roch towards Charles River. The houses of the *habitants*, the General Hospital, and the Intendant's Palace were thronged with soldiers, who found their tents poor protection against the rigours of a winter campaign. A six-gun battery was erected within three hundred paces of St. John's Gate, a battery of two guns thundered from the bank of the St. Charles, while a third belched impotent fire across the river from Point Lévi. From the cupola of the Intendant's Palace a body of riflemen continued to pick man after man off the ramparts, until Sir Guy Carleton at last trained his guns upon it. It was a hard thing for the Governor to destroy perhaps the finest building of all Quebec, but the rigours of the siege seemed to leave him no alternative; and soon the venerable building lay in ruins, having witnessed the chequered history of the city since the days of the great Talon.

Day and night the cannon on the ramparts
answered the enemy's howitzers, and once again the
river gorge echoed back the roar of artillery. Shells
and grenades burst continually in the streets, and as
weeks wore away the citizens became inured to the
dangers of battle or sudden death by roundshot,
grape, and canister. Outside the walls, the enemy
suffered in like manner, running the gauntlet of
Carleton's artillery and exposed to the musketry of
the garrison. One day as Montgomery dashed over
the snow-covered plain in a carriole his horse was
killed by a cannon shot. Such casual dangers,
however, were the least cause of his anxiety, which
was especially due to the prolongation of the siege.
His men were ill-clothed, depending for rations
largely upon the goodwill of the *habitants*, who
anxiously weighed the chances of British prowess.
Moreover, desertion and sickness thinned his ranks ;
and at last, having resolved upon a *coup de main*,
he formed his plans and awaited a dark night for
their execution.

Meantime, the wary Carleton neglected no means
of informing himself of the enemy's intentions.
When this latest resolution of the invader came to
his ears, the night watches of Quebec were doubled,
and he and his devoted officers slept in their clothes
at the Récollet Convent, whence, at a moment's
notice, they could hasten to a threatened quarter.

On the 30th of December a deserter from Montgomery's camp, being allowed within the gates,
confirmed Carleton's suspicions by affirming that
the Continental army had received final instructions,
with permission to plunder the city on its capture.
Once more the Governor inspected the fortifications
and the barriers of the Lower Town, and anxiously
awaited the assault.

Having accurate knowledge of the city's defences, Montgomery saw but one plan promising
success to his enterprise. This was to divide his
force and attack the Lower Town from two
directions. From St. Roch Arnold was to
force the barrier below the Sault-au-Matelot, while
he himself should creep along through Près-de-
Ville, at the base of Cape Diamond, carry the
barrier and blockhouse standing in his way, and
reach the foot of Mountain Hill. Uniting at
this point, the two columns would gain the Upper
Town and overpower the garrison, the real assault
being conducted under cover of a simulated attack
upon the ramparts from the Plains. The plan was
desperate, but at least not more hopeless for the ill-
conditioned troops of the invaders than a long and
cruel siege.

It was the last night of the year 1775, the stars
were winter bright, but the fleecy clouds of im-
pending storm were driven across the sky. Silently

the guards paced the ramparts of the watchful
city, gazing eagerly over the glimmering Plains
of Abraham, and across the river where the
lights of the Lévi outposts twinkled against the
dark sky. Midnight passed, the stars were
obscured, and snowflakes began to fall, at first
slowly, then swiftly blown upon the rising wind.
Presently, as the clock in the guard-house struck
four, two rockets shot up from the enemy's camp
and burst in a fiery shower beyond the Cape.
Captain Malcolm Fraser of the Highlanders stopped
short in his round of inspection: " Guard, turn
out!" he shouted. Having raised the guard, he
rushed down St. Louis Street sounding the alarm,
and at the Récollet Convent found General Carleton
and his staff. In five minutes every bell within
the walls was ringing, drummers were beating the
assembly, and every soldier of the fort was at his
post.

Meanwhile, the two forces of the Continental
army were marching to the attack. Arnold's
division, having the shorter distance to traverse,
reached its objective first. " When we came to
Craig's house, near Palace Gate," writes a participant,[1]
" a horrible roar of cannon took place, and a ringing
of the bells of the city, which are very numerous
and of all sizes. Arnold, leading the forlorn hope,

[1] *Siege of Quebec*, 1775, 1776, by John Joseph Henry.

advanced perhaps one hundred yards before the main body. . . . The snow was deeper than in the fields, because of the nature of the ground; and the path made (by the advance guard) was almost imperceptible because of the falling snow. Covering the locks of our guns with the lappets of our coats, holding down our heads (for it was impossible to bear up our faces against the imperious storm of wind and snow), we ran along the foot of the hill in single file. . . . In these intervals we received a tremendous fire of musketry from the ramparts above us. Here we lost some brave men, when powerless to return the salutes we received, for the enemy was covered by his impregnable defences. . . . They were even sightless to us; we could see nothing but the blaze from the muzzles of the muskets. . . . We proceeded rapidly, exposed to the long line of fire from the garrison, for now we were unprotected by any buildings. The fire had slackened in a small degree. The enemy had been partly called off to resist the General (Montgomery), and strengthen the party opposed to Arnold in our front. Now we saw Colonel Arnold returning, wounded in the leg and supported by two gentlemen. . . . (He) called on the troops in a cheering voice as we passed, urging us forward, yet it was observable among the soldiery, with whom it was my misfortune to be now placed, that the Colonel's

2 A

retiring damped their spirits. . . . Thus proceeding, enfiladed by an animated but lessened fire, we came to the first barrier, where Arnold had been wounded at the onset. This contest had lasted but a few minutes, and had been somewhat severe, but the energy of our men prevailed. The embrasures were entered when the enemy were discharging their guns. The guard, consisting of thirty persons, were either taken or fled, leaving their arms behind them. . . . From the first barrier to the second there was a circular course along the sides of the houses and partly through the streets. . . . This second barrier was erected across and near the mouth of a narrow street adjacent to the foot of a hill which opened into a larger, leading soon into the main body of the Lower Town. Here it was that the most serious contention took place. . . . Confined in a narrow street, hardly more than twenty feet wide, and on lower ground, scarcely a ball, well aimed or otherwise, but must take effect upon us. . . . A crowd of every class of the army had gathered into the narrow pass, attempting to surmount the barrier, which was about twelve feet or more high, and so strongly constructed that nothing but artillery could effectuate its destruction. . . . Within the barrier, and close into it, were two ranges of musketeers, armed with musket and bayonet, ready to receive those who might venture the dangerous leap. . . .

Sir John Cope Sherbrooke.

Governor General of Canada. 1816-1818.

This was near daylight, . . . and all hope of success having vanished, a retreat was contemplated. . . . The moment (however) was foolishly lost when such a movement might have been made with tolerable success . . . and Captain Laws, at the head of two hundred men, issuing from Palace Gate, most fairly and handsomely cooped us up. Many of the men, aware of the consequences, and all our Indians and Canadians, escaped across the ice which covered the Bay of St. Charles. . . . This was a dangerous and desperate adventure, but worth while the undertaking, in avoidance of our subsequent sufferings. Its desperateness consisted in running two miles across shoal ice, thrown up by the high tides of this latitude ; and its danger, in the meeting with air-holes, deceptively covered by the bed of snow. . . ."

With the other wing of the invading army, the issue was even less doubtful and far more tragic. Montgomery had pushed through the storm, along the base of the cliffs from Wolfe's Cove to the base of Cape Diamond. Deep snow covered the rocky pathway, and spray from the fretting river had rendered it slippery with ice. Every man in the chosen company knew the peril of the enterprise, and moved forward stealthily. Soon the advance guard led by Montgomery in person could discern through the driving snow the first straggling houses

of the Lower Town.   A barrier crossed the roadway,
but no sight or sound gave evidence that the guard
was on the alert.   Forward they crept, silent and
full of desperate purpose.   Suddenly, when they
were within thirty yards of the barrier and counting
fully upon the surprise of the outpost, four cannon
and a score of muskets pounded forth a deadly fire.
Itself taken by surprise, the Continental army broke
and fled.   No sound reached the wakeful guard save
the groans of the wounded who had gone down
before that fatal barrier; but, distrustful even of the
silence, their battery continued to sweep the pass.

At dawn a reconnoitring party ventured forth
from the guard-house.   Thirteen bodies lay half
buried in the snow, and the only remains of the invading army were General Montgomery, his two aides-
de-camp, Cheeseman and M'Pherson, a sergeant, and
eight men.   All but the sergeant were dead, and he
too died within an hour.   As for the General, only an
arm appeared above the snow, and a drummer-boy
picked up his sword close by.   The English soldiers,
uncertain whose body it was, fetched a prisoner, one
of Arnold's forlorn hope, who could not restrain his
grief for the brave General who had been the idol of
his troops.   Widow Prentice, of Freemasons' Hall,
also recognised Montgomery by the sabre-cut upon
his cheek; and Sir Guy Carleton having no
further doubt as to his identity, gave orders that

CAPE DIAMOND
(Près-de-Ville, where Montgomery fell)

the slain General should have honourable burial.
Up Mountain Hill they bore him to the small house
in St. Louis Street, still known as Montgomery
House, and later in the same day he was laid in a
coffin draped with black, and borne by soldiers to
a new-made grave in the gorge of the St. Louis
bastion. A brass tablet now marks the spot near
the present St. Louis Gate.

Although both divisions of their army were
defeated, over four hundred prisoners taken, and
their General slain, the invaders were yet unwilling
to give up the struggle against the grim walls of
Quebec. They were sore beset by cold, hunger,
and the hardships of active warfare; and small-pox
carried off nearly five hundred of their number.
On the death of Montgomery, Arnold had succeeded
to the chief command, but it was April before his
wound was healed. Meanwhile, they had quickly
erected a new battery at Point Lévi, and once again
the guns of the citadel entered upon an artillery
duel with that historic ravelin. From time to time
rockets sent up from the enemy's camp threw the
defenders of the city into unusual alarm, and once or
twice, when the signals seemed more pregnant, the
whole force turned out and swiftly took up their
assigned positions. General Carleton on the other
side, not having enough soldiers to dislodge the
besiegers, had been content to hold fast and wait

until spring should bring him reinforcements from England. No vigilance on the part of the garrison was relaxed, and throughout the cold and dreary winter the sentries marched night and day upon the ramparts.

Towards late spring the increased activity of the besiegers caused a corresponding restiveness among the many prisoners within the city. Sir Guy Carleton had treated them with as much liberality as was possible under the circumstances; but on an attempt on the part of some of the officers to bribe the guard, he speedily placed the offenders in irons. On the last day of March a large number of prisoners made an attempt to escape from the Dauphin barracks, just inside St. John's Gate. Their plan was to overpower the guard, whose strength was necessarily small, capture the adjacent city gate, and hold it open for their comrades on the Plains. The plot was discovered, however, and the prisoners were transferred to the British gun-boats in the harbour.

As the weeks went by, the anxiety of an ever threatened attack told heavily on the garrison, and even the convalescent were called upon for guard-house duty. A blockade extending over four or five months was exhausting their provisions; and for fuel they were at length reduced to tearing down wooden houses in the suburb of St. Roch. For half a year the Richelieu, Montreal, and Three Rivers, in fact the whole of Canada, had been virtually in the enemy's hands; Quebec alone remained, but, commanded by Carleton, Quebec was a fortress in the most real sense.

It was the evening of the 3rd of May, and in the gathering darkness a ship rounded Point Lévi and drew near to the ships in the basin. Cheers rose from the garrison and a saluting gun boomed from the citadel. Still the strange craft made no salute, and a heavy crash of artillery burst from the Grand Battery. For answer, flames leaped up the rigging and along the bulwarks of the approaching schooner. It was the *Gaspé*, which the enemy had fitted up as a fire-ship and sent into the harbour. The crew, being disconcerted by the alert challenge of the garrison, hastily lighted the fuses and escaped in small boats, but only to see the impotent fire-ship carried down the river by the ebbing tide.

Meanwhile, the invading army had drawn near to the ramparts, intending to assault the town under the confusion caused by the *Gaspé*. To these dogged troops, steeled for their last great effort, the failure of the fire-ship was a severe blow. Moreover, their slight remaining hope vanished a day or two later when the British frigate *Surprise*, arrived in the harbour, having boldly forced its way through the ice-packs which still beset the lower river. Not long afterwards the *Isis*, fifty guns, and the sloop-of-war *Martin* also rounded Point Lévi.

After six months of toil, privation, and suspense the brave garrison was at last relieved. Once more in Quebec numberless joy-bells rang out, and artillery crashed triumphantly across the tide. Flags ran up on every bastion and parapet within the walls, and the cheers of the reinforced garrison carried dark despair to the enemy's camp across the Plains.

The siege was immediately raised, the invaders thinking only of escape. General Carleton, with a force of only a thousand men, marched out by the city gates and tried to fall upon the enemy's flank. So rapid had been their flight, however, that only the van of his column was able to come up with the Provincials, who, in their hurried retreat, had not only abandoned their artillery, ammunition, and scaling-ladders, but had left their sick and wounded in the tents of Ste. Foye. Once more the invader had failed to seize the key of all Canada; and another successful conflict was written in the annals of Quebec. Never again was a hostile army to beset those grim grey walls. "Twice conquered and thrice conquering" became the pregnant summary of two centuries of the history of the fortress, and the lapse of still another hundred years makes no amendment necessary. Like her younger sister, New Orleans, the city upon the St. Lawrence had often been the battlefield of the nations, but, for both, the centuries have brought prosperity and peace.

CHAPTER XVIII

SOCIAL AND POLITICAL PROGRESS

QUEBEC had passed through her last ordeal of fire and sword, and for many years the 31st of December was celebrated with enthusiasm as the anniversary of the victory. But although the effort to detach the French Canadians from their allegiance to Great Britain resulted miserably in the defeat of Montgomery and Arnold, the Thirteen Colonies did not quite relinquish the hope of accomplishing their end. Instead of an army, Congress now despatched commissioners to Canada, Benjamin Franklin, Samuel Chase, and Charles Carroll of Carrollton being of the number. The mission, however, was without success; for the ancient capital, although the most foreign in speech and custom of all places in British North America, remained steadfast under the temptation to swerve from her allegiance. Franklin, indeed, added nothing to his reputation by his general relations with the settlements on the St. Lawrence. For twenty-four years he had held the position of Deputy-Postmaster-

General for the English colonies, Quebec being regarded as in some sense within his jurisdiction; and the unsatisfactory monthly service between Quebec and Montreal as well as the absence of intermediate post-offices, had made him unpopular along the Canadian river. It is not surprising,

BENJAMIN FRANKLIN
(One of the four American Commissioners to Canada in 1776)

therefore, that he failed to arouse the enthusiasm of the French, especially for a cause which their strong monarchical principles failed to approve.

It is estimated that more than twenty-five thousand United Empire Loyalists crossed the border at the end of the American Revolutionary War to live under the British flag. These, for the most part, went to Upper Canada, the settlements along Lake Ontario and the Bay of Quinte, being centres of vigorous life and progress; while not a few settled in Quebec, adding to the sound character of its sturdy population.

A further accession, moreover, was made by the arrival of two regiments of Hessians and Brunswickers, who came out to garrison the citadel. Many of these presently obtained their discharge in order to marry and settle down in Quebec. The current directory discloses many names of German origin, names now high up in the roll of citizenship, but once in the books of the Hanoverian regiments of George III.

A memorable figure passes across the stage of Quebec history just at this time. In 1782 the frigate *Albemarle*, twenty-eight guns, lay in the harbour, and her brilliant, handsome commander was Horatio Nelson. This paragon of fortune had entered His Majesty's Navy as a child of twelve; at fourteen he was captain's coxswain on the expedition of the *Carcass* to the North Pole; and now, with an astonishing experience crowded into a life of twenty-four years, he dropped anchor before the rock of Quebec.

The sober Haldimand was Governor, and the *Sturm und Drang* of the American Revolution had cast a cloud upon the social life of Canada. For if Quebec was not what it had been in the days of Sir

Guy and Lady Carleton, the sterner *régime* of Haldimand had deeper influences behind it than the

CHARLES CARROLL OF CARROLLTON
(One of the four American Commissioners to Canada in 1776)

militarism of a rigid soldier. Nevertheless, Nelson
and his gay company helped to lighten the
heavy cloud, and for the space of a few weeks
dinners and dances, on shore and on board the

Albemarle, enlivened the autumn season in the capital. Southey's *Life of Nelson* contains rather a quaint picture of the commander of the *Albemarle* about this time. Prince William Henry, then known as the Duke of Clarence, regarded him as the merest boy of a captain he had ever seen. Dressed in a full-laced uniform, an old-fashioned waistcoat with long flaps, and his lank, unpowdered hair tied in a stiff Hessian tail of extraordinary length, he made altogether so remarkable a figure that, to use the Prince's own words, " I had never seen anything like it before, nor could I imagine who he was nor what he came about. But his address and conversation were irresistibly pleasing; and when he spoke on professional subjects, it was with an enthusiasm which showed he was no common being."

Freemasons' Hall, at the top of Mountain Hill, was the fashionable rendezvous ashore, and not since the days of Murray's garrison had the old stone hostel been so merrily possessed. One Miss Mary Simpson appears to have been a *belle* of the period; and Sir James Le Moine, the antiquary, has identified her as the lady whose charms might have changed the course of history. "At Quebec," writes his biographer, " Nelson became acquainted with Alexander Davison, by whose interference he was prevented from making what would have been called an imprudent marriage. The *Albemarle* was about

The Fourth Duke of Richmond.
Governor General of Canada 1818-1819.

to leave the station, her captain had taken leave of
his friends, and was gone down the river to the place

SAMUEL CHASE
(One of the four American Commissioners to Canada in 1776)

of anchorage, when, the next morning, as Davison
was walking on the beach, to his surprise he saw
Nelson coming back in his boat. Upon inquiring
the cause of his reappearance, Nelson took his arm

to walk towards the town, and told him he found it utterly impossible to leave Quebec without again seeing the woman whose society contributed so much to his happiness, and then and there offering her his hand. 'If you do,' said his friend, 'your utter ruin must inevitably follow.' 'Then let it follow,' cried Nelson; 'for I am resolved to do it.' 'And I,' replied Davison, 'am resolved you shall not.' Nelson, however, on this occasion was less resolved than his friend, and suffered himself to be led back to the boat." [1]

It is not clear why Nelson's utter ruin should "inevitably follow" his marriage with Mary Simpson. Was it on account of his youth? Or was the statement due to Davison's distrust of marriage in general? If this was the reason, it is evident that Nelson was not greatly moved by his friend's pessimism; for not much more than a year later we find him making an unsuccessful proposal of marriage to Miss Andrews, the daughter of an English clergy-man at St. Omer, France, a rebuff for which, in the following year, he found consolation in an alliance with Mrs. Nesbit.

The settlement of the United Empire Loyalists in Canada greatly altered the political complexion of the conquered country. The terms of the Quebec Act of 1774, though necessary in the circumstances,

---

[1] Southey's *Life of Nelson*, chap. i.

BREAKNECK STEPS TO-DAY

were distinctly opposed to the views of the English minority, who strongly resented the employment of French civil law. And now these newcomers greatly increased the strength of this English faction, the peculiar conditions under which they chose to throw in their lot with Canada giving them a claim upon the Home government which could not be disregarded. The continuous agitation for parliamentary government which marked the years from 1783 to 1790, was not confined to the English section of the population. With the English, however, it took the special form of a demand for a separate province west of the river Beaudette, the capital of which should be Cataraqui,[1] "with the blessings of British laws, and of British Government, and an exemption from French tenures."

In the midst of this political turmoil, Sir Guy Carleton, who, for his distinguished services, had been raised to the peerage with the title of Lord Dorchester, returned to Canada as Governor-General; and on the 23rd of October, 1786, Quebec welcomed her former deliverer at the landing-stage, the whole population, French and English, uniting to give him an honourable and joyous reception. Every one felt indeed that Dorchester was the man to solve the political difficulty of the period; and with these omens of success he set to work forthwith, dividing

---

[1] Now the City of Kingston, Ontario.

the province into four administrative districts on an English pattern, and preparing for the English government a careful report on the social, political, and judicial conditions of his province, to facilitate remedial legislation.

In the spring of 1791 the younger Pitt introduced into the British House of Commons a Bill providing for the political needs of Canada. It proposed the division of the country into two provinces, the special character of each being preserved through the medium of an elective assembly. This naturally raised strenuous opposition among the English minority whom this division would still leave in the province of Lower Canada. It was all very well, they declared, for the English of Upper Canada to be accorded representative government, but for themselves this measure would mean a further decrease of influence in Quebec. On behalf of the English section of the population, Adam Lymburner, an influential merchant of the city, proceeded to England, and was heard at the bar of the House of Commons. The debate was keen and fierce. Pitt supported the Bill in its original form, contending that the territorial separation would put an end to the strife between the old French inhabitants and the new settlers from Britain and the New England colonies. Edmund Burke, whose speech related mainly to the French Revolution, was of opinion that " to attempt

Admiral Viscount Nelson

to amalgamate two populations composed of races of men diverse in language, laws, and customs, was a complete absurdity." Fox, opposing the division of the province, accused Burke of irrelevancy in his address, and made a speech which provoked a memorable quarrel and brought to an end the friendship of the two greatest Parliamentary orators of the century.

At last, however, the Bill became law under the title of the Constitutional Act; and on the 17th of December, 1792, the first legislature of Lower Canada assembled in the chapel of the Bishop's Palace, which had been fitted up as a council chamber. From the seventeenth century this hoary structure of stone had overlooked the Grand Battery from the top of Mountain Hill, commanding a view of the basin and the attenuated Côte de Beaupré, of which from the time of Laval it had been the seigneurial manor-house. In appropriating the episcopal palace for legislative purposes, the Imperial government recompensed the Catholic see of Quebec by an annuity. The old French building was demolished in 1834, and the new House of Parliament, soon afterwards erected on the same site, served to indicate the wonderful political development of the French province as an integral part of the British Empire.

The proclamation of the Constitutional Act, on

the 26th of December, 1791, was the signal for great
public rejoicings in Quebec. During the day the regimental bands played to the trooping of the colours
on the Esplanade, and in the evening the streets
were ablaze with lights and torches, while fountains
of fireworks broke from the high bastions of the
citadel. A public dinner, attended by one hundred
and sixty gentlemen, brought the *fête* to a close.

An unusual feature of these celebrations was the
presence of His Royal Highness Prince Edward,
Duke of Kent, son of George III., who had come to
Quebec in the preceding summer as colonel of the
Seventh Fusiliers. The transfer of this gay regiment
from the Gibraltar of the Old World to the Gibraltar
of the New did more than merely decorate the social
annals of Quebec ; for the visible presence of a prince
of the blood contributed not a little to crystallise
the loyalty of a French province not quite beyond
the influence of the great revolutionary fires of
Europe. Although he was but twenty-five, Prince
Edward had the tact and *savoir faire* of riper years ;
and during his three years' residence in the garrison,
exerted a great and far-reaching influence on the
fidelity of French Canada. The reception of the
gallant Prince when he landed at the head of his
regiment in August 1791 was marked by all that
enthusiasm which the Gallic city had learned of
old. Long since, in 1665, the Marquis de Tracy

Lord Dalhousie.

Governor General of Canada 1820-1828.

OLD PARLIAMENT HOUSE, QUEBEC

Map of
CANADA
(Upper & Lower)
illustrating events until the campaign
of 1814.
English Miles

0   50   100   150   200

Q   u   e   b   e   c

R. Saguenay

Tadousac

(Lower) (Stad) (Canada)

Laurentine Mts.

Mal Baie

(Ottawa) mond

Ottawa R.

i   o

Lake of Two Mountains

wrence

Three Rivers

Batiscan

R. St. Lawrence

Sorel

Vercheres

Peter

Orleans

R. St. John

Montreal (Hochelaga)

Lachine

Ft. Chambly

St. Louis Rapids

St. Therese

R. Richelieu

LaColle

I. aux Noix

Lake Champlain

The Valley of the river
ST. LAWRENCE.

English Miles

0   10   20   40   60   80

52°

L. Mistassini

Anticosti

C   A   N   A   D   A

Egg I.

Gulf of St. Lawrence

Gaspé B.

Newfoundland

R   e   (c)   Mts.

Cabot Str.

R. Saguenay

R. St. Lawrence

Ile Royale

L. St. John

Tadousac

(C. Breton I.)

Laurentine

A   c   a   d   a

L. of St. John (Pr. Edward I.)

Louisbourg

Quebec

R. Chaudiere

Orleans

R. St. John

Three Rivers

Ft. Beausejour

L. St. Peter

Sorel

R. St. Croix

Nova Scotia

Port Royal

Halifax

Richelieu

Chebucto Harb.

heal

Annapolis

Lacolle

B. of Fundy

C. La Hève

44

Lake Champlain

N   E   W   Y   O   R   K

Crown Pt.

Carillon

Ticonderoga

Ft. Loyal

Casco B.

enry

gal

Ft. Edward

Salmon Falls (Portsmouth)

dy

Albany

Haverhill

Hudson R.

Boston

Nantasket

Massachusetts

A T L A N T I C   O C E A N

New Hampshire

Merrimac

Kennebec

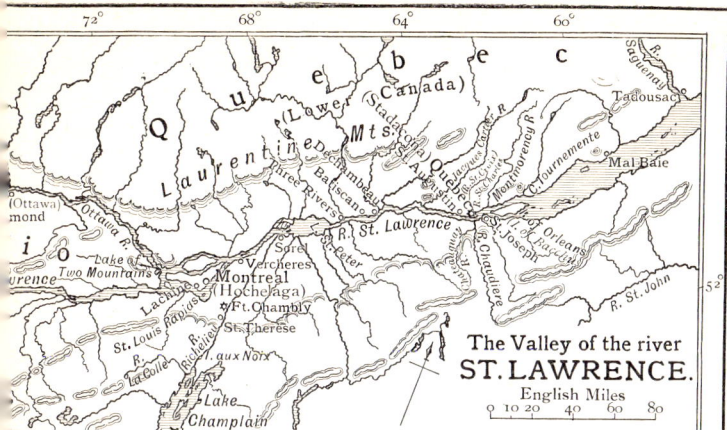

Walker & Cockerell sc.

had schooled her in these august pageants, and now
when Commodore Sawyer's squadron, consisting of
the *Leander*, the *Resource*, the *Ariadne*, the *Thisbe*,

HIS ROYAL HIGHNESS THE DUKE OF KENT, K.B.

the *Ulysses*, and the *Resistance*, dropped anchor in
the basin, Quebec was streaming with flags and
bunting and resounding with music.   Next day

his Royal Highness held a *levée* at Château St. Louis, where the civic authorities assembled to do him honour.

Prince Edward established himself at Kent House, the sombre mansion in St. Louis Street, which Bigot had built for the fascinating Angélique des Meloises almost half a century before. Here he held his court; but his heart was in the country, and except upon public occasions, he preferred the stately retirement of Haldimand House, a rustic retreat still standing near the brink of Montmorency Falls. Gaily he made his promenade along the Beauport Road, or shot over the marshes of La Carnardière; and at his own or the neighbouring homestead of M. de Salaberry, the genial company whiled away many an evening with whist. Frequent balls and receptions in the old Château recalled the days of Frontenac's merry court;. or, still further back, that night of Canada's first ball, the 4th of February, 1667, when the courtly soldiers of the Carignan-Salières regiment led the grand dames of New France through the mazes of a Versailles quadrille. From a child, indeed, Quebec had conned the worldly wisdom of Fontainebleau. Her wholesome reputation for the social graces is reflected in the compliment paid by George III. to the first Canadian lady who had the honour to be presented at the Court of St. James's: " Madame,

ST. LAWRENCE RIVER FROM THE CITADEL

if the ladies of Canada are at all like you, I have indeed made a conquest!"

It was among these gracious spirits that Prince Edward's lines were fallen; and within the space of three years the large-hearted Duke had bound the hearts of French Canada more firmly to the throne upon which his own daughter was to sit as Queen Victoria.

Meanwhile, in Europe, the feudalism which had lost Canada to France was in its mortal throes. The shock of the French Revolution was quivering through the hemisphere, and the convulsion was felt heavily in the New World. In the United States, Washington was President, Hamilton was at the Treasury, and Jefferson was Secretary of State, with Madison as a colleague in the Cabinet. In the early stages of the Revolution the United States had given enthusiastic sympathy to the movement; but as it grew in violence, all but the mob and Jefferson and Madison were alienated. No degree of tyranny appeared to offend the sensibilities of these latter statesmen; and when the French Convention declared war against England, their approval of that measure all but committed the United States to the principles of red republicanism. Genet, the French Ambassador to the United States, with an insolence that defeated itself, carried on unblushing intrigues until his recall was requested. For a time, moreover, the populace cried out for war with England, and only the calm resolution of Washington averted such a catastrophe. John Jay was presently despatched to England to negotiate the "Treaty of Amity and Commerce," but it required all the weight of the sober-minded portion of the population to secure its final ratification.

This, however, did not prevent M. Adet, the new French Ambassador to the United States, from sending an address to the French Canadians, informing them of the success of the arms of France against the allied powers of Europe, and calling upon them to rally round the standard of the Republic. The response to this appeal in the Province of Lower Canada was absurdly feeble. The greatest power in all Canada — the Church — shrank in horror from the blood-stained banner of regicide France; and zealous always for the monarchy, the Catholic hierarchy indignantly spurned the overtures of a republic whose most cherished principle was atheism — which had abandoned the worship of God for the cult of Reason. "For God and the King" had been the priestly motto from time immemorial, and the new Republic repudiated obligation not to one only but to both. Accordingly, the vast influence of the Church was exerted on the side of loyalty to Great Britain.

It must not be assumed, however, that the intrigues which the French Republic carried on by way of the United States, found no response whatever in Lower Canada ; for naturally enough there were some whose habitual discontent made them ready for treasonable enterprise. Yet the promoters of disaffection miscalculated the numbers and strength of their party, and the resulting demonstration was factitious and puerile.

Lord Dorchester was withdrawn from Canada in the midst of this small and abortive mutiny. For sixteen years, all told, this gallant soldier of Wolfe's army had administered the country he helped to conquer, and no Governor before or since has earned a more deserving fame. Quebec and Montreal strove to outdo each other in the protestations of loyalty and regret marking their valedictory addresses. On the 9th of July, 1796, the frigate *Active* embarked the veteran Governor, and sailed for England. The vessel was wrecked, however, off the island of Anticosti, fortunately without loss of life; and in small boats Lord Dorchester and his companions reached Isle Percée, where they were afterwards picked up by a ship from Halifax and conveyed to England.

General Prescott, who succeeded to the governorship, was a man of harsher temperament. But although his anxiety for the loyalty of the French

2 c

province was much increased by the intrigues of revolutionary agents, he soon perceived their plans to be fatuous and their enterprise devoid of importance. While the forward spirits in Quebec were leavening the mass of the *habitants* with specious reports of a French fleet ready to co-operate with them, a force composed for the most part of ill-disposed Americans was to percolate into Canada from Vermont. This so-called fleet consisted of a ship, ironically called the *Olive Branch*, which had sailed from Ostend bound for Vermont with twenty thousand stand of arms, several pieces of artillery, and a quantity of ammunition. She had not got far on her way, however, before a British cruiser seized her and bore her into Portsmouth harbour.

Meanwhile, Du Millière, an alleged French General, was scattering money about on the borders of Vermont, while a plausible American was intriguing at Quebec. With timber cutters and the simplest of artisans as his confederates, this misguided revolutionist hatched his theatrical conspiracy in the neighbouring woods. He proposed to overcome the city-guard with laudanum ; and fifteen thousand men were only awaiting the uplifting of his hand ! These and similar illusions possessed a poor dupe named M'Lane, until the Government having decided upon the apprehension of the leading conspirators, M'Lane was arrested and charged with high treason.

Chief Justice Osgoode presided at the trial, and a jury condemned him to death.

On the 21st of July, 1797, above two thousand troops were drawn up in the streets of Quebec as the chief conspirator was led forth to his execution on the *glacis* just outside St. John's Gate. "I saw M'Lane conducted to the place of execution," writes

PERCÉE ROCK

De Gaspé excitedly. "He was seated with his back to the horse on a wood-sleigh whose runners grated on the bare ground and stones. An axe and a block were on the front part of the conveyance. He looked at the spectators in a calm, confident manner, but without the least effrontery. He was a tall and remarkably handsome man. I heard some women of the lower class exclaim, whilst deploring his sad fate, ' Ah, if it were only as in old times, that handsome man would not have to die! There would be plenty of girls ready to marry him in order to save his life!' And even several days after the execution I heard the same thing repeated. This belief, then universal among the lower class, must, I suppose, have arisen from the fact that many French prisoners, condemned to the stake by the savages, had owed their lives to the Indian women who had married them. The sentence on M'Lane, however, was executed in all its barbarity. I saw all with my own eyes, a big student named Boudrault lifting me up from time to time in his arms so that I might lose nothing of the horrible butchery. Old Dr. Duvert was near us, and he drew out his watch as soon as Ward the hangman threw down the ladder upon which M'Lane was stretched on his back, with the cord round his neck made fast to the beam of the gallows. . . . 'He is quite dead,' said Dr. Duvert, when the hangman cut down the body at the end of about twenty-five minutes. . . . The spectators who were nearest to the scaffold say that the hangman then refused to proceed further with the execution . . . and it was only after a good supply of guineas that the sheriff succeeded in making him execute all the sentence, and that after each act of the fearful drama his demands became more and more exorbitant. Certain it is that after that time Mr. Ward became quite a personage, never walking in the streets except with silk stockings, a three-cornered hat, and a sword at his side. Two watches, one in his breeches pocket and the

HON. WILLIAM OSGOODE
(First Chief Justice of Upper Canada)

other hanging from his neck by a silver chain, completed his toilet."

With Black, the ship-carpenter who turned king's evidence against M'Lane, the reward was far different. Blood-money failed to solace him for the contumely heaped upon him; and, according to the historian Garneau, he was so overcome by public contempt that after some years he was reduced to begging his bread in the streets of Quebec.

Since the enactment of this gruesome tragedy more than a century ago, the steep declivity which joins the Lower to the Upper Town, just outside St. John's Gate, has retained the name of Gallows Hill. No other executions appear to have taken place upon

NEW ST. LOUIS GATE

the spot, a well-known hillock upon the Plains of Abraham having been for many years the Golgotha of Quebec, while Gallows Hill only served this purpose during a transition period. By 1814 we find an execution taking place from the gaol erected four years before in St. Stanislaus Street within the walls. On the 20th of May in this year, Patrick Murphy paid the extreme penalty of the law for the

wilful murder of Marie Anne Dussault of the Parish
of Les Escuriels. Four years later Charles Alarie and
Thomas Thomas were executed at the same place,
" for stealing to the value of forty shillings in a vessel
on a navigable river." The same register chronicles
the dire fate of John Hart, a Nova Scotian who,
for larceny, was sentenced to six months' imprison-

OLD MARKET SQUARE, UPPER TOWN

ment, and to be publicly " whipt between ten and
twelve in the market-place." Hart had no stomach
for this ignominy, and escaped from gaol on the
14th of February, 1826. Having been recaptured
three days later, in November of that year he stood
with the noose about his neck upon the fatal door.

It is doubtful, indeed, whether the unfortunate
creatures behind those stout walls on the Côte St.

Stanislaus ever breathed the prayer contained in a quaint inscription which till lately survived upon the lintel of their prison-house : " *Carcer iste bonos a pravis vindicare possit.*" [1] To-day the building itself serves a more kindly purpose, though the pious legend over the doorway might need but slight revision.   Morrin College occupies one wing,

FRONTENAC TERRACE TO-DAY

and the other contains the well-stocked library of the Literary and Historical Society of Quebec.   Valuable manuscripts have taken the place of useless male-factors in the donjon keep, and the vaults are full of the gold and myrrh of history.

The punishment of crime undoubtedly underwent more change in the last half of the nineteenth century

---

[1] " May this prison cause the wicked to bear testimony to the just."

than during several of the preceding centuries.
There is, for instance, a striking resemblance between the public whipping of John Hart and the
chastisement of offenders so long before as the time
of Frontenac. In the year 1681, one Jean Rattier
was condemned to death, but his sentence was
commuted on condition of accepting the post of
public executioner. Fourteen years afterwards
Rattier's own wife was apprehended for theft, and
according to her sentence, she was publicly whipped
in the Lower Town Market-place by the dutiful
husband.

CHAPTER XIX

THE STORY OF THE GREAT TRADING COMPANIES

But now to leave the fortress city for a little space, and see its influence working in the wilds which it had commanded by the valour of its adventurers and traders. While England and France had been contending on the St. Lawrence for mastery, and the struggle to gain or to retain the Gibraltar of America had dragged its length through generations, far off in the white north another strife between the civil energies of both nations was being waged. The English explorers — Frobisher, Davis, Hudson, and Baffin — had been the first to reach the northern coast from the sea, giving their names to water and territory which have since become familiar to the civilised world. Theirs was the old dream—a north-western route to India and China. No such vision, however, had presented itself to the French explorers who, about the same time as the English, planted their flag upon those barren shores, and pushed up from the south, partly to explore, but more certainly

Gen. Lord Aylmer.
Born in 1775.
Governor General of Canada.
1830-1831 — 1831-1835.

to develop the trade in furs which the *Compagnie des cents Associés*, founded by Richelieu in 1627, had already worked to advantage. The charter of this Company, indeed, did not include the regions of Hudson's Bay, but was confined to the province of Canada alone. To-day, Canada comprises all the vast territory north of the 49th parallel of latitude, even to the pole; then its sphere of influence stretched westward to the Missouri and the Mississippi, and southward to Louisiana; while those regions now called Manitoba, Saskatchewan, Athabasca, Assiniboine, and the Klondike were as yet unknown. When Hearne, the Hudson's Bay Company explorer, pushed his way northward and westward to the copper mine on the Copper River, it seemed as if the ultimate ends of the world had been reached, and that the vast region of ice and snow, inhabited by wandering tribes of Indians, would be for ever the property of a trading company.

So far back as 1630 an agency of commerce and exploration was founded in Quebec, under the name of the Beaver Company. This was forty years before the Hudson's Bay Company received its charter from the second Charles. The French went so far in their eagerness for territory that they even claim to have discovered Hudson's Bay, through one Jean Bourdon, in 1656. This claim is not admitted, however, in the *Jesuit Relations*, where, in

1672, Father Albanel writes: " Hitherto this voyage
had been considered impossible to Frenchmen, who,
after having undertaken it three times, and not
having been able to surmount the obstacles, had seen
themselves to abandon it in despair of success." The
claims of England to the territory were undoubted;
but there can be no question that Frenchmen were
the first traders in the vicinity of Hudson's Bay.

The names of two stand out clearly, first as agents
of French enterprise, and afterwards of successful
English adventure, in this early commercial history
of the far north; where, for nearly two centuries and
a half, British energy and justice, and the honesty
of English rule has, through the Hudson's Bay
Company, worked southward to meet the ever
increasing territory owned by the French until 1759.
The Frenchmen whose names are so identified with
the early history of Hudson's Bay were Medard
Chouart, called also Groseilliers, and Pierre Radisson.
They had emigrated from France as young men in
the middle years of the century, and settled at first
in Three Rivers. After a somewhat intricate matrimonial experience, Radisson had established relations
which afterwards stood them both in good stead,
at the same time typifying the ambiguous nature
of international relations in the far north. On the
French side he was son-in-law to Abraham Martin,
whose name was given to the Heights of Abraham;

MR. SAMUEL HEARNE

(Explorer of the Hudson's Bay Company and Chief Factor at Prince of Wales Fort, Hudson's Bay)

The Territory of the
HUDSON'S BAY
COMPANY,
1670 to 1870.

English Miles

0 100 200 300 400

Walker & Cockerell sc.

Hudson's Strait

James Bay

HUDSON'S BAY

Arctic Circle

Rupert's Land

Albany R.

Ft. Charles

Lower

Upper

Canada

Sault Marie

L. Superior

L. Nipissing

R. Ottawa

Ft. Severn

York Factory

Ft. Churchill

Churchill R.

Nelson R.

Sturgeon Lake

Lake Winnipeg

Cumberland Ho.

Saskatchewan

Assiniboine R.

Ft. Ellice

L. of the Woods

Ft. Rouge
(Winnipeg)

Red R.

(Assiniboia) Manitoba

N. Saskatchewan R.

S. Saskatchewan R.

Missouri R.

Ft. Reliance

Great Slave Lake

Ft. Resolution

Coppermine R.

L. Athabasca

Athabasca R.

Ft. McMurray

Ft. Chippewan

Ft. Vermilion

A t h a b a s c a

R o c k y   M o u n t a i n s

Great Bear Lake

Mackenzie R.

Ft. Franklin

Ft. Simpson

Fraser R.

Vancouver I.

Ft. Yukon
(Klondike)

Ft. Selkirk

Longitude West 110° of Greenwich

60°

70°

80°

90°

100°

110°

120°

140°

60°

50°

100°

120°

he was also son-in-law to Sir John Kirke, a brother
of the English admiral to whom Champlain surrendered Quebec; while to bind him closer to the
companion of his adventurous life, he was brother-
in-law to Groseilliers.

Thus allied by disposition and relationship the
two enterprising Frenchmen, allured by visions of
fortune and adventure in the unknown regions
of the north, soon abandoned the safe comforts
of town life; and having served a probation in
several short expeditions, they at last applied to
the reigning powers in Quebec for leave to oper-
ate on a larger scale. The existing Company, however, jealous for its monopoly, hedged them round
with such difficult conditions that the young men
broke impatiently from all control and plunged into
the wilds of the West, penetrating at least as far as
Lake Winnipeg. But Quebec was a stern step-
mother, and when they returned, instead of meeting congratulation, they were arrested and fined for
illicit trading. After a vain appeal to Paris, finding themselves rejected and discredited among their
own countrymen, the two adventurers performed the
first of those political somersaults which made them
a nine days' wonder alternately in London and Paris,
and finally brought to one, at least, an inglorious
competency of £10 a month. Fifty eventful years
were, however, to roll past before that anti-climax

to the drama of their lives. To begin with, when
they had shaken off the dust of New France, they
repaired to Boston, propounding to the New England traders the novel scheme for furnishing an
expedition to be sent round to Hudson's Bay by
way of the sea; at the same time offering their
own experience for service in the undertaking. Although disposed to favour the proposal, the Boston
merchants had no available ships of their own,
but advised an application to the English Court.
Arriving in England in 1667, the two friends were
introduced by Lord Arlington, then ambassador in
Paris, to Prince Rupert, the natural patron of all
adventurers at the time, and who, moreover, was then
expecting a grant of territory in America as a reward
for his services to the royal cause. Already the
merchants of London had been roused to the
possibilities of this trade by the recent arrival of
the first cargo of furs from New Amsterdam; and
now when the two impartial Frenchmen pointed
out to them that the trade was being choked in
Quebec, and that England had a golden opportunity of profitable enterprise, two vessels, the
Nonsuch and the *Eagle*, were fitted out without delay,
and one Captain Gillam received instructions to in-
vestigate and report.

Such was the beginning of the Hudson's Bay
Company. Having spent a winter at Fort Charles,

PRINCE OF WALES'S FORT, HUDSON'S BAY, 1777

the first fort on the Bay, so named after the royal
patron, the adventurers returned to England in 1670
with such solid proofs of the soundness of the

PRINCE RUPERT

speculation, that the new Company received a charter
from the King under the title of "*The Governor and
Company of Adventurers of England, Trading into
Hudson's Bay.*" The Company were constituted
lords and proprietors of the territories round Hud-

son's Bay, now called Rupert's Land, having powers
like those of the feudal lords of an earlier time —"to
employ ships of war, to erect forts, to make reprisals,
to send home English traders who neglected their
licenses, and to declare war or make peace with any
people not Christian." Although the Declaration of
Rights in 1689 limited the rights granted by exclusive charters, and allowed British subjects to trade
freely to any quarter, yet the Hudson's Bay Company had in the twenty years previous to that date
obtained such a hold upon the new territory, especially by the erection of forts, that they easily left
all competitors behind.

The spirit of discovery was never so alive
among the French as during those years following the expulsion of Radisson and Groseilliers;
yet the Government in Quebec was slow to realise
the serious nature of the menace in the north; and
from the official papers afterwards prepared for the
British delegates at Utrecht, their easy confidence is
thus described : —

" Mr. Bailey, the Company's first Governor of
their factories and settlements in that Bay, entertained a friendly correspondence by letters and
otherwise with Monsieur Frontenac, then Governor
of Canada, not in the least complaining, in several
years, of any pretended injury done to France by
the said Company's settling a trade and building a

fort at the bottom of Hudson's Bay, nor making pre-
tensions to any right of France on that Bay, or to the
countries bordering on it, till long after this time."

Trouble, however, came in due course. With a
natural distrust of renegade Frenchmen, Governor
Bailey suspected the two friends of being concerned
in a plot set on foot by certain Jesuit agents of
the Intendant Talon in 1673, by which the loyalty
of the Indians was to be alienated from the English
traders. After scenes of personal violence, the alleged traitors justified the suspicions of the Governor
by severing once more the slender tie of their
allegiance and returning to the service of France.
Nor was it long before new fruits of their restless
energy appeared. In 1681 the *Compagnie du Nord*
was organised as a rival to the "Adventurers of
England"; and in the same year the Intendant
Duchesneau complained to his Government of the
aggressions of the English traders.

"They" (the English), he wrote, "are still in
Hudson's Bay on the north and do great damage to
our fur trade. . . . The sole means to prevent them
succeeding in what is prejudicial to us would be to
drive them by main force from that Bay, which
belongs to us. Or, if there would be an objection in
coming to that extremity, to construct forts on the
rivers falling into the lakes, in order to stop the
Indians at these points."

From this time to the peace of Utrecht there was war between the Hudson's Bay Company and the French. A veiled expedition set out from Quebec in 1682, under the guidance of Groseilliers and Radisson, to attack the forts on the Bay; and by their effrontery and good generalship they at last became possessed of the newly built Fort Nelson, with Bridgar its Governor, and returned next year with their prisoners and spoils to Quebec. But this triumph was soon converted by their lawless temper into disgrace and condemnation; and to escape penalty for misappropriating large quantities of fur, the two leaders were compelled to fly from New France for the second time, and once more take refuge in Paris.

But now the English Company decided to make another bid for the services of these versatile bush-rangers, who once more proved their graceful facility for playing a double game. Radisson was sent by the English ambassador to London, where he became a lion of society, and was presented to Charles II. John Selwyn thus describes his appearance:[1] —

"To the Duke's Playhouse, where Radisson, the American fur-trader, was in the royal box. Never was such a combination of French, English, and Indian savage as Sir John Kirke's son-in-law. . . . He was not wont to dress so when he was last here,

[1] Quoted by Beckles Willson, *The Great Company*, vol. i. p. 141.

The Earl of Durham.

Governor General of Canada May-Oct. 1838.

but he has got him a new coat with much lace upon it, which he wears with his leather breeches and shoes. His hair is a perfect tangle. It is said he has made an excellent fortune for himself."

Radisson's star, however, was almost set, for although he enriched his new masters with fresh cargoes of spoil from the north, his reckless disposition had again involved him in a quarrel with a powerful agent of the Company, and on returning to England he found himself discredited and neglected. With a pension of ten pounds a month, paid by the Company only after the strenuous Radisson had had recourse to law, he continued to live in obscurity until 1720, his friend Groseilliers having died ten years before. He had paid dearly for his lack of patriotism. An affected or assumed distrust of him on the part of the Hudson's Bay Company, who had profited enormously by his services, was the unconvincing reason given for mean neglect and an injustice only at last set right by the law invoked through Sir William Young and Richard Cradock, members of the Company. Brigand or traitor though he was, as such he had been the agent of the Hudson's Bay Company, and his bold services were worthy of reward.

Meantime the Company's servants were being hard pressed in the Bay, confronted as they were by one of the best commanders of the time, the famous

Sieur d'Iberville, who gained his first laurels in this obscure conflict. Although the glory of the campaign was reaped by their French assailants, who, between the years 1682 and 1688, inflicted losses on the Company to the extent of seven ships with their cargoes, and six forts and factories, yet the material advantages turned out in the end to be on the side of the English traders. Among other indiscretions, the conquerors fell to quarrelling with the Indian tribes, who soon made their position on the shores of Hudson's Bay intolerable ; while the *coureurs de bois*, spreading out from their headquarters at Michillimackinac, diverted the Indian trappers from French and English forts alike.

On the other hand, the Hudson's Bay Company were able, in 1690, to declare a dividend of seventy-five per cent on their original stock ; and on the accession of William III. they presented him with a substantial proof of the progress of their undertaking : —

" On this happy occasion," so their address ran, " we desire also most humbly to present to your Majesty a dividend of 225 guineas upon a £300 stock in the Hudson's Bay Company . . . and although we have been the greatest sufferers of any Company from those enemies of all mankind, the French, yet when your Majesty's just arms shall have given repose to all Christendom, we also shall enjoy our share of these great benefits, and do not doubt but to appear often with this golden fruit in our hands, under the happy influence of your Majesty's most gracious protection over us and all our concerns."

William acknowledged this manifestation of loyalty by granting the Company a confirmation of their charter, and by including a statement of their grievances in his first declaration of war against France; but it is evident that the Home Government at that time took little real heed to the interests of this distant dependency, and by a casual clause in the Treaty of Ryswick the most important ports on Hudson's Bay were ceded to the French.

The Company's prospects after that surrender were indeed gloomy; shares fell low, indifference and ignorance prevailing in high places; and the faithful remnant could only hope for a renewal of the war. But at last Fortune began to smile again; for although no important battles were ever afterwards fought in the region of the Bay, the brilliant campaigns of Marlborough in Europe reflected glory upon the struggling traders in the New World, and gave them prestige and power; until finally, by the Treaty of Utrecht in 1713, the huge undefined domain of Hudson's Bay was unconditionally yielded up to Great Britain. After many years one more hapless attempt was made to capture the forts of the north ; but thenceforth the French put forward no regular claim to the territory so long disputed.

Although the merchants of New England in due course made efforts to secure a share of the fur trade, the only real competition, from first to last, was offered by the French explorers. In 1684 Du Lhut had been sent westward by Governor La Barre to counteract the influence of the Hudson's Bay Company with the Indians, and he had only reported to his master that in two years not a single savage would visit the English at Hudson's Bay. Iberville's victories in the north, however, had distracted the attention of the Government from this enterprise, and the work was left to be carried on by independent traders. A profitable trade in furs sprang up on the lines of La Vérendrye's discoveries, and the forts of Michillimackinac and Sault Ste. Marie continued to flourish until the traders were finally withdrawn from all the outlying regions to defend Quebec against the English.

It had been a gallant fight, in which the native qualities of both races had been seen to advantage. Ardent, brave, adventurous, the Frenchman had ever been the best of pioneers. With a faculty for acquiring languages and dialects, he quickly adapted himself to the ways of the Indian, won their sympathy, and treated them with an equality and freedom which made their path of peaceful conquest easy and trade a cheerful jugglery. From first to last there entered into the life of the French trader and adventurer an element of patriotism and romance — conquest for conquest's sake and for the glory of French enterprise. He must ever remain the more eloquent, the more picturesque figure, the more admired pioneer of the Far North. But his rival, the Briton, had qualities which outwore him, and the patriarchal and stable methods of the Hudson's Bay Company prevailed in the end.

The heroic age of the Company had passed away; and now a long and uneventful period began, in which, as in the Middle Ages, the energies of men were slowly gathering for the more strenuous activity of modern conditions.

"*Pro pelle cutem*," the chosen motto of the Company, was perhaps humorously understood as conveying loosely the notion of an exchange of peltries; for certainly the vindictive principle, "a skin for a skin," did not mark their dealings with the Indian tribes. From the first they were fortunate in encountering more peaceable races than those opposing the colonists further south; and a regular trade was conducted upon the basis of a fixed scale of values, the unit of calculation being one beaver skin. Thus a gun could be procured for eight, or ten, or twelve winter beavers, according to the classification of the skin by size and weight. One beaver was the equivalent of a hatchet, or four pounds of shot, or half a pound of beads, or a pound of tobacco. A laced coat was worth six beavers, and a looking-glass and comb cost two beavers ; and so on through all the luxuries and necessities of Indian life, other pelts being always reduced to the terms of beaver skins.

A traveller [1] who visited the country at a some-what later period of the eighteenth century has drawn a picture of the ornate ceremony, which, on the Indian side at least, transformed barter into a solemn function, and provided the exiled traders with a comedy of manners. He describes how, salutes having been fired on both sides, the Indians are elaborately welcomed within the fort, where, after long silence and much tobacco-smoking, the subject of the visit is distantly broached, and the chief receives propitiatory gifts of brightly coloured apparel : " A coarse cloth coat, either red or blue, lined with baize, and having regimental cuffs ; and a waistcoat and breeches of baize. The suit is ornamented with orris lace. He is also presented with a white orris shirt; his stockings are of yarn, one of them red, the other blue, and tied below the knee with worsted garters ; his Indian shoes are sometimes put on, but he fre-quently walks in his stocking feet; his hat is coarse,

[1] Umfreville, *Present State of Hudson's Bay*, 1790.

and bedecked with three ostrich feathers of various colours, and a worsted sash tied round the crown ; a small silk handkerchief is tied round his neck, and this compleats his dress."

The Chief thus gaily equipped is conducted back from the fort to his own tent. " In the front a halbard and ensign are carried ; next a drummer beating a march ; then several of the factory servants bearing the bread, prunes, pipes, tobacco, brandy, etc. Then comes the Captain [Chief], walking quite erect and stately, smoaking his pipe, and conversing with the Factor."

Afterwards came the smoking of the sacred calumet, the pledge of peace and unity, followed by the inspection of the merchandise, and a speech from the Chief in this wise : —

" You told me last year to bring many Indians to trade, which I promised to do ; you see I have not lied ; here are a great many young men come with me ; use them kindly, I say ; let them trade good goods ; I say ! We lived hard last winter and hungry, the powder being short measure and bad, I say ! Tell your servants to fill the measure, and not to put their thumbs within the brim ; take pity on us, take pity on us, I say ! We paddle a long way to see you ; we love the English. Let us trade good black tobacco, moist and hard twisted ; let us see it before it is opened. Take pity on us, take pity on

us, I say! The guns are bad; let us trade light
guns, small in the hand and well shaped, with locks
that will not freeze in the winter, and red gun cases.
Let the young men have more than measure of
tobacco; cheap kettles, thick and high. Give us
good measure of cloth; let us see the old measure;
do you mind me? The young men love you, by
coming so far to see you; take pity, take pity, I say;
and give them good goods; they like to dress and
be fine. Do you understand me?"

By such yearly functions, by gifts, and a sober
friendliness never dissociated from the authority of
the ruling race, the English company held its sway
after the French had retired.

About this time, however, loud complaints were
heard on all hands of the want of enterprise of the
Hudson's Bay Company in not seizing the opportunities afforded by the charter. Its trade was
lethargic, its traders were timid or slothful, its people
possessed none of that audacity and adventure which
had sent Frenchmen like Du Lhut and La Vérendrye
into the wilds intent on territory or trade. They
yawned and were content with the trade which came
their way. It seemed as though they smugly counted
on their business virtue to attract, and their yearly
gifts and patronage to allure the fur-hunting tribes.
A world lay spread around them, and they remained
at the doors of their posts and forts. No joy of the

woods possessed them, no faith in the future drew them on; they followed the makers of Empire, guessing nothing of what Empire meant, hating their rivals for gifts they neither possessed nor desired. One Joseph Robson, who worked as surveyor in the

SIR ALEXANDER MACKENZIE
(Celebrated North-West explorer)

northern forts in 1744, relates a conversation held that year with the captain at York Factory : —

" I expressed my surprise," he writes, " that the Company did not send Englishmen up the rivers to encourage and endear the natives, and by that means put a stop to the progress of the French. . . . He said that he believed the French would have all the country in another century. To which I could not help immediately replying that such an alienation could only be effected through the remissness of the English." Robson next requested leave to travel inland; and "this brought on dismal tales of the difficulties to be encountered in such an expedition; and when I talked of going up rivers, I was told of stupendous heaps of ice and dreadful waterfalls, which would not only obstruct my passage but endanger my life. To confirm this, he said that Governor Maclish once attempted to go a little way up Nelson River to look for timber in order to build a factory, but found such heaps of ice in the river that they were discouraged from proceeding any higher." [1]

Umfreville, the writer and traveller already quoted, likewise challenges the Company for its "total want of spirit, to push on its work with that vigour which the importance of the contest deserves. The merchants from Canada," he continues, "have been heard to acknowledge that were the Hudson's Bay Company to prosecute their trade in a spirited manner, they must be soon obliged to give up all thoughts of penetrating into the country; as from the vicinity of the Company's factories to the inland parts, they can afford to undersell them in every branch."

This advantage enabled the older Company to reach the stations on the Bay at an earlier season of

[1] Robson, *Six Years' Residence in Hudson's Bay*, 1752.

Sir John Colborne.
(afterwards Lord Seaton)
Governor General of Canada 1838-1841.

the year than was possible for their rivals by the overland route. Yet such was the zeal animating the Canadian companies that, conquering all difficulties of season and situation, they delivered goods to the Indians in their villages and tepees, thus anticipating their journey to the north; and some time after the Conquest forty canoes of about four tons burden each left the St. Lawrence every year for the interior.

The fall of Quebec marked a crisis in the affairs of the Hudson's Bay Company, and for a time indeed it seemed as if it also would pass away with the old *régime*. Their foes at this time began to multiply; for while the veteran *coureurs de bois* of Canada were ready enough, after the Conquest, to take service under their new masters, the Colonial forces were now further augmented by a large body of Scotch settlers, partly Jacobite refugees, and partly soldiers of the Highland regiments of Amherst and Wolfe. With vitality thus renewed the Canadians now turned to the west, their emissaries penetrating as far westward as Sturgeon Lake on the Saskatchewan, where a trading station was erected to divert the Indians from the forts at Hudson's Bay. But suddenly the "Adventurers of England" awoke from their long sleep, and Hearne, their agent, was forthwith sent to open up new territories, across which a chain of stations soon marked the successive stages

2 E

of their progress, from Cumberland House to distant
Athabasca. The spirit of competition was now
aflame, and on many occasions in the course of the
next fifty years it caused the opposing Companies
to pass the limits of commercial strife and contend
in open warfare, until mutual interest and vice-regal
authority at last combined to reconcile them.

A great and threatening rival to the Hudson's
Bay Company had come. The North-West Company, founded at Montreal in 1782, under the
leadership of Simon M'Tavish, was founded on
principles which made it a power against the older
organisation, its agents receiving a stimulus to enterprise from a share in the profits of the undertaking
and pay double that given by the English Company.
These advantages proved so potent, that soon after
beginning operations the North-Westers were able to
send abroad skins to four times the value of those
exported by their great rival.

But this zeal was met in a new and robust spirit
which held the issue of the conflict long in doubt.
The beginning of the new century saw its force
increase — a civil war carried on beyond the vision of
the nations in the vast forests of the north. The
story of this Homeric struggle, however, with its
romantic episodes and opposing heroes — Cuthbert
Grant, Colin Robertson, Duncan Cameron, and the
rest — the battle of Greys against Blues, in which the

chiefs of the north, issuing with their wild *bois brûles* from the stronghold of Fort William,[1] raided and harried the despised "old countrymen," the "Pork-eaters," the "Workers in gardens," or suffered reprisals from these underestimated rivals; the history of Lord Selkirk's settlement in the Red

SIMON M'TAVISH
(Founder of the North-West Company in 1783)

River, around which the final battle wound in the year when Europe was witnessing the last great effort of Napoleon — all this does not fall within the scope of the present work.

In 1821, under pressure from the Duke of Richmond, the Greys and Blues agreed to merge

1 Founded in honour of William M'Gillivray in 1805.

their forces in an equal partnership, which, retaining
the name of the older Company, was framed on
the co-operative principle so effective in the success

EARL OF SELKIRK
(Founder of Selkirk Settlement, 1820)

of the North-Western concern. Having received a
fresh charter from the Government, the new Company began a peaceful and not less profitable career,
until in exchange for an indemnity of three hundred
thousand pounds, and a grant of seven million acres

in the best districts of the North-West Territories, the feudal rights of the Hudson's Bay Company were at last taken over by the Dominion of Canada. The Company, however, still pursues its prosperous way. Its forts and posts are sources of influence, centres of safety; its officers and men a devoted and upright band who have proved their right to the gratitude of the empire — unliveried policemen of good government and national integrity.

CHAPTER XX

QUEBEC entered upon the nineteenth century equipped with the machinery of constitutional government, which was, however, clogged in action by unhappy divisions within the city. The four years of Sir James Craig's rule were disturbed by a truceless war between the Legislative Assembly and the Governor, whose arbitrary temper ill qualified him to lead a people still groping for standing-ground within the area of their new constitution. He looked at popular institutions with the distrust natural to an old soldier, and the period of his administration became known in the annals of the province as "the reign of little King Craig." Born at Gibraltar, he had entered the army at the tender age of fifteen, and having earned rapid promotion on many battlefields, he finally reached the rank of major-general at the close of the American revolutionary war. Further experience in India and the Mediterranean increased his reputation, and

in the autumn of 1807 he arrived in Quebec full
of military honours, and imbued with the high
political views then held by the most exclusive
wing of the Tory party. The members of the
Legislative Council and the administrative clique
drew close about the person of this new champion,
and in the same degree the French majority in

FERRY-BOAT ON THE ST. LAWRENCE

the Legislative Assembly held aloof. The burning
questions of the day, whether the judges should
sit and vote in Parliament, whether the Assembly
could communicate directly with the Home Government — these were but the occasions of an antagonism
really due to diversity of race and temperament;
for, as Lord Durham discovered a generation later,
" this sensitive and polite people " revolted, not so

much against political disability, as against the exclusive manners and practices of a ruling class far removed from themselves by language and mode and code, who ruffled their racial pride at every turn.

The new Governor was now the forcible instrument of this unsympathetic power. With an undue sense of the importance of the vice-royalty, the *ipse dixit* of " the little king " dissolved Parliament on more than one occasion. On the other side, *Le Canadien*, the journal of the French party, rhetorically stood for liberty, fraternity, and equality as against arbitrary government. Moderate men, wavering for a time, were at last scandalised by its editorial violence, and rallied to the side of the Governor. The situation quickly became acute, and stringent measures of repression were adopted by Sir James Craig and his councillors. The offending journal was suppressed ; five recalcitrant officers of militia were relieved of their command ; and, finally, the city guards were strengthened to meet the peril of a possible insurrection. Soon a new element of danger appeared in the threatened war between England and the United States, offering to the aggrieved party a tempting occasion for redress. Fortunately, however, neither the unwisdom of the English Government nor the neighbourhood of a hostile power availed to drive or lure the Canadians into the

Lord Sydenham.

Governor General of Canada 1839-1841.

crooked path of rebellion. As the past had already
proved, their country's peril was sufficient to
unite in hearty concord all parties, French and
English, in the defence of the common heritage;
the experience of half a century of British rule
having convinced even the survivors of the *Ancien
Régime* that however haughty or aloof officials
might be, security, order, and justice prevailed
under the British flag.

Considering the especial temptations to treason
bearing upon the French population at this crisis,
such loyal conduct is the more praiseworthy. In the
first place, it was maintained throughout a war which
was part of England's life-and-death struggle against
France, the mother-country of French Canadians.
Again, apart from this natural affinity with the
chiefest enemy of England, material causes operated
yet further to strain their faith ; for the enterprise of Montgomery and Arnold was about to be
resumed; and the French must choose either to suffer
the terrors of a hostile invasion, or to join the armies
of the United States in driving the British power
for ever from the Continent. Finally, as if these tests
of loyalty were not enough, the port of Quebec was
invaded by English press-gangs, who terrorised the
quays of the Lower Town and kidnapped able-
bodied youths of both races. But notwithstanding
so many temptations to swerve from allegiance,

when news came in June, 1812, that the Americans had declared war against England, the loyal sentiment of the Canadians was unanimous, the Maritime Provinces joining their forces with those of Lower and Upper Canada to repel the invaders; and Major-General Isaac Brock, the Lieutenant-Governor, in his speech to the Legislature of the Upper Province, thus expressed the feeling of the entire country : —

" We are engaged," he declared, " in an awful and eventful contest. By unanimity and despatch in our councils, and vigour in our operations, we may teach the enemy this lesson, that a country defended by free men enthusiastically devoted to the cause of their king and constitution can never be conquered."

Thus, instead of the support on which they calculated, the invading army was to encounter a resolute and united foe. Nor were the causes of Canadian loyalty far to seek. The French population, by nature loyal and content, were unwilling to sever the ties of noble monarchical tradition binding them to the past, and embark upon the troubled seas of American politics, there to be lost among loose and powerful majorities out of sympathy with their conservative ideals, their temperament, and those racial rights so fully acknowledged by England after the Conquest. Also east and west, the Maritime Provinces and Upper Canada contained an element already devotedly attached to the Crown. The sacrifices of the

United Empire loyalists made almost sacred the soil
of Upper Canada, now Ontario.   Men who had
already braved the anger of their fellow-citizens in
the American Colonies, and abandoned their homes
to witness to the ideal of a united empire, were

SIR GORDON DRUMMOND
(Lieut.-Governor of Upper Canada, December 1813 to April 1815)

not likely at the last to throw away their crown of
service and stultify themselves before the world.

Upper Canada was already a flourishing colony,
containing at the outbreak of this American war
about a quarter of the population of the two
provinces combined.   To balance inferiority in
point of numbers, the peculiar circumstances of the
English colonists — affinity of race to the mother-

country, a fertile territory, the memory of special
benefits received — combined to bring the zealous
British sentiment of the new province into special
prominence at this crisis. Inspired by the wise
counsels of Sir Guy Carleton, the British Government had there formerly pursued a generous policy
now about to bear opportune fruit; for when, at the
end of the War of Independence, the loyalist refugees
were crowding to the appointed places of rendezvous
along the northern frontier, facing the future unpro-
vided, the large sum of £3,000,000 sterling had
been granted to recompense their losses, in addition to further help allowed more needy settlers.
Under the four years of Colonel Simcoe's sympathetic rule (1791–95), the province had trebled its
population, a vigorous immigration policy enticing
crowds of wavering loyalists or enterprising specu-
lators from the south. "Where," asks Brock in his
proclamation at the opening of the war, "where
is to be found, in any part of the world, a growth
so rapid in prosperity and wealth as this colony
exhibits?"

Yet the inhabitants of Upper Canada, for all their
special interest in the British connection, hardly ex-
ceeded the Lower Province in the zeal with which
they rose to meet the new invasion. Indeed, the
United States had entirely miscalculated the strength
of this spirit of loyalty, which proved a more potent

inspiration than their own vaunted superiority in resources and population : for, on the American side, recruits came slowly forward, and the movement had none of the spontaneity evident among their adversaries. The " Loyal and Patriotic Society," established by Bishop Strachan, then rector of York, undertook to provide for the national wants of Canada created by the war. The sum of £120,000 was raised in Upper Canada and the Maritime Provinces, while the Quebec Legislature contributed no less than £250,000 towards preparations for defence. At the same time, the colonials were zealously enlisting, all men between the ages of sixteen and forty-five being required to serve in the militia; and their strength was further supplemented by more than four thousand regulars, scattered throughout the country.

The Commander-in-Chief of these forces was Sir George Prevost, who had come to Quebec as Governor in succession to Sir James Craig, a change much welcomed by the French Canadians; for although the new Governor was not an able general, he possessed the gentle art of conciliation, a gift of almost equal value at that critical time. As the New England States had been averse to war from the beginning, the adjoining Maritime Provinces of Canada were spared the trial of invasion, and the quarrel was fought out along the southern border of Upper and Lower Canada.

The American Commander, General Dearborn, divided his army of invasion into three parts, intending first to secure a base of operations at the

MAJOR-GENERAL SIR ISAAC BROCK, K.B.
(Administrator of Upper Canada, 1812)

three important points of Detroit, Niagara, and Queenston, and thence to overrun the Upper Province. He was confident that, with the help of the disaffected colonists, these columns would

soon be able to converge and march together upon
the capital. General Hull, of Michigan, commanded
the army of the west; Van Rensselaer led the
army of the centre against Niagara and Queenston; while the army of the north, under Dearborn
himself, moved from Albany by Lake Champlain
towards Ontario.

On the Canadian side, Major-General Brock
appeared to realise most clearly the need for decided
measures. His commanding presence — he was six
feet three inches in height — and his immense
muscular strength were joined to an intense and
chivalrous spirit which was a deciding influence in
uniting the colonists to energetic defence. His
practical sense appears in an order directing officers
" On every occasion when in the field to dress in con-
formity to the men, in order to avoid the bad consequence of a conspicuous dress," — an expedient only
lately adopted in more modern warfare, and not
until bitter necessity forced it.

In other respects, however, we have outgrown the
ideas entertained at that time on the subject of
martial appearance, for the writer of the *Ridout
Letters* [1] says, immediately after the battle on Queenston Heights —

" The American prisoners, officers, and men are

---

[1] *Ten Years of Upper Canada in Peace and War*, 1805–1815, *being the Ridout
Letters, with Annotations*, by Matilda Edgar, 1891.

the most savage-looking fellows I ever saw. To
strike a greater terror in their enemies they had
allowed their beards on their upper lips to grow.
This, however, had no other effect upon us than to
raise sensations of disgust."

Brock was a native of the Island of Guernsey, and
had served with the armies of Britain in many parts
of the world, being also present with Nelson at
Copenhagen ; but had already served officially in
Canada for ten years before the war. He
now found himself opposed to the vainglorious
Hull ; nor was it long before he justified his reputation and won glory for the arms of Canada by
capturing the American General at Detroit, together
with 2500 troops and thirty-three cannon. Brock's
ally on this occasion was the Chief Tecumseh, an
Indian of reputed supernatural birth, the natives
having been induced to throw in their lot with the
British colonists in consequence of the seizure of the
old port of Michillimackinac by a small force of
regulars and Canadian voyageurs. Following his
career of victory, Brock was soon afterwards confronted by the army of the Centre, consisting of
six thousand Americans, and engaged in the memorable battle on Queenston Heights. Here, after a
long and doubtful fight, the colonial forces were
once more successful, though they paid a heavy price
for victory in the loss of their wise and brave

commander, whose name is endeared to all Canadians, and whose renown grows with succeeding generations.

Meanwhile General Dearborn had undertaken the invasion of Lower Canada with the army of the north, setting out from Albany to attack Montreal by way of Lake Champlain; and to oppose him Colonel De Salaberry, at the head of the French Canadian regiment of Voltigeurs, together with three hundred Indians and a force of rural militia, held an advanced post on the River Lacolle. De Salaberry was distinguished by long experience of foreign service in the British army, having already confronted the Americans, when as a mere boy-subaltern he had covered the evacuation of Matilda. In 1795 he commanded a company of Grenadiers in the expedition to Martinique; and some years later held the post of honour with the Light Brigade at the capture of Flushing. And now at last he brought his experience to the defence of his native province, where his name and fame are not more deeply venerated than in the English provinces.

Reaching the outpost of Lacolle late in November, a strong force of Dearborn's army found the Canadian militia securely intrenched at Blairfindie. But the season was already far advanced; and now successive blows fell in the news of Hull's surrender at Detroit and of the defeat on the Queenston Heights; so that

2 F

at last the American commander despaired of success against the spirited defenders of Lower Canada, and decided to abandon the plans against Montreal and to fall back forthwith on Albany. Thus, apart from some successes won by the United States upon the sea, the result of the first campaign was altogether favourable to the Colonies.

The second year of the war put the loyalty of Lower Canada to more crucial tests. Once more the Americans planned and exploited a threefold attack, in the west, centre, and east. In the west, they were repulsed at Frenchtown by General Proctor; but in the centre this loss was more than counterbalanced by the control of Lake Ontario by American vessels, leading to the capture of Fort York,[1] the capital of the Upper Province, and of Fort George, near Niagara, the Canadian generals, Sheaffe and Vincent, being compelled to fall back upon Kingston and Burlington Heights. In following up these successes, however, the Americans were severely checked at Stoney Creek, near Hamilton; while another blow was inflicted upon them by the skilful strategy of Lieutenant Fitzgibbon, who, having been warned of the enemy's advance by the heroic Laura Secord, devised a trap in which, with a handful of Canadians and Indians, he captured a large force under Colonel Boerstler, at Beaver Dams.

[1] Now Toronto.

Sir Charles Bagot.

Governor General of Canada 1842-1843.

But the tide of war turned once more against
the Canadians, when the British fleet on Lake Erie
surrendered to Commodore Perry, and Proctor, the
victor of Frenchtown, met with a humiliating defeat

DE SALABERRY
(1778-1829)

at the hands of General Harrison, a future President
of the Republic, Chief Tecumseh being among the
slain. On the ocean, however, British naval prestige
was restored, and among the events of this year was
the celebrated duel between the *Shannon* and the
Chesapeake. But while, in the west and centre, the

issue was hanging thus in doubt, events more decisive were happening in the east.

The army of the north was sent once more against Montreal and Quebec, this time in two divisions, the first of which was to march northward from Albany, and at Châteauguay to effect a junction with the second division, coming down the St. Lawrence in three hundred boats from Sackett's Harbor. The St. Lawrence army, commanded by General Wilkinson, was intercepted by a force of French Canadians, and sustained a memorable defeat at Chrystler's Farm, near Long Sault Rapids; and the force from Albany was now to meet a similar fate. Late in September this first division, under General Hampton, crossed the Canadian frontier south of the historical outpost of Isle-aux-Noix; but as De Salaberry was once more in command of the advanced line of defence, again holding a strong position at Blairfindie, the enemy, in order to effect the necessary junction with the other division, was compelled to make a long detour by way of the Châteauguay River. In spite of the difficulties of the route, they pressed forward towards the shore of Lake St. Louis. De Salaberry was not dismayed by this new movement, and hastening westward from Blairfindie, he ascended the Châteauguay and took up a strong position on ground intersected by deep ravines. The same tactics which had destroyed Braddock's legion at

A BEGGAR OF CÔTE BEAUPRÉ

Monongahela in 1775, were now brought to bear
with equal effect upon the Americans themselves.
The Canadian general, having destroyed the bridges,
erected a triple line of defence, under cover of
which he held his force, consisting of only three
hundred Canadians, a band of Indians, and a few
companies of Highlanders. Early in the morning
of October 26th, the American army advancing to
the ford, the banks of the river suddenly blazed with
musketry fire. For four hours the invaders strove
in vain to force the passages of the river in the face
of De Salaberry's death-dealing trenches, bravely
attempting to outflank the Voltigeurs; but before
those unyielding breastworks, numbers and impetuosity were both unavailing; and, at last, after heavy
losses, Hampton was constrained to recall his men
and retire from the field. This victory, nobly fought
and won by the French Canadians, ranks with Carillon
in the annals of the Lower Province, and the bullet-
riven flags of both engagements are still shown among
the trophies of Quebec. The loyalty and courage
of the French population had decided the issue of
another campaign in favour of Great Britain.

In 1814 the chief events of the war in Canada
happened once more about Lake Champlain and
Niagara. The invaders were again driven back with
loss at Lacolle Mill; but at the end of the season
they recovered ground in this quarter by dispersing

the British army and the fleet of Lake Champlain at Plattsburg, an engagement which led to the recall of Sir George Prevost, whose bad generalship was blamed for this reverse. Meanwhile, the hottest battle of all the war had been fought in the Upper Province, when the American armies, planning to reach Kingston,

ST. LOUIS STREET, PLACE D'ARMES, AND NEW COURT HOUSE

and having won some minor successes, were finally scattered at Lundy's Lane, near Niagara Falls, and compelled to fall back upon Lake Erie.

But apart from the fortunes of war, when peace was finally proclaimed by the Treaty of Ghent in 1814, the chief gain to the British cause, so far at least as Canada was concerned, lay not so much in the undoubted advantage held throughout those three

trying years, but rather in the sure knowledge that
the people of French Canada had remained loyal at
a crisis when their disaffection would have turned the
scale and lost to England her remaining North
American colonies. As De Salaberry wrote to the
House of Assembly, in reference to the victory at
Châteauguay : " In preventing the enemy from
penetrating into the province, one common sentiment
animated the whole of my three hundred brave companions, and in which I participated, that of doing
our duty, serving our sovereign, and saving our
country from the evil of an invasion. The satisfaction arising from our success was to us adequate
recompense. . . ."

Temptations to treason had been multiplied ;
for besides many grievances at home, the French
inhabitants were constantly exposed to the emissaries
of the United States, who preached specious doctrines
of liberty throughout the parishes of Quebec; and
it was indeed fortunate that the unique influence of
the Catholic clergy, powerfully led by Bishop Plessis,
was actively exerted on the side of loyalty, just as
at a later time they earned a sincere tribute from
Lord Durham, and "a grateful recognition of
their eminent services in resisting the arts of the
disaffected."

" I know of no parochial clergy in the world,"
wrote Lord Durham, " whose practice of all the

Christian virtues, and zealous discharge of their clerical duties, is more universally admitted, and has been productive of more beneficial consequences. . . . In the general absence of any permanent institutions of civil government, the Catholic Church has presented almost the only semblance of ˚stability and organisation, and furnished the only effectual support for civilisation and order."

But the loyalty of the French population, which would not permit them to take advantage of the foreign difficulties of their rulers, was soon to be further tried and shaken through a prolonged period of political agitation.

General Earl Cathcart.

Governor General of Canada 1846-1847.

CHAPTER XXI

THE MODERN PERIOD

THE history of Quebec in the period succeeding the war of 1812 is a long record of internecine strife, due to certain conditions of the Canada Act of 1791, a measure halting midway between military rule and responsible government. The Act had been well intended, and it was, maybe, a necessary stage in constitutional development; but its immediate result was to organise opposing factions into formal assemblies, each bent on checking the policy of the other, and bringing the government of the country to a deadlock. On one side, the interests of the English were identified with the Legislative Council, a body appointed by the King for life, and owing no responsibility to the suffrages of the people; while, on the other, a French majority ruled in the popular assembly, whose authority, powerful in influence, impotent in administration, controlled neither the executive officers nor financial affairs. Accordingly, the dispute between the Assembly and the English ascendency, or "Family Compact," soon resolved itself into a struggle for and against responsible government.

An insoluble problem was now presented to successive governors — Sherbrooke, Richmond, Dalhousie, Kempt, Aylmer, Gosford. All in turn addressed themselves to the work of pacification, and all retired baffled by that racial egotism which granted favours with airs of patronage, or met con-

CITY HALL, QUEBEC

tinued concessions with ever increased demands. The English were naturally apprehensive of a French dominance, which might prove dangerous to the security of constitutional union; the French Canadians were too keenly alert for signs of tyranny, too suspicious of a power sullied by nepotism and greed of office. Of all the long series of viceroys, perplexed, discomfited, yet honourably bent on doing their duty to both races and to the constitution, one of the wisest was Sir John Cope Sherbrooke, to whom Prevost resigned the reins of government in 1815. He early saw the expediency of liberal measures, and his wise administration led moderate men to believe that a peaceful era of constitutional progress was forward. Unhappily, however,

LIEUT.-COLONEL JOHN BY, R.E.
(Founder of Bytown, now Ottawa)

these hopes were dashed by the succession of the Duke of Richmond two years later — a chivalrous but uncompromising advocate of the extreme views of his party in England. The Duke, however, almost atoned for the political narrowness of his administration by the stimulus he brought to the social life of the capital and the sincerity of his belief that by personal influence he could harmonise contending factions. Under his magnificent patronage Château St. Louis became once more the scene of lavish hospitality. Dinners, dances, and theatricals were the order of the day ; and fashionable officers, issuing from their quarters in the citadel, found distractions in St. Louis Street and the Grande Allée, due compensation for all they had left at home. For the exiled sportsman, too, there was the racecourse on the Plains of Abraham, riding to the hounds on the uplands of Lorette, snipe at Sillery Cove, and ducks on the St. Charles Flats.

With pomp and circumstance the Duke of Richmond made progress through his dominions, everywhere speaking, entertaining, endeavouring to conciliate. He travelled up the St. Lawrence by steamer and thence by canoes along the shore of Lake Ontario to Toronto and Niagara. Next, he undertook the more arduous journey in the course of which he was to meet a tragic end.

The little settlement of Richmond, named after the Governor himself, lay thirty miles from Perth, at some distance west from the Ottawa river. Here, following the trail through the woods, the Duke had penetrated in search of adventure. That night he and his small staff stayed at the village inn, and the next day they started in canoes on their way down to the junction with the Rideau river. Hardly had they commenced their journey, however, when the

Duke's actions began to excite alarm. The attendants sought in vain to restrain his violence, and the boats drawing in to shore the party landed. Breaking loose from all control, the Duke plunged into the woods, and was found soon afterwards lying exhausted in a fit of hydrophobia, the result of a bite by a tame fox two months before at Sorel. He died the same night; and the body was presently carried back to Quebec, where for two days it lay in state at the Château. An impressive service was held in the English cathedral, and the body of one who had been Canada's most splendid governor since the days of De Tracy and Frontenac, was deposited in the cathedral vault. Minute guns boomed forth from the citadel, and Quebec was plunged from gaiety into mourning.

The social brilliance of the Duke of Richmond's rule, however, could not blind the popular party to the inadequacy of the policy for which he stood; and discontent soon began to take a bitter and dangerous form. The concessions grudgingly doled out by Dalhousie and Kempt, succeeding governors, did not touch the main issue of the question, and even when Lord Aylmer removed the last serious grievance, only withholding from the Assembly the right to vote upon the salaries of civil officers, it might have seemed that there was no further ground for agitation. But the essential grievance lay not so much in material disabilities as in the limitation of the abstract right to self-government; and Joseph Papineau, the eloquent and ardent leader of the movement, summed up his party's political creed in the new watchword — *La nation Canadienne*. Parry and thrust, the fight grew faster, and the temper

SIR PEREGRINE MAITLAND

(Lieut.-Governor, Upper Canada, Aug. 1818 to Nov. 1828; also Administrator as Governor for Canada in 1820)

of the combatants became heated. Papineau was elected to the speakership of the Assembly, a challenge the Governor answered by prorogation. Next, the Progressives demanded an elective council, and the Government replied that such a step would mean abandoning the province wholly to the French, who were yet unprepared to wield complete popular

power, and would moreover endanger the interests
of the English minority.   The demand was formally
rejected by Lord John Russell on the return of Lord
Gosford's commission in 1835.

The fiery eloquence of Papineau now led the more
ardent of his followers to the point of rebellion;
and for a time it seemed as if Lower Canada would

TRAPPISTS AT MISTASSINI

throw away the name for steadfast loyalty she had
earned through so many years.   The rebellion of
1837, however, met with no serious support throughout the Province of Canada ; and, except as an
original centre of agitation, Quebec did not figure in
it at all.   At the same time defensive measures were
not omitted, the leading citizens, both French and
English, forming themselves into a regiment at the

2 G

disposal of the Governor-General. Parliament House was set apart for a drill-hall and guard-house, and garrison duty was performed here during the whole of an anxious winter. Montreal, however, suffered violence at the hands of a misguided mob; and in the country parishes the *habitants* were harangued after Mass on Sunday by deputies of the *Fils de Liberté*. Yet, while they punctuated these fervent addresses with shouts of "*Vive Papineau*" and "*Point de despotisme!*" they neither knew nor cared what the struggle for responsible government really meant. In the parishes along the Richelieu, indeed, Papineau and his followers made a greater commotion; but, except in Bellechasse and L'Islet, the contented *habitants* of the St. Lawrence forgot the seditious procession almost as soon as it passed. These ingenuous *enfants du sol* had no political aspirations beyond the preservation of their religion, their language, and their ancient customs; and, in spite of the bitter prophecies of peripatetic agitators, they refused to believe that their peace and comfort and quiet life were in any real danger from English oppression. The Government easily coped with this factitious rising, which nowhere reached the importance of an organised revolt. But while the military problem was soon solved, important political results followed hard upon such palpable tokens of discontent. English ministers now turned most serious attention to the constitutional defects of the colony, and decided to make a full and authoritative inquiry. Gosford's successor, Sir John Colborne, was now re-called ; and

THE HON. LOUIS JOSEPH PAPINEAU

on April 24th, 1838, the Earl of Durham sailed for Canada as High Commissioner, and he proved to be the keenest statesman, save Frontenac, who had figured in the history of the country.

Lord Durham was at this time forty-six years of age, and into that comparatively short life he had already crowded a remarkable political record. At twenty-one he entered the House of Commons as member for the county of Durham, at once identifying himself with the party of parliamentary reform — indeed, he is even credited with the drafting of the first Reform Bill. An experience of five years in the cabinet with Grey and Palmerston, and of two years as ambassador at St. Petersburg, marked him out as a politician and diplomatist of the first rank. A certain stateliness and formality of character appears, however, to have made him many enemies in England, and they did not scruple to gratify their dislike or jealousy during his mission to Canada. Their enmity is echoed in a trivial paragraph in *The Times*, describing an incident which happened on the outward journey : —

" A letter from Portsmouth states that on the evening of Lord Durham's arrival in Portsmouth, his lordship and family dined at one table and his staff at another, in the same room and at the same hour. We suppose we shall soon hear of Lord Durham's reviving the old custom of arranging his guests above and below the salt-cellar." [1]

On the 27th of May, 1838, H.M.S. *Hastings* and a squadron of gunboats and frigates dropped anchor in the harbour of Quebec. Flags were flying gaily

[1] *The Times*, 3rd May, 1838.

The Earl of Elgin.

Governor General of Canada 1847-1854.

from tower and bastion to welcome the High Commissioner, who was attended ashore by a retinue
eclipsing in brilliance even that of the Duke of
Richmond, and further guarded by two cavalry
regiments, on their way to reinforce the regular
forces in the country. As such a suite could not be
accommodated in the old Château, Parliament House
was fitted up as a residence; and here Lord Durham
established himself with a magnificence suitable to
a monarch, but unusual in a viceroy of Quebec.
On his daily drives he was accompanied by three or
four equerries in scarlet and gold, who galloped
before his carriage to clear the road; and at his
frequent entertainments guests received only the
most stately hospitality. It is not unnatural that this
large ceremony in a new and poor country impaired
his influence, and at first increased the difficulties of
his mission.

The situation was indeed one requiring the
wisdom of a ripe diplomatist. Previous to the rebellion of 1837, government had become impossible
owing to the antagonism of the racial elements
existing together in the province; and on Lord
Durham's arrival he found the constitution of the
Colony suspended, supreme power being lodged
in his own person as High Commissioner, whose
slightest indiscretion might lose the vast territory to
the Crown. That he was keenly alive to the

delicacy of his task is shown by the chivalrous,
almost romantic generosity with which he met the
natural prejudices of the French, and tolerated their
utmost bitterness against his own compatriots; and
although this imaginative and liberal spirit met with
disapproval from the ruling powers in England, and
was finally the cause of his withdrawal, his concilia-
tory policy was amply justified by the event.   Indeed,
it is certain that the insular assurance — by no means
absent from subsequent public life in England —
which prompted Lord Gosford, the previous Governor, to declare that the ulterior object of the
French Canadian politicians was " the separation of
this country from England, and the establishment
of a republican form of government," and who met
the imaginary demand with a sharp and scornful
negative, would soon have brought Canada to the
verge of a revolutionary war.

The proclamation published immediately on Lord
Durham's arrival in Canada gave promise of fair
dealing to all parties. " I invite from you," he
assures them, " the most free, unreserved communi-
cations. I beg you to consider me as a friend and
arbitrator, ready at all times to listen to your wishes,
complaints, and grievances. If you, on your side,
will abjure all party and sectarian animosities, and
unite with me in the blessed work of peace and
harmony, I feel assured that I can lay the founda-

ENGLISH CATHEDRAL

tions of such a system of government as will protect the rights and interests of all classes. . . .

" In one province the most deplorable events have rendered the suspension of its representative constitution, unhappily, a matter of necessity ; and the supreme power has devolved upon me. The great responsibility which is thereby imposed on me, and the arduous nature of the functions which I have to discharge, naturally make me most anxious to hasten the arrival of that period when the executive power shall again be surrounded by all the constitutional checks of free, liberal, and British institutions." [1]

The problem to be solved is stated and partly solved in the famous report on the affairs of Canada subsequently published by the High Commissioner — perhaps the most remarkable document in British colonial history. It showed the keenest insight into knotted complications, and at the same time it made practical and far-seeing suggestions, which reduced the problem to its simplest terms, and prepared the way for a legislative union upon a sovereign scale, and with a provincial autonomy having the happiest results.

" I expected," he declared, " to find a contest between a government and a people ; I found two nations warring in the bosom of a single state."

[1] *Quebec Gazette*, 29th May, 1838.

Nor could any lasting reform be accomplished unless the hostile divisions of Lower Canada were first reconciled.   As far as the French population were concerned, he found an explanation of their antagonism, not so much in their unjust exclusion from political power, as in the grudging and churlish patronage with which privileges were one by one conceded ; while, on the other hand, the Loyalists were intolerant to a degree, regarding every favour shown to their rivals as a slight put upon themselves, and professing principles which were thus summed up by one of their leaders : " Lower Canada must be *English* at the expense, if necessary, of not being *British*."   Elsewhere Lord Durham confesses the overbearing character of Anglo-Saxon manners, especially offensive to a proud and sensitive people, who showed their resentment, not by active reprisal, but by a strange and silent reserve.   The same confession might still be made concerning a section of English-speaking Canadians, who seem to consider it a personal grievance that French Canadians should speak the French language.   Lord Durham would probably have reminded them that conquest does not mean that birthright, language, and custom, spirit and racial pride, are spoils and confiscations of the conqueror.

As for the grievances he came to remedy, Lord Durham dwells upon the circumstances which practi-

Lord Lisgar.

Governor General of Canada 1868-1872.

cally excluded French Canadians from political power,
leaving all positions of trust and profit in the hands
of the English minority; for although they numbered only one in four of the inhabitants, this
privileged class claimed both political and social
supremacy as though by inherent right. Owing
no responsibility whatever to the legislature, they
could afford to smile at the protestations of that
superfluous body, and pursue their own wilful
course.

Coming to practical counsel, the High Commissioner pointed out that there was no need for
any change in the principles of government, or
for any new constitutional theory to remedy the
disordered state. The remedy already lay in the
British constitution, whose principles, if consistently
followed, would give a sound and efficient system
of representative government. His first suggestion
was the frank concession of a responsible executive.
All the officers of state, with the single exception of
the Governor and his secretary, should be made
directly answerable to the representatives of the
people; these officers, moreover, should be such
as the people approved, and should therefore be
appointed by the Assembly. He further advised
that the Governor should be forbidden to employ
the resources of the British Constitution in
any quarrel between himself and the Legislature,

resorting to imperial intervention only when imperial interests were at stake.

His second recommendation was to bring the Upper and Lower Provinces together by a legislative union. He met the threatened danger of a disaffected people endowed with political power by an appeal to arithmetic: "If the population of Upper Canada is rightly estimated at 400,000, the English inhabitants of Lower Canada at 150,000, and the French at 450,000, the union of the two provinces would not only give a clear English majority, but one which would be increased every year by the influence of English emigration. . . . I certainly shall not like," he continues, " to subject the French Canadians to the rule of the identical English minority with which they have so long been contending ; but from a majority emanating from so much more extended a source, I do not think that they would have any oppression or injustice to fear."

This plea for unity among all the elements of political life in Canada, premature as it was, marked, perhaps, the limitation of Lord Durham's scheme. But although he was mistaken in the degree of allowance to be made for the distinct individuality of the French province — a defect afterwards made good on Dominion Day — the work he did, the counsel he gave, made an epoch in the progress of

Canadian nationality, and prepared the ground for the completer measures of the future.

The treatment of rebels was the most critical question with which Lord Durham had to deal, and

THE MARQUIS OF LORNE (DUKE OF ARGYLL)

it was ultimately the cause of his withdrawal, so timid and unchivalrous was the Government of the day in the face of political and journalistic criticism. While granting a general amnesty to the rank and file of the offenders, the High Commissioner offended

constitutional pedants by deporting eight of the
leading revolutionists without trial to Bermuda ; and
although this measure was taken advisedly, with the
purpose, as it turned out, of saving the prisoners
from the heavier penalty they would certainly have
received from a regular court, the Viceroy's numerous
enemies did not scruple to use this technical omission
as a basis for attacks upon his policy.   Moreover,
when he was bitterly denounced in the House of
Lords by Brougham and Lyndhurst, the ministry of
Melbourne offered but a feeble defence of their
representative ; with the result that Durham, on
hearing of this desertion by the Cabinet which had
appointed him, sent in his resignation.

The departure of the High Commissioner was
deeply regretted by those who were able to appreciate
the wisdom and sincerity of his administration, though
indeed it was otherwise regarded by the leaders of
that social clique in Quebec whose family compact
he had resolutely condemned.   Yet he had builded
better than England or Canada or himself then knew,
and his tireless energy and imagination left behind
him the material for a sound structure.   Besides the
masterly report of his commission, a visible, if less
important, monument to his beneficent work for
Canada still stands in the magnificent terrace at
Quebec, known to-day under an improved form and
by another name, yet in a larger measure his con-

ception and his achievement. He sailed from Quebec on the 1st of November, 1838, the ceremony of his departure being hardly less imposing than that marking his arrival five months before. Troops lined the streets from the Governor's residence to the Queen's wharf, the bands playing " Auld Lang Syne " to express the regret felt at parting from a sincere and strong administrator, thus sacrificed to his enemies by a vacillating Ministry. At this last evidence of sympathy and appreciation the *hauteur* of the Viceroy relaxed, and, as he passed on board the frigate *Inconstant* homeward bound — as he himself records — his heart went out towards the people of Canada, by whom, at least, his motives were understood and honoured ; and this feeling of gratitude to perhaps the most simple and sincere of all British peoples remained with him to the end.

By an act brought forward by Lord John Russell, the provinces of Upper and Lower Canada were formally united, and the first Parliament of the two Canadas was opened in the city of Kingston in June, 1841. This experiment partly meeting the needs of the country, and satisfying that high civic and national sense which make Britishers confident that they can govern themselves, opened up the way for that freer union which has since 1867 made a nation of a series of scattered territories.

The legislative union of the Upper and Lower

Provinces had not been concluded without sharp opposition; for the citizens of Quebec foresaw that her influence must inevitably wane under the new conditions, and they set themselves strongly to defeat the measure. However, the ancient city lay too far east to remain the capital of the expanding territories, and with an almost exclusively French population it could not remain the political pivot of a British dependency. Opposition was overborne in due time, and the Act of Union shifted the national centre of gravity farther west.

Canada was now embarked upon a course of self-government, and was never again to feel the hand or obey the voice of England in her internal politics. So much the union had accomplished. The problems of the succeeding period concerned Canada alone, and she was now free to seek a better way to her national organisation. A responsible legislature had been conceded, yet with defects in constitution bearing hardly upon the character and traditions of the French element. Thus, although the population of the Lower Province numbered two hundred thousand more than that of her partner, the two provinces were allowed an equal number of representatives in the new house; the French language was cast aside; and the united assembly was saddled with the heavy debts previously contracted by the western province. It was not long

before an agitation was started to readjust the
relations between Upper and Lower Canada, and
free the French from conditions which pressed heavily
upon their material interests and racial sentiment.
The new problem was, to find a way by which the

SIR GEORGE CARTIER

principle of self-government recently conceded to
Canada as a whole might be reconciled with the free
action and growth of its component provinces; and
for twenty-five years this question engaged the politicians of the country.

Time, however, brought a decided change in the

2 H

attitude of the two opposing sections of the legislature, as one by one the grievances of the French were removed. In 1848 the restrictions placed upon the use of their language in the Parliament were done away ; and by the surprising advance of the West, the hardship of disproportionate representation was taken over by Upper Canada. Twenty years after the Union, the Western Province had already a population greater by three hundred thousand than that of her rival. In the later period of the discussion, therefore, the position of parties was reversed, the French defending the existing order, the Upper Province calling out for reconstruction. But statesmen on both sides now began to aim at larger and more patriotic ends than the exclusive advantage of their own province ; and in 1860 a scheme for a federal government was proposed by George Brown, a Liberal statesman, intended to bring the interests of the provinces into line with those of the country at large. The movement was premature ; but four years later a convention met at Quebec to discuss the union of all the provinces of British North America, the chairman being Étienne Paschal Taché, who died before the work was consummated. There met the fathers of Confederation, John A. Macdonald, chief of them all — George Brown, George Étienne Cartier, Alexander Galt, Thomas D'Arcy M'Gee, William M'Dougall, Alex-

The Marquis of Dufferin.

Governor General of Canada 1872-1878.

ander Campbell, Hector Langevin, James Cockburn
— together with Charles Tupper and other representatives of the Maritime Provinces.   It was agreed
that " the system of government best adapted under
existing circumstances to protect the diversified interests of the several provinces, and secure harmony
and permanency in the working of the Union, would

SIR JOHN A. MACDONALD

be a general government charged with matters of
common interest to the whole country ; and local
government for each of the Canadas, and for all the
Provinces of Nova Scotia, New Brunswick, Prince
Edward Island, charged with the control of local
matters in their respective sections."

These proposals were well received in London, and
in 1866 the Canadian Legislature met for the last

time under the old conditions.   The British North
America Act became law in March of the following
year, the Earl of Carnarvon being Colonial Secretary;
and on the 1st of July the new Dominion, under
command of John A. Macdonald, was launched by
Governor-General Viscount Monk on that prosperous course which still conducts the premier colony
of England into an ever brighter future.

Valiant in asserting her predominance there was,
however, a siege against which the fortress and
bastions of Quebec were of no avail.   Left behind
in the march of progress, commercial and political,
her prestige as a centre of national influence slowly
declined, and Montreal and Toronto took over that
pre-eminence which had been hers for centuries.   Yet
nothing could rob the city of her maternal grandeur.
She saw no longer in the West the wild prospects
and the fertile wastes, but a sturdy nation settling
down to its destiny, and spreading out over half a
continent; so realising her ancient prophecy, so
fulfilling her laborious hopes, the reward of zealous
toil and martyrdom.   Colbert's dream was now come
true, save for the flag which floated over the happy
homesteads in the peaceful land.   These homesteads
of the West, in the region of the great lakes, were
indeed to be centres of growth and progress and vast
wealth; yet the venerable fortress on the tidal water
ever was, and still remains, the noblest city of the

American continent.   There still works the antique
spirit which cherishes culture and piety and domestic
virtue as the crown of a nation's deeds and worth.

SIR WILFRID LAURIER

There still the influence of a faithful priesthood, and
a university in some respects more distinguished than
any on the American continent, keep burning those
fires of high tradition and a noble history which light

the way to national grace of life, if not to a sensational prosperity. Apart from the hot winds of politics — civic, provincial, and national — which blow across the temperate plains of their daily existence, the people of the city and the province live as simply, and with as little greedy ambition as they did a hundred years ago.

The rumble of the calèches and the jingling of the carrioles in the old streets are now pierced by the strident clang of the street-car ; and the electric light sharpens garishly the hard outlines of the stone mansions which sheltered Laval, Montcalm, and Murray ; but modern industry and municipal emulation sink away into the larger picture of fortress life, of religious zeal, of Gallic mode, of changeless natural beauty. No ruined castles now crown the heights, but the grim walls still tell of

> " Old, far-off, unhappy things,
> And battles long ago."

The temper of the people is true. Song and sentiment are much with them, and in the woods and in the streams — down by St. Roch and up by Ville Marie — chansons of two hundred years ago mark the strokes of labour as of the evening hour when the professional village story-teller cries " *cric-crac* " and begins his tale of the *loup-garou*, or rouses the spirit of a pure patriotism by a crude epic of some valiant atavar ; when the parish fiddler brings

them to their feet with shining eyes by the strains of
O Carillon. They are not less respectful to the British
flag, nor less faithful in allegiance because they love
that language and that land of their memories which
they know full well is not the Republican France
of to-day when their Church suffers at the hands
of the State. If ever the genius of the Dominion
is to take a high place in the fane of Art, the
soul and impulse of the best achievement will
come from Old Quebec, which has produced a
sculptor of merit, Hébert; a renowned singer,
Albani; a poet crowned by the French Academy,
Louis Fréchette; and has given to the public life of
the country a distinction, an intellectual power, and
an illuminating statesmanship in the persons of
Étienne Taché, Sir George Cartier, and Sir Wilfrid
Laurier. Enlarged understanding between the two
peoples of the country will produce a national
life marked by courage, energy, integrity, and
imagination. Though Quebec has ceased to be an
administrative centre of the nation, the influence of
the people of her province grows no less, but is
woven more and more into the web of the general
progress. The Empire will do well to set an en-
during value on that New France so hardly won
from a great people, and English Canada will reap
rich reward for every compromise of racial pride
made in the interests of peace, equality, and justice.

APPENDIX I

GOVERNORS OF CANADA

Early Viceroys and Lieutenant-Generals.

Sieur de Roberval, 1540.

Marquis de la Roche, 1598.

Charles de Bourbon, Comte de Soissons, 1612 (Champlain Governor).

Henri de Bourbon, Prince de Condé, 1612.

Duc de Montmorency, 1619.

Henri de Lévis, Duc de Vantadour, 1625.

Governors under the Company of One Hundred Associates.

Samuel de Champlain, 1633.

M. Bras-de-fer de Chastefort, 1635.

M. de Montmagny, 1636.

M. d'Ailleboust, 1648.

M. Jean de Lauson, 1651.

M. Charles de Lauson, 1656.

M. d'Ailleboust, 1657.

Viscomte d'Argenson, 1658.

Baron d'Avaugour, 1661.

Governors-General under Royal Government.

M. de Mézy, 1663.

Seigneur de Courcelles, 1665.

(Marquis de Tracy, Viceroy, 1665–67.)

473

Count Frontenac, 1672.

M. de la Barre, 1682.

M. de Denonville, 1685.

Count Frontenac, 1689.

M. de Callières, 1699.

Marquis de Vaudreuil, 1703.

Marquis de Beauharnois, 1726.

Count de Galissonière, 1747.

Marquis de la Jonquière, 1749.

Marquis du Quesne, 1752.

Marquis de Vaudreuil-Cavagnac, 1755.

Governors of the Province of Quebec.

Gen. Sir Jeffrey Amherst, 1756.

Gen. James Murray, 1763.

Gen. Sir Guy Carleton, 1768 (Lieutenant-Governor from 1766).

Gen. Sir Frederick Haldimand, 1778.

(Henry Hamilton and Col. Henry Hope Lieutenant-Governors, 1785–87.)

Lord Dorchester (Sir Guy Carleton), Governor-General of British North America, 1787.

Governors-General during the Fifty Years when Canada was divided.

Lord Dorchester, 1791.

Gen. Robert Prescott, 1797–1805 (Lieutenant-Governor, 1796).

Sir James Craig, 1807.

Sir George Prevost, 1811.

Sir John Cope Sherbrooke, 1816.

Duke of Richmond, 1818.

(Hon. James Monck and Gen. Sir Peregrine Maitland administrators, 1819–20.)

Earl of Dalhousie, 1820.

Sir James Kempt, 1828.

Lord Aylmer, 1830.

Lord Gosford, 1835.

Sir John Colborne, 1838.

Lord Durham, 1838.

Hon. C. Poulett Thompson (afterwards Lord Sydenham), 1839.

Governors-General from the Union of the Canadas until Confederation.

Lord Sydenham (C. P. Thompson), 1841.

Sir Charles Bagot, 1842.

Lord Metcalfe, 1843.

Earl Cathcart, 1846.

Earl of Elgin, 1847.

Sir Edmund Bond Head, 1854.

Viscount Monk, 1861–67.

Governors-General of the Dominion.

Viscount Monk, 1867.

Lord Lisgar (Sir John Young), 1868.

Earl Dufferin, 1872.

Marquis of Lorne, 1878.

Marquis of Lansdowne, 1883.

Earl of Derby (Lord Stanley of Preston), 1888.

Earl of Aberdeen, 1893.

Earl of Minto, 1898.

APPENDIX II

LEADERS AND PREMIERS AFTER THE UNION OF 1841

Hon. Robert Baldwin and Louis H. Lafontaine, 1841.

Sir Dominick Daly, 1843.

Hon. W. H. Draper, 1844.

Hon. H. Sherwood, 1847.

Robert Baldwin and Hon. Louis H. Lafontaine, 1848.

Sir Francis Hincks, and Hon. A. N. Morin, 1851.

Sir Allan M'Nab and Sir E. P. Taché, 1855.

Sir John A. Macdonald, 1856.

Hon. George Brown, 1858.

Sir George E. Cartier and Sir John A. Macdonald, 1858.

Hon. John Sandfield Macdonald and Hon. Antoine A. Dorion, 1861.

Sir E. P. Taché, 1864.

Sir N. Belleau, 1865.

Prime Ministers since Confederation, 1867.

Sir John A. Macdonald, 1867–73.

Hon. Alexander Mackenzie, 1873–78.

Rt. Hon. Sir John A. Macdonald, 1878–91.

Sir J. J. C. Abbott, 1891–92.

Rt. Hon. Sir J. S. D. Thompson, 1892–94.

Sir Mackenzie Bowell, 1894–96.

Sir Charles Tupper, Bart., 1896 (April — July).

Rt. Hon. Sir Wilfrid Laurier, 1896.

APPENDIX III

LISTE DES GOUVERNEMENTS DE LA PRO-VINCE DE QUEBEC DEPUIS L'ÉTABLISSE-MENT DE LA CONFÉDÉRATION 1867

Ministère Chauveau	1867
Ministère Ouimet	1873
Ministère de Boucherville	1874
Ministère Joly	1878
Ministère Chapleau	1879
Ministère Mousseau	1882
Ministère Ross	1884
Ministère Taillon	1887
Ministère Mercier	1887
Ministère de Boucherville	1891
Ministère Taillon	1892
Ministère Flynn	1896
Ministère Marchand	1897
Ministère Parent	1900

INDEX

479

.